WORLD WAR II

AND THE

AMERICAN INDIAN

WORLD WAR II

AND THE

AMERICAN INDIAN

KENNETH WILLIAM TOWNSEND

University of New Mexico Press

Albuquerque

Library of Congress Cataloging-in-Publication Data

Townsend, Kenneth William, 1951–
    World War II and the American Indian / Kenneth William Townsend. — 1st ed.
        p.   cm.
Includes bibliographical references and index.

  ISBN 0-8263-2039-2 (alk. paper)
  1. World War, 1939–1945—Indians. 2. Indians of North America—Cultural
assimilation. 3. Indians of North America—Ethnic identity. I. Title.
D810.I5 T69 2000
940.53′089′97—dc21

                                                            99-050786

With love,
To my wife, Diann,
and to our children,
Danielle, Brandon, and Dustin

Contents

Acknowledgments

The path taken by a manuscript from its inception to its final book form is one determined principally by its author, but a permanent mark is imprinted on the project by those who aid the writer's research and by those who read early drafts of the work and offer their insightful comments. *World War II and the American Indian,* then, is certainly the product of numerous voices that offered service, advice, and encouragement.

I am grateful for the direction provided by faculty in the history department at the University of North Carolina at Chapel Hill, particularly that given by Robert Moats Miller and Roger Lotchin. Each of these respected historians encouraged me to analyze fully the material I unearthed and to place my findings into the broader context of the era. Moreover, their keen insight led me to consider points that I had not previously contemplated. I must also thank George Tindall. His passion for the art of writing remained an invisible force behind each draft of this book.

I appreciate the cooperation given me by archivists and library staff members at the National Archives in Washington, Yale University, the University of North Carolina, and the Virginia State Library and Archives. My appreciation is further extended to the staff of the United States Department of Justice, which, under the provisions of the Freedom of Information and Privacy Act, located, printed, and forwarded documents held by the Federal Bureau of Investigation. Given the tremendous number of FOIPA requests they receive and must work through annually, I am struck by their thoroughness and their rapid response to my own search for information. A special note of thanks must be given to Coastal Carolina University in Conway-Myrtle Beach, South Carolina. Most recently, the university granted me sabbatical leave for the purpose of making final revisions to the manuscript. Without release time from classroom responsibilities, completion of the book would have been substantially delayed. Special thanks is given to Ms. Sharon Tulley and Ms. Marchita Phifer, whose combined efforts in the Interlibrary Loan Section of Kimbel Library provided me with numerous government documents, journal articles, unpublished manuscripts, and archival material that otherwise would have required extensive travel to some extremely remote locations.

My gratitude also extends to Thomas A. Britten, professor of history at Briar Cliff College in Iowa, whose sound comments proved beneficial to the final product. And, to David Holtby and the staff of the University of New Mexico Press, I must express my greatest thanks. Mr. Holtby's encouragement, support, and guidance throughout the process of moving an unpublished manuscript to published book form made the effort an extremely pleasant experience. I am delighted and honored to have this book published under the University of New Mexico banner.

Finally, I will forever be grateful to my family. My parents, Margaret and Dallas Townsend, have never wavered in their support of me. The grounding in life they gave me, and the occasional financial aid they provided toward this project, proved much more valuable than they have ever imagined. For my wife Diann, and my children, Danielle, Brandon, and Dustin, I reserve my most profound gratitude, for they were surrounded by my work daily from the book's conception to its completion. Their patience and their understanding for my many trips and the hours I spent on the manuscript over so many years has been nothing less than remarkable. It is a debt that cannot be repaid.

World War II
and the
American Indian

Introduction

As the train chugged from the station, Corporal Virgil Wyaco peered through the passenger car window at the urban landscape of New York City, and within a short time even the tallest building was but a faint sight. For the next three days, the train rumbled over the lush, green summer countryside of Pennsylvania, past Midwestern farmlands that brimmed with crops nearly ready for harvesting, and crossed the parched prairies of the lower Great Plains to Fort Bliss in Texas. Wyaco studied the nation that only one year earlier sent him to war in Europe. He viewed a natural beauty that consoled his heart and surveyed a population whose prosperity was unmistakable—both images conflicting eerily with the sights and sounds of war now lodged in his memory. He had fought the Germans along the Ziegfried Line east of Metz, jumped the Saar River, battled the enemy in Bastogne, crossed the Rhine into Germany under heavy fire, witnessed the destruction of Stuttgart and Frankfurt, and participated in the liberation of Jewish prisoners at Dachau, just outside Munich. The suffering and death he encountered in less than twelve months defied understanding. Now, the veteran was returning home to Zuni Pueblo in New Mexico.

The war drew Virgil Wyaco into a brotherhood of men forever shaped by their overseas experiences and plagued by their haunting memories of combat. In battle, he, like his comrades, had fought not for political ideals or patriotism but for self-survival, for the lives of his fellow soldiers, and, in some instances, for revenge. He knew that in close combat he personally took the lives of several German soldiers, but he also knew that he was probably responsible for the deaths of many more Germans. The corporal admitted openly his role in the execution of captured soldiers. Despite the numerous bodies he stepped over in battle, "I'd seen nothing like Dachau," he recalled. "There were dead people piled everywhere, sometimes in neat rows the way Germans like things, sometimes all twisted. . . . [They] looked like juniper firewood just unloaded from a pickup truck, no more human than that, all naked and skinny. . . . And

I

I'd never been more angry in my life. Nor have I been since," he said. Sixty ss camp guards had surrendered to the American troops who entered Dachau and were themselves now under close supervision when Wyaco's commanding officer gathered him and several other GIs together. "He led us up to the ss troops and ordered 'Shoot them!'" "I didn't wait for another order," Wyaco confessed, "nor did any of the other men. The dozen of us all emptied our clips, shooting into the Germans. It took less than half a minute before they were like the same jumbled pile of bodies we'd found inside [the camp]." Recounting the experience many years after the war, Wyaco added, "I've never felt any remorse for my part in that execution. Those ss guards were more like witches than like men. They'd already lived too long."[1]

In this particular incident, and in the battles he fought across Europe, Wyaco's behavior was the same as most other American soldiers, but being Indian carried with it some differences. Reared at Zuni Pueblo, not far from Albuquerque, he had spent much of his childhood and adolescent years herding sheep, like many Indian children in the Southwest, and worked numerous odd jobs for whatever cash was offered, occasionally on temporary projects funded by the Bureau of Indian Affairs. With a life steeped in traditional Zuni culture and based in the pueblo community, he fully expected to continue sheep ranching as an adult. But Wyaco's educational experience, although limited by BIA financial constraints and tribal responsibilities, linked him to the non-Indian world. The ideas he absorbed from white teachers and a curriculum that still encouraged assimilation with mainstream society left him with a desire to see and to experience life beyond his community. Wyaco's thoughts and emotions drifted between two worlds—one world grounded in Zuni traditions and another that tempted him to break with his cultural identity.

World War II served as a crossroads in Wyaco's life. The nation's manpower needs presented the young Zuni with the opportunity to move into the non-Indian world, learn from his experiences, gain new skills, and perhaps secure profitable employment in mainstream society following the war. Restless, and uncertain about himself and his future, Wyaco tried to enlist in the United States Navy in 1941 but failed to pass the physical examination. A year later, however, the army found his health acceptable and inducted him at Fort Bliss.[2] For Wyaco, then, military service was perceived as an appropriate path on which he would learn more of the surrounding world, satisfy his own restlessness, and perhaps resolve the "two worlds" dilemma he felt.

The twenty-five thousand Indians who served in America's armed forces during World War II and the forty-thousand who secured civilian employment in the nation's defense industries all held their own individual motives for participating in the war. Like Virgil Wyaco, many expected their experiences would resolve an uncertain identity or channel their lives in a new direction. For some, military service or work in urban defense plants promised travel and the experience of seeing the nation and world outside their own communities. Wartime employment held the potential for higher-than-usual wages and job training not previously available on reservations, money desperately needed for themselves and to be shared with families back home. Many young men hoped to renew a warrior spirit that had nearly vanished within their tribes and attain personal honor in a manner consistent with Indian traditions. Many more Indian men and women perceived their involvement in the nation's war effort as the final step toward full assimilation with white society, and more than a few believed their involvement was a patriotic duty as American citizens.

There was, then, a myriad of reasons for Indian participation in World War II, and for each man and woman the war served as a personal crossroads. Armed with improved health, a firmer educational base, specialized job skills, and a record of military service, many Native Americans hoped to make a successful transition into mainstream society once peace returned. The prospect seemed dim but possible before the war, partly because of the training afforded to many American Indians under the Indian Reorganization Act and the unintended direction toward assimilation the act included, but war brightened the prospect and directly offered the opportunity to take the step toward inclusion. For others, pre-war federal Indian policy revitalized traditional Indian cultures; developments during the war affirmed for many Native Americans the value of a renewed, reinvigorated Indian identity apart from mainstream society. Whether bound for assimilation or retrenchment, World War II was the crossroads for Native Americans and, ultimately, for federal Indian policy.

One

Native Americans: A Vanishing Race?

Through **the wilderness** of woodland America and across the windswept prairies, a forgotten minority that contributed eight thousand young men to the Great War quietly straggled home without fanfare or tickertape parades. Unlike the all-black 369th Infantry Regiment, which triumphantly marched down New York's Fifth Avenue, preceded by martial music and applauded by William Randolph Hearst and Governor Alfred E. Smith, American Indians returned from the war virtually unnoticed to resume the lives they left nearly two years earlier.[1]

Indians were indeed a forgotten minority, a people apart from mainstream American life. For most Americans, Indians belonged to a bygone era of cavalry soldiers, war parties, and savagery. They remained wrapped in stereotyped images of horses, war bonnets, and tepees, which had no relevance to modern America except on the silver screen of movie houses nationwide. The image was further burdened with the misconception that Indians constituted a vanishing race as a result of increasing death rates and their melding with the general population. With extinction looming in the shadows, few Americans expressed concern for Indians.

Thomas Britten effectively argues in his recent book *American Indians in World War I: At Home and at War* that "service during World War I was a defining moment" in the lives of Indian "doughboys." A heightened pride in tribal identity emerged among those Indian men who served overseas, but the meeting of Native Americans from other tribes and from other regions of the United States and the sharing of common concerns in civilian life "fostered a Pan-Indianism among [Indian] veterans." For many, a commonality among Indian veterans as Americans surfaced, rather than the continuation of a strict tribal identity. Moreover, Native American servicemen in World War I had learned "mechanical and clerical skills, hygiene, and the English language." With overseas travel, Indians encountered "different lifestyles and cultures," and in combat alongside America's white soldiers Indians were "treated as equals," received respect, and gained a "firsthand look at how the majority society worked and thought." "Service in the war," argues Britten, "tended to de-villainize and de-mythologize popular misconceptions and helped foster a realistic appreciation and understanding" of Native Americans among white soldiers.[2] Their wartime experiences, then, led many Indians to assume assimilation with the general population to be more readily available should veterans choose that course.

For white veterans, military service alongside Indians in the trenches and mud-soaked battlefields of France cultivated a widely held assumption that Native Americans were finally on the precipice of total inclusion with white society. That premise was accepted in higher echelons, as both the United States Army and the Bureau of Indian Affairs expressed little interest in preserving native cultures in the postwar years. Assimilation of Indians into white society was, after all, the stated goal of federal Indian policy since the 1880s, and the Indians' voluntary participation in World War I seemed to confirm some success in reaching that goal. And, as Britten also reveals, Commissioner of Indian Affairs Cato Sells "viewed the war as an unexpected but welcomed opportunity to advance the cause of [Indian] assimilation" into the white mainstream.[3] In concert with long-standing integrationist policies of the federal government and the Indians' involvement in the European war, Native Americans were deemed to be a vanishing race.

Along with these sentiments, the public's indifference toward reservation realities in the 1920s underscored American society's implicit understanding that native cultures were indeed vanishing. Almost unobserved by the general population and without congressional debate, Indian veterans plodded through mounds of bureaucratic paperwork to receive citizenship, and in 1924 Congress extended the status to all Native Americans. Although New Mexico and Arizona still refused to enfranchise Indians, the Citizenship Act of 1924 constituted the anticipated final act of assimilation.

Assimilation, however, had not achieved the reality assumed by many Americans in the early 1920s. Of the nation's 244,000 Indians, only 15,000 resided in urban centers by 1920.[4] Most Native Americans continued to live on reservations scattered across the country, tucked into the isolated reaches of the United States, and those communities exhibited the antithesis of progress. Rather than a sign indicative of assimilation, the movement of Indians to urban environments was minimal and more often than not a sign of desperation. It represented an absence of economic opportunity on reservations and a personal revulsion toward inadequate living standards commonplace on Indian lands. It further indicated tribal rejection of those who, through the boarding-school experience, now seemed alienated from their homes. And, to some extent, it was an effort among some veterans to secure inclusion in a postwar society by those who had earlier accepted them in wartime settings. The migration of Indians to urban settings at this date was certainly not the result of a successful, federally sponsored, assimilationist program.

Following the Great War, economic opportunity and reservation living standards actually worsened, especially in the late 1920s. Reservation lands seldom provided subsistence, and total acreage continually shrank from Indian ownership. Between 1920 and 1928, Indian land holdings dwindled from 55,792,000 acres to 47,285,000 acres—a consistent pattern from the 1880 figure of 241,800,000 acres of reservation land. Although the Dawes Act of 1887 accounted for a portion of the lost acreage, many additional measures were equally responsible. The opening of western Oklahoma to white settlement in 1892 relinquished thousands of acres from Native American control, and additional lands fell from Indian ownership under the Curtis Act of 1892, the Jerome Agreement of 1900 (sustained in the Supreme Court ruling *Lone Wolf v. Hitchcock*), the Burke Act of 1906, and congressional authority granted in 1907 for the sale of allotments owned by "noncompetent" Indians. Moreover, hundreds of thousands of acres were ceded to white owners through lease arrangements, invalidated wills, and sales of individual allotments by Indians themselves. As land withered from Indian possession, the number of reservation-based farmers likewise declined. By 1920, 16,680 Indians were actively engaged in agriculture, whereas 24,251 Indians farmed the land only ten years earlier.[5]

With an annual per capita income of two hundred dollars among Indians nationally, as compared with two thousand dollars for whites, and faced with agricultural recession in the early 1920s, frustration was followed with despair, especially when reservation conditions were contrasted with booming urban prosperity. It was little wonder that deteriorating living conditions on reservations encouraged an increased migration of Indians to urban communities throughout the decade. By 1930 approximately thirty-three thousand Native Americans lived in the nation's cities and towns, a figure more than twice the 1920 finding.[6]

Despite the general indifference of white society and the federal government toward further degeneration of Indian living standards, a small number of progressive reformers in the middle 1920s discovered the reservations to be a new field in which to press their energy and rally behind a new cause. While some individuals such as anthropologists Franz Boas and Frank Speck were familiar

with Indian cultures and history, most reformers were educators, social workers, and other progressive "holdovers" who previously involved themselves with
inner-city, immigrant community improvement. Of these, John Collier soon
commanded the most visible attention.

A young man at the opening of the twentieth century, Collier served as a social worker in New York City, securing direct aid and providing direction for
immigrant families. Through his work, he developed a genuine appreciation for
the unique qualities and characteristics to be found in the various cultural
groups that resided in the city's numerous wards. Here were traditions and
traits which, he felt, should be preserved rather than lost in a supposed melting-
pot society. What emerged within Collier was a personal advocacy for cultural
preservation.

Shortly after relocating to southern California in 1919, Collier toured southwestern Indian communities and visited Taos Pueblo. There he became enam-
ored by the appearance of peaceful cooperation among the community's
residents, the prevalent concern for the common good, and a spiritual awareness that seemed to exceed his encounters with other cultural groups. Still, he
reeled from the extent of the poverty he encountered. As witness to cultural disintegration among Indians across the Southwest, Collier commenced a thirty-
year crusade for tribal revitalization. His primary target became the Bureau of
Indian Affairs, which, he believed, was ultimately responsible for the deterioration of Indian communities and cultures. From his own research and his interviews with individual Indians and tribal leaders, Collier became convinced that
the bureau's central purpose was the destruction of a distinct Indian identity in
America. He concluded that, "the bureau leaves the family intact, or physically
tears it apart," whichever is preferred by federal policy or white influence at any
particular moment. Should an Indian leave a will, "the bureau may heed it or
destroy it, and the heirs have no recourse. In 1926," he added, "the bureau actually destroyed one-fifth of the Indian wills on which action was taken that
year." He further noted that "if Indian allotted land is coveted by white men,
the bureau may, and does, lease it to them." Moreover, "land belonging to the
allotted Indian who dies is sold to white men" and the "heirs are made landless."[7] One thing seemed clear to Collier and other observers: continued loss of
land and little effort to provide direct aid to Indian reservation communities
would only guarantee the disappearance of Native Americans. Existing programs and organizations failed to alter the perceived direction.

The melding of American Indians into the general population was the expressed goal of the Indian Rights Association since its inception in the early
1880s. Founded firmly on the precepts of Christianity, individualism, and pa-

triotism, the association called for the full assimilation of Native Americans into white society. Convinced of the value of cultural pluralism, John Collier challenged the Indian Rights Association; he and other progressives took steps to organize themselves into a unified front against established federal policy framed by the association and to concentrate their effort toward the preservation of a separate, distinct, Indian identity. In 1924 Collier secured the support of Harold Ickes, himself a former progressive among New York's poor. With Hamlin Garland and William Allen White, they founded the American Indian Defense Association (AIDA). It first moved to counter the government's reduction of Pueblo Indian land holdings, but AIDA soon broadened its direction and championed a variety of Native American issues nationally, such as the end of allotments in severalty, better health and education programs, and the right of Indian self-determination.[8]

As AIDA procured mounds of information to document the deterioration of Indian reservation living standards, its members lobbied Congress and publicly railed against the Indian Rights Association and Washington's long-standing policies. Collier personally launched a series of scathing assaults against the Bureau of Indian Affairs, Congress, and the Indian Rights Association. The combined attack caught the attention of progressive politicians and generated pressure on Washington officials, at the very least, to survey Indian reservations to determine the accuracy of AIDA's allegations. In 1926 Secretary of the Interior Hubert Work commissioned the Institute of Government Research to conduct an investigation of reservation conditions. Early the following year, the Institute appointed Lewis Meriam as coordinator for a team of experts then being assembled for the task, and for the remainder of the year investigators toured reservations, interviewed individual Indians, and assessed their findings. On February 21, 1928, Meriam presented Secretary Work an 847-page report titled *The Problem of Indian Administration.* Most often referred to simply as "the Meriam Report," the document extensively detailed the conditions of Indian health, education, economics, and family life and concluded with a penetrating indictment of bureau and federal policies to date, without singling out any individual for blame. The sheer force embodied in the statistical analysis shattered the complacency of many people within Congress and stung the bureau's conscience with the realization that Native Americans were not simply vanishing but instead were slowly being strangled into nonexistence on the reservations.

Although painfully aware of the extremely poor living conditions to be found in most reservations, reformers themselves staggered under the voluminous and incriminating figures that illuminated a depth of poverty, disease, and illiteracy among Indians more serious than even they expected. The Meriam Report revealed a tuberculosis mortality rate of 26.2 percent—a level seven times greater than the general white population. Second only to tuberculosis was trachoma with a contraction rate that hovered between eighteen percent and twenty-one percent for all Native Americans. The rate of infant death further compounded the dismal picture as the Meriam team discovered that fully twenty-six percent of all Indian deaths occurred among children under one year of age. For total deaths under the age of three, the team uncovered a rate of thirty-seven percent, compared to sixteen percent for the general population. Also, venereal diseases, typhoid, pneumonia, and dysentery commonly sifted through tribes with greater frequency than among whites.[9]

Investigators cited improper diets, poorly prepared food, ignorance of preventative medicine, a lack of personal hygiene, and a general absence of sanitation on reservations as causative agents for the infection and mortality figures. Few physicians and nurses were available for Indian service, and among these men and women there was a preponderance of poorly trained, poorly paid, unconcerned, and, in some instances, unqualified personnel. Trachoma examinations witnessed by Meriam's team found doctors checking only one eye for the blinding disease. Children were "rushed through so rapidly that it is impossible to make careful diagnoses," complained one team member. Medical facilities were generally inadequate, and chest x-ray equipment was rarely on site. Indian boarding schools proved to be a microcosm of reservation health problems—hot water seldom available, soap often inaccessible, and soiled towels the rule rather than the exception. At one school, eighty girls shared two toilets. In the kitchens, dirty cooks prepared and served food on unclean dishes and "everything was covered with flies." Frequently, spoiled food was given to the children.[10]

Beyond the dismal report regarding Indian health, Meriam's team detailed a system of education that proved equally devastating. Illiteracy averaged thirty-six percent among Native Americans nationally, with some reservations peaking at sixty-seven percent of its total residents; this was in contrast to a six percent illiteracy rate for the general population. As in health care, educational facilities were declared grossly inadequate, plagued with unqualified teachers, administrators more committed to the maintenance of a strict daily regimen with severe punishment for students who crossed the boundary of established proper behavior, and a curriculum cluttered with antiquated instructional programs not immediately transferable to urban employment. The consequence was a system incompatible with the realities of the surrounding world.[11] For those who truly desired movement into mainstream white society, the academic program provided at boarding schools precluded a successful transition to the white labor force, and those who wished to return home soon discovered that the curriculum held no relevance to the reservations.

More important for immediate survival, continued loss of tribal lands reduced the already limited economic potential of most Indians who attempted farming or ranching enterprises. Acreage removed from reservations in the Northwest concurrently devalued the worth of timber and fishing industries among Indians in that region. And, tied to the problem of vanishing lands, inadequate job skills training among those young men and women returning from boarding schools to reservations guaranteed poverty. The Meriam team reported that eighty-four percent of all Indians lived on less than two hundred dollars annually. This figure did not include the earnings of child laborers under the age of fourteen, who netted between nine and fifteen cents per day. As desperate as these conditions were, Meriam's investigators projected a further decline in Indian earnings for the following decade.[12] Needless to say, *The Problem of Indian Administration* confirmed many of John Collier's earlier allegations and those offered by earlier proponents of reform such as Francis E. Leupp and Charles Rhoads. The report clearly startled members of Congress.

Meriam's findings were compounded the following year with the onset of the Great Depression. The economic crisis that crept upon the nation's agricultural communities in the early 1920s and was partially responsible for a decline in Indian income now enveloped America's industrial and manufacturing sectors. Factory closures in cities coast to coast funneled millions of workers into the long lines of the unemployed. With each passing year from 1929 to 1933, the number of banks, retail stores, professional agencies, movie houses, restaurants, and other businesses that shut their doors increased beyond comprehension for the average American. Community resources were severely strained to provide even limited relief to the growing ranks of the jobless and homeless. Under the disabling weight of massive, record-setting unemployment rates, thousands of urban Indians returned home to their reservations in search of work or to be in more familiar surroundings only to find their families more strapped by poverty than ever before. Decreasing market prices for agricultural products and cattle required many Indians to sell herds, grazing lands, and even tools simply to obtain some income. Pine Ridge and Rosebud Sioux earnings fell twenty-five percent in the opening years of the depression, from about $200 annually to $153. Much of that income resulted from service as day laborers and through the sale of handicrafts. Families sold household items such as pots, pans, blankets, rugs, furniture, and extra articles of clothing. Only these acts of desperation, along with some relief from the American Red Cross, averted outright starvation.[13]

At the local and state levels of government, Indian requests for aid often met deaf ears. Clinton Rickard, a chief among the Tuscaroras of New York, lashed out at the absence of government relief for Indians living in the state. "After all the lobbying in Congress the New York state officials had done in the past years to obtain complete jurisdiction over the Indians," he complained, "the Albany government now showed itself none too eager to provide assistance to Indians in time of crisis."[14] Rickard did not concede state jurisdiction over the Iroquois Confederacy, but he showed New York's bid for jurisdiction to be conveniently set aside during economic calamity. "All we asked [for]," he added, "was equality of opportunity with whites and other[s] in getting useful jobs so that we could support ourselves." He reminded the state legislature that historically Native Americans had provided aid and comfort to white Americans in desperate times. "When the white men first came to this continent, they were few, weak and feeble. . . . We gave them land to plant corn on for their women and children; we gave them many plant foods unknown to them such as corn, squash, beans, and many more," he said. "When famine walked among them and their little ones cried for bread, it was the Indian who gave them meat, corn, and fish. The hand that fought for the white man in all his wars was now open to him for relief," Rickard added.[15]

Albany responded with only limited aid, principally in the form of government-sponsored jobs in which a small minority of Indians gained employment. New York also collected food and clothing, and it earmarked surplus goods for the Iroquois reservations. However, Indians who found jobs with state offices were denied surplus items, and the planned general distribution of government owned garments and foodstuffs did not materialize. "During the winter," Rickard recalled years later, "some of our men suffered frozen feet and hands while working out in the cold, but this clothing sat unused in boxes" in state-controlled warehouses. Had it not been for friends and the Boy Scouts of America, he said, who "without thought of gain, collected shoes and other clothing for needy Indians, we would have been in even more desperate circumstances than we already were."[16]

Although state governments nationwide provided little relief to their native populations, or to anyone else, Washington did become more attentive. The stern, sad evidence set forth in the Meriam Report loosened the congressional hold on budget allocations. In 1930, Congress authorized additional appropriations totaling $1,440,000 for medical services on reservations. The funding provided 183 physicians, 13 trachoma specialists, 11 dentists, 149 "graduate nurses," 8 practical nurses, and 92 hospitals with a combined bed capacity of three thousand.[17]

With reservations spread from the Atlantic to the Pacific, increased facilities and personnel allowed for only a thin coverage of health care. Still, improvements in health care were visible. Late in 1931, a government survey of 17,320 Indians across twenty-four reservations concluded that the infection rate for trachoma had been reduced to eight percent, from the eighteen percent rate listed in the Meriam Report. The glowing statistic, however, proved misleading. A rate of thirty percent was discovered among Arizona Navajos, twenty percent among the Flathead and Blackfeet, and nearly thirty percent among the Apaches of San Carlos and Fort Apache, Arizona. The survey's low incidence of infection resulted principally from the inclusion of the Eastern Band of Cherokees in North Carolina, the Jicarilla Apaches, Florida's Seminoles, and several Indian communities in Wisconsin and Minnesota that showed a complete absence of the disease.[18] Positive gains did appear in the quality and quantity of health service to Native Americans as a result of rising appropriations, but, clearly, the improvements were not as sweeping as the report suggested. It was equally clear, however, that the Meriam Report had inspired a substantial body of congressmen to support increased funding for medical care on Indian reservations.

Washington officials also moved to redress the educational imbalance between Native Americans and the general population. In response, the Bureau of Indian Affairs in 1930 hired Will Carson Ryan as director of Indian Education. A nationally respected educator, Ryan previously served the United States Bureau of Education and taught at Swarthmore College. More importantly, he had personally directed Meriam's inquiry into Indian education. That document's findings and recommendations reflected his own outrage over the state of Indian education and his expectations for rapid, fundamental redirection.

Ryan initiated a three-pronged reform package: the gradual elimination of boarding schools, the establishment of reservation-based community day schools, and the development of federal-state contracts to finance Indian education programs. The new director believed that "provisions for the care of Indian children in boarding schools are grossly inadequate." Therefore, his first efforts were aimed at the closure of those institutions.[19] He planned to utilize the appropriations formerly given to boarding schools to finance the construction and operation of educational facilities on the reservations and placing children in school settings close to their families and familiar surroundings. More cost-efficient reservation day schools would also permit the purchase of modern equipment, recently published texts, and the acquisition of properly trained teachers and administrators.

Ryan further realized that the standard curriculum had to be scrapped for a more practical one reflecting the needs and experiences of Indian students and one that promised the development of job skills in a depressed national economy. With this in mind, Ryan called for a vocational training program available to Indians on each reservation with cross-cultural instruction that would make movement into white society more possible, should Indians choose to pursue assimilation. By the end of 1931, boarding-school enrollment dropped from 69,000 children to 21,677.[20] Without question, the imprint of economic depression on state and local economies curtailed funding for transportation services, school supplies, teachers and supervisory personnel, food, and utilities at boarding schools and therefore was responsible for the closure of some schools completely and a reduced program at other institutions. Nonetheless, reservation day schools were constructed with federal dollars and commenced operation under the direction Ryan provided.

The day schools were aimed at the education of both children and adults. For the older students, Ryan envisioned courses related to home budgeting, food preservation, sewing, personal hygiene, community sanitation, first aid, English language development, and job-skill training. Such facilities functioned as community centers for each reservation, which brought the entire tribe into the educational experience.

Although motivated by a sincere desire to provide Indians with a viable educational framework suited for movement into urban areas or continued residency on the reservation, Ryan's work garnered only minimal gains in the early 1930s. Of nearly 250 boarding schools in operation at the time of his appointment, only six were completely closed by 1933. Ryan faced an Indian Bureau reluctant to make fundamental change and a national economic crisis that limited funding and kept most reservation day schools on the drawing board. Within the boarding-school structure itself, Ryan faced an imposing wall of resistance. Administrators generally refused to implement the curriculum dictated by Ryan and maintained established discipline and food service practices in defiance of Ryan's directives. Most administrators were entrenched in their positions and resented the director's interference with standard operating procedures. His policies were frequently viewed as impediments to the schools' objectives of instilling patriotism, discipline, and Christianity. With administrators hostile to Ryan's goal of cross-cultural and practical instruction, little change emerged within boarding schools.[21]

Without a strong, pan-Indian movement to pressure the bureau into addressing their most serious concerns and with no expectation of an economic remedy to the national financial crisis by the Republican administration in Washington, Native Americans watched the presidential campaign of 1932 with cautious optimism. Preceding administrations had either ignored reservation conditions or provided superficial reforms. As a result, Franklin Delano Roosevelt's vague promise of a new deal swayed few Indians. Still, his recognition of America's forgotten man in the midst of economic uncertainties, along with his assurance of immediate federal intervention to aid all segments of society, did stimulate some hope among Indians for a Democratic victory in November. As election day drew closer, a defeat for the Hoover administration seemed to hold the only possibility for substantial improvements in Indian living conditions; it would have been quite difficult in 1932 for conditions to deteriorate further.

Roosevelt's march into the White House heightened Indian expectations for some measure of relief, especially once the new president announced Harold Ickes as his choice for secretary of the Interior. Ickes was a nationally recognized progressive reformer, cofounder of the American Indian Defense Association, ardent critic of the Bureau of Indian Affairs, and advocate for a fundamental redirection in federal Indian policy. Findings presented in the Meriam Report horrified him, and he relentlessly called on Congress to raise appropriations for Indian programs along with greater scrutiny of bureau officials who handled federal dollars. Now, as secretary of the Interior, Ickes soon provided evidence of his intention to "clean house" within the BIA. He appointed John Collier as commissioner of Indian Affairs, and, once confirmation was granted by the Senate in April 1933, Indians had two outspoken proponents for radical change in key federal positions.

Collier wasted little time in formulating a new direction for the BIA; his ideas for reform were first laid in the early 1920s. Throughout spring and summer, the commissioner honed his objectives and took cues from Roosevelt's evolving economic strategy. Patterned after the president's national program for relief, recovery, and reform, Collier laid the foundation for an "Indian New Deal" specifically to address Native American issues. Under this overarching banner, the commissioner intended to advance reform through two separate channels. The first, and perhaps the easier, was to lobby Congress for increased appropriations and solicit supplemental funds from other federal agencies in order to finance reservation reconstruction. Money secured from these sources would be used to purchase additional acreage for tribal communities, reforest lands, lay irrigation systems, provide a network of roads on reservations, construct health centers capable of serving most Indians, and expand Ryan's vision of reservation day schools.

At the same time, Collier promoted congressional passage of a bill that would structurally alter the very foundation of federal Indian policy. Late that summer, Collier met with Senator Burton K. Wheeler of Montana and Congressman Edgar Howard of Nebraska, both Democrats who served on the Indian Affairs Committee in their respective houses. He explained his long-standing opposition to the BIA, highlighted findings cited in the Meriam Report, and encouraged the two men to co-sponsor a bill to end the damaging impact of previous federal Indian policy. Convinced of the urgent need to improve Indian living conditions, both men agreed to support Collier's direction and to introduce the commissioner's plan to Congress under their sponsorship.[22]

The Wheeler-Howard Bill recommended an immediate end to the system of individual land allotments passed by Congress in 1887 and a halt to further reduction of Indian land holdings under powers granted by congressional acts and court decisions.[23] Under the proposed legislation, Indian lands would be entrusted to the tribal unit and dispersed according to local preference. Connected to this feature, congressional appropriations for the purchase of additional acreage and a revolving credit fund through which tribes could borrow money for agricultural development were guaranteed. The bill also proposed that federal dollars provide for land reclamation, improvements in health-care services, an education system conducive to Indian needs, and full utilization of Indian resources for the direct benefit of Native Americans. While many of the specific items to be financed were also planned for in Collier's supplemental funding design, the weight of federal law in the form of the Wheeler-Howard Act would allow the commissioner to extend his influence into outside sources of money. Politically, the plan permitted each tribe its own constitution and the legal status of a semi-autonomous, incorporated unit when dealing with state and federal levels of government.

The proposed legislation, titled the Indian Reorganization Act (IRA), marked a radical departure from previous federal Indian policy and represented a culmination of earlier reform efforts. The extent of funding planned for individual Indians and reservations surpassed earlier allocations. A complete overhaul of government services was intended through increased appropriations. The bill's provision for self-determination granted Indians a measure of control over their own destinies—assimilation or the retention of tribal structures. Most striking of all, and directly counter to historic bureau procedures, the bill allowed each individual tribal organization to accept or to reject the legislation once passed by Congress. At no other time in their relations with the United States had Native Americans been permitted the opportunity to deny the implementation of any policy.

A complete redirection in Indian affairs was outlined in the Wheeler-Howard Act. It intended to destroy the "vicious circle" in which American Indians historically found themselves—a circle of stereotyped images, insufficient skills for employment off the reservation, and a constant loss of land and resources that precluded tribal economic security. This vision had been with Collier for nearly a decade by the time he assumed the position of commissioner, and in 1933 he confidently asserted that the IRA provided the organization, money, and "invention" necessary to accomplish the goal.[24]

When presented to the United States Senate, the bill was passed without amendments or deletions. The House of Representatives, however, took exception to the provision that sanctioned the consolidation of Indian lands into tribal ownership. Such a move, voiced a majority of congressmen, denied the opportunity for private-property ownership among the more acculturated, assimilationist-bound Indians. Moreover, common ownership countered traditional American values. After the removal of that one section, the bill received approval in the House and became law in June 1934.[25]

Collier expected the Indian Reorganization Act to receive a ringing endorsement from Native Americans nationally; instead, Indians answered with mixed responses. In discussions among some Arapahos, the IRA was lauded as a "better governmental break than ever." The act allowed the Indian the opportunity "to participate actively in his own problems and in the common good." Said one tribal council member, the new policy would create "the first intelligent system of Indian education . . . ever offered" and a "practical method of guaranteeing to all tribes the ability to learn to run their own affairs."[26] Indians recognized and welcomed the elevated appropriations promised under the act, the reclamation of reservation lands, the addition of acreage to tribal holdings, expanded health and educational services, Collier's validation of traditional culture and values, and the unique opportunity to accept or reject the new policy. On these points, few Indians could oppose the IRA.

Nonetheless, the widespread enthusiasm Collier expected among Indians failed to materialize. Federal Indian policy over the preceding century seldom benefited the native population; altered directions in policy typically signaled further loss of land and cultural disintegration among tribal communities. Not surprisingly, then, passage of the IRA spawned considerable cynicism throughout the Indian population nationwide. "There is some big wolf circling around to see its way to take what we have got," said one Arapaho. A desire "to be left alone just where we are" manifested itself from the moment the bill first appeared on the congressional floor.[27] Given the historic relationship between Indians and whites and the lengthy list of broken treaties, it seemed unlikely that the IRA was anything but another disguise through which Washington could erode further the position of Indians in America.

Collier's contention that the IRA validated traditional cultures and values was also challenged by many Indians. The Iroquois Confederacy argued, as did many tribes, that having a written constitution itself countered the very tradition of self-government that the commissioner promised to protect. Beyond this, the political structure to be erected in tribal groups that accepted the IRA was not of Indian origin and, therefore, demonstrated the act's contradictory position on self-government.[28] A constitution and political system created under the guidance of white structures, one that required federal government approval, could not accurately represent tribal values. In addition, left intact by the IRA would be the reservation system, superintendents appointed by the Interior Department, and the Bureau of Indian Affairs' continued management. Retained would be the paternalism of Congress and federal agencies. "The IRA did not allow the Indians their independence. . . . It did not protect their sovereignty," complained Rupert Costo, a Cahuilla from California and later president of the American Indian Historical Society.[29]

The maintenance of established treaties seemed to be the preferred course for many tribal groups. The Quapaw of Oklahoma battled the IRA and held firm to the position that "We have a treaty with the United States, describing by metes and bounds the size and shape of our allotments, and it states that its purpose is to provide a permanent home for the nation." The Yakima tribal council drafted a statement of opposition to the IRA that sounded a similar rebuttal to the new policy. "We feel that the best interests of the Indians can be preserved by the continuance of treaty laws" entered into with the United States. Yakima Indians demanded the Treaty of 1855 not be circumvented by the IRA. Farther east, in New York, the Oneida Indians of the Iroquois Confederacy insisted that Washington honor "the terms of the Treaty of Canandaigua between our nation, our confederacy, and the United States of November 11, 1794."[30] In their rejection of the IRA, the assumption was that existing treaties with the United States government would remain in force; when America entered World War II, Indians learned that Congress held the authority to invalidate all treaties at will.

The most vocal opposition centered on another issue. Although Collier's program was putatively intended for the Indians' benefit, it actually ignored realities of Native American life. Traditional American Indian cultures had been supplanted by the reservation system one century earlier. Numerous ceremonies had long vanished under the constraints of Christian education and denominational oversight of reservations, and many Native Americans had accepted the Christian religion as their own. Traditional values such as community welfare and the common use of land faded under the strictures of individualism and the system of land allotment. This was extended into America's territorial possessions as well. Alaskan natives had never experienced a reservation system, but their long-standing relationship with whites resulted in a widely held affinity for the individual work ethic and assimilation. For many Native Americans, there was no return to traditional forms; only through assimilation could Indians survive.

Among the earliest Indian critics of the IRA to express such a perspective was the Navajo Jacob C. Morgan. Active in tribal affairs on the Navajo Reservation, creator of the Navajo Progressive League in 1918, and an avowed assimilationist, Morgan viewed the IRA as a means for continued subjugation of the native population. Rather than a forward movement for Indians, the act pushed tribal groupings "a step backward," he said. Morgan based his contention on the realities of current Navajo existence. The tribal population had increased from about eight thousand to forty-three thousand over the preceding sixty years. During that time, land holdings remained constant—fully two-thirds of which included desert land. As the man-to-arable-soil ratio declined, poverty only worsened. Housing proved insufficient and usually consisted of a single room, dirt floor, and no window. Ignorance of basic health care and sanitation prevented longevity rates similar to other minorities. By promoting the revitalization of traditional cultural values rather than assimilation, the IRA would perpetuate Navajo poverty. "Our future under this plan," Morgan asserted, "is a sunset" for the Navajo people.[31]

Morgan and others believed that the Indians' only avenue for ending the stagnant condition in which they existed rested in education and off-reservation employment. Boarding schools armed Indian children with the English language, job skills, and indoctrination into white values—all necessary for self-improvement and the anticipated movement into white society. The commissioner's plan for an educational system that would "begin at home, in relation to tribal needs . . . and start from the base of the Indians' own traditions, culture, and pride" would, Morgan contended, halt Indian movement into mainstream America and force continued residency on poverty-ridden reservations. Additionally, the act's focus on self-government, herd management, farming, mineral extraction, and forestry by "local effort and initiative" generated little possibility for actual advancement. Some white opponents of the

Wheeler-Howard Act concurred with Morgan and his supporters; Collier's IRA "does not give Indians much leeway not to be Indian, and to walk Main Street like the rest of us."[32]

Despite the amount of opposition lodged against the IRA nationally and within individual tribal councils, the majority of tribes responded favorably to the act. Of the 263 councils voting on the measure, 192 accepted it. Two distinct patterns emerged. First, acceptance of the IRA was typically by a narrow margin, a margin based more on hope than on any single feature of the IRA and one achieved due, in part, to widespread nonparticipation in the voting process. Among the Arapahos, for example, one-third of the voting Indians rejected the IRA. It was argued at the time that if all eligible voters had cast their ballots, the IRA could have been defeated. Among the Shoshones, a one-vote margin in favor of policy redirection kept the issue alive until absentee ballots were tallied. Once the ballots were counted, the IRA met defeat.[33]

Second, those who voted to reject the act generally feared the loss of something valuable to the larger tribe. Tribes that had experienced minimal contact with white society and remained more tightly wedded to traditional values generally denounced the IRA. With limited interference from Washington over the years, their cultures remained virtually unchanged. The revitalization of traditional native customs and values as promised in the IRA seemed irrelevant. An improved educational and health program, increased federal appropriations, and self-government had little importance to communities that, without interruption, had cared for themselves and directed their own affairs. In this environment, many Native Americans suspected a darker objective in the IRA, feared Washington's creeping hand into their relatively autonomous lives, and decided not to accept Collier's program. On both coasts were tribes that preferred the continuation of established treaties with the federal government, and Indians who had prepared themselves for assimilation saw in the IRA a virtual return to the blanket and a wall impenetrable for movement into mainstream American society.

Collier personally visited reservations where passage seemed doubtful. He availed himself for questions, clarified specific provisions within the IRA, and reassured councils that the act permitted both the revitalization of traditional culture and a pathway for assimilation, whichever the tribe or individuals within the tribe preferred. The commissioner's presence often tilted the balance in favor of the IRA in tribal elections. Equally important, councils that delayed voting witnessed the implementation of reform programs and IRA provisions among other tribal groups. With federal dollars flowing more freely into those communities and redevelopment of tribal resources commencing, many Indians soon accepted the sincerity of Collier's reform movement and voted to approve the IRA.

Between 1934 and 1940, Collier and the Indian Reorganization Act advanced reservation-based health-care services and initiated a concentrated effort to educate Indians in personal hygiene. Substantial change materialized. By the end of the decade, the Indian Health Service employed two hundred full-time physicians in reservation residency, one hundred seventy-five part-time doctors, and numerous specialists and consultants. Eight hundred graduate and public health nurses worked in the field, with an additional thirteen hundred employees who provided health education and management of medical facilities. Moreover, ninety-seven full-service hospitals operated with a bed capacity of five thousand. By 1940, an estimated sixty-four thousand Indians received inpatient care annually with another one million visits as outpatients.[34]

In a 1938 *Scientific Monthly* article, Dr. James G. Townsend reported that in the first year of Collier's administration, the tuberculosis infection rate on reservations dropped from twenty-six percent to fifteen percent. Further decreases occurred in each of the three succeeding years. Townsend noted that late in 1937 and throughout much of 1938 the TB infection rate did reverse course and inch upwards, but the pattern reflected positive development. Rather than a resurgence of tuberculosis, the increase actually reflected the expansion of medical service and equipment capable of detecting the disease where no such ability previously existed. This confirmed the Indian Bureau's success in spreading health care to Indian populations.[35] Similar patterns of improvement surfaced among trachoma patients and Indians saddled with diabetes and other health problems.

Dr. J. R. McGibony, assistant surgeon general of the United States and director of health for the Office of Indian Affairs, concurred with Townsend's assessment. A "greater proportion of Indians had x-ray examinations of the chest," he explained, "because of the availability of facilities and a continuous education campaign." Like Townsend, McGibony was not alarmed by the upturn of infection rates but was instead delighted that the movement illuminated a pattern of improved health care among Indians.[36]

On the eve of America's entry into World War II, the state of Native American health nationally more closely resembled the general population than ever before; medical exams for Indians being inducted into the armed forces showed a marked closure of the gap between whites and Native Americans. For the year 1941, 37.5 percent of all Indians called into military service were rejected for health related reasons. This compared favorably to a thirty-two percent rejection rate for white recruits. Only thirteen percent of Native Americans failed entry medical examinations for tuberculosis or trachoma.[37] The gross disparity between whites and Indians in personal health had narrowed significantly during Collier's first seven years as commissioner of Indian Affairs and highlighted the achievements made under the IRA's banner.

Partially responsible for the improvement of reservation health standards was education. Much effort had been expended in providing reservation Indians with basic knowledge of personal and community hygiene, sanitation, and food preparation. But Collier hoped the emphasis on health-related instruction could be extended to the broader education program itself as a standard course of instruction in the boarding schools and reservation day schools. By the time the United States entered World War II, the Indian Education Service required students to complete coursework related to personal and community health.

The Indian Education Service had already experienced some redirection under the leadership of Will Carson Ryan before Collier's appointment as commissioner. Collier initially retained Ryan as director of Indian Education, but the director's determination to replace boarding schools with a reservation-based day-school program and his plan to alter significantly the curriculum of Indian education only hardened the resistance to change among entrenched school administrators. To press his program for educational reform, Collier recognized the need to replace Ryan with a director more capable of confronting hard-liners and compelling redirection. The commissioner selected Willard Walcott Beatty, whose forceful character and sharp administrative skills promised control over recalcitrant Indian school administrators.

Aware that immediate and complete closure of all boarding schools was impractical, Collier and Beatty laid plans to reduce their number gradually and to improve the quality of education in those left operational. Coupled with the overhaul in boarding schools was the continuation of community day-school construction initiated by Ryan, the expansion of services to Indians living in remote regions, and a determination to create cross-cultural and bilingual programs. Collier believed that each of these components was essential to bring the full impact of the Indian Reorganization Act to the native population.

The commissioner and new director wasted little time. By the end of 1935, ten boarding schools had either closed their doors permanently or had been transformed into community day schools. Among those transformed was Haskell Institute, located in Kansas. Beatty replaced its superintendent with Henry Roe Cloud, the first of many Indians who assumed administrative posts in the education division under Collier. Rather than maintain the institute's military regimen and classical education, Henry Roe Cloud charted a curriculum of practical instruction for the development of future Indian leaders. Among his earliest actions was the dismissal of the school's football coach, noted for his harsh disciplinary tactics, and the severance of Haskell's ties with the National Guard, which had supplied officers, instructors, uniforms, dummy weapons, and a military code of conduct.[38]

Other boarding schools soon followed the example set by Haskell. In 1936 the Santa Fe Boarding School ceased its military connections, after which, according to interviewed students, the institution became "more tolerable." The Boy's Advisor at the Albuquerque Indian School sounded a similar note stating that "we find a different atmosphere through the entire plant; there is more home life and more student participation." Of primary importance was the introduction of practical education—teaching those subjects that would permit students to assimilate into white society or return to reservations armed with skills and knowledge beneficial to their Indian communities.[39]

On reservations, Collier and Beatty extended educational services to adult men and women under the Community Day School Program. Local facilities offered training in the English language, personal hygiene, cooking, sewing, farming, and job skill development. Often, the schools served as the center of tribal activity. As day-school construction increased and the number of student programs expanded, children began to receive the same basic practical education presented in boarding-school settings but within the reservation environment. This allowed children to remain at home with their parents and not break the family bond.

Contrary to critics, community day schools proved cost-efficient. The child living in a boarding school required a four-hundred-dollar annual expense, while day-school costs totaled half that amount. Collier's program resulted in an increased educational opportunity for more Indian children and adults. Two hundred twenty-six community day schools were in service by 1940. Among the Navajo alone, Collier and Beatty's program allowed six thousand more children to receive an education.[40]

Expanded services required a larger number of teachers and trained personnel. In 1936 Beatty implemented an instructor-training course to cultivate recent college graduates for positions in the Indian Education Division. Funded directly by Congress, recruits entered a two-year training period during which time prospective teachers studied Indian cultures, history, and language in addition to progressive education methods and field techniques. Many new teachers, caught in the spirit of reform, far exceeded the expectations of reservation superintendents by working longer hours, traveling to remote areas to reach individual families, and creating mobile libraries.

Not all tribal groups experienced the same depth of reform. Congressional appropriations, although much greater than under previous administrations, still fell short of actual need. This was compounded by a numerical rise within the Indian population during the 1930s, a growth that reflected improved medical care and a reduction of infant mortality. The population increase surpassed the bureau's ability to provide educational services. An added problem surfaced. Low salaries forced many teachers and school administrators into private industry and discouraged others from entering service in Indian education. In spite of these difficulties, more progress had been realized in Collier's first seven years as commissioner than under any previous commissioner. As Americans steeled themselves for war in 1941, Indians found greater opportunities in specialized military training because of the educational foundation laid under the IRA and its support programs.

To supplement health and education reform, Collier hoped to stimulate economic development of the reservations as well. As the IRA made its way through Congress in 1934, the Indian Bureau encouraged and funded instruction in the marketing of crops and homemade items, home management, and basic budgeting skills. "I recall thinking at the time," said Fools Crow, a Sioux, "that we have been living on less than a budget already. Poverty of the worst kind was our daily companion." The commissioner's program, however, energized reservation economies and elevated both personal and tribal income.[41]

Specialized courses surpassed simple instruction in domestic matters; the commissioner moved to include Indian participation in President Roosevelt's Civilian Conservation Corps (CCC), which won congressional support in the spring of 1933. Collier urged Secretary of the Interior Harold Ickes to present the matter to FDR personally and to encourage the formation of a separate, Indian-only, subdivision. Ickes complied with the commissioner's request and stressed to the president the Indians' immediate need for economic rehabilitation. In particular, Indian reservations desperately required reforestation, soil erosion controls, and the restoration of grazing lands. He cautioned Roosevelt that the employment of white workers on Indian lands might net the desired physical changes, but the exclusion of Indian workers might also spawn tribal resentment. Direct Indian participation in the Civilian Conservation Corps would result in vital training conducive to reservation maintenance and possible employment off the reservation. As a subdivision of the CCC, a separate Indian division would accommodate cultural variances and special needs faced by Indian men. President Roosevelt sanctioned the creation of the Civilian Conservation Corps—Indian Division (CCC-ID) exclusively for Indian participants, although administrative posts would initially be held by whites. Funding permitted 14,400 Indian enrollees for the first six months, with appropriations fixed at $5,875,000.[42]

The CCC-ID fit well into Collier's broader reform package. Its purpose was to supply immediate financial relief to participants and vocational training, which could be utilized on or off the reservation. Money earned through the federal works program would stimulate tribal economic ventures, and the conservation efforts would directly contribute to the revitalization of Indian lands. In addition, tribal councils would have direct input in determining which projects were most necessary on the reservation, a feature that generated widespread enthusiasm among Indians.

By July 1933, fifty-six reservations commenced project work. To compensate for the peculiar needs of its enrollees and to accommodate as many Indians as possible, CCC-ID requirements governing enrollment proved less restrictive than the parent organization's governance of white and African American enrollees. Marital status was no barrier for Indian participation in the program. Individual camps bypassed the 200- to 225-man limit imposed on the national organ. Age restrictions, eighteen to twenty-five years in the CCC, were waived for Native Americans, as was the limitation to a single, six-month period of enrollment. As with the national organization, the CCC-ID operated a "boarding camp" for Indians in which workers resided on the project site, received room and board, and had paychecks mailed home. However, the CCC-ID also sponsored "family camps" and "commuting projects" that enabled a participant to work and gain job-skills training yet retain his home and any source of income his land provided.[43]

Between 1934 and 1941, nearly eighty thousand Indians worked under the direction of the CCC-ID. Their labor resulted in the creation of 6,200 springs and small reservoirs, 1,350 wells, 1,064 impounding dams and large reservoirs, 900 vehicle bridges, 7,000 miles of truck trails, 2,500 miles of fire breaks, and ninety ranger lookout stations. More than 6,500 miles of telephone lines had been stretched, one million acres received pest control treatment, and two hundred fifty thousand acres were cleared of poisonous weeds. Seventy reservations participated in the program, and they benefited from improved irrigation systems, revitalized grazing lands, a reduction in timber loss from forest fires and insect damage, and less soil erosion. Individuals learned specific job skills and took classes to strengthen their abilities in math, home finance, and English. Supervisory and administrative talents emerged as more than two-thirds of such positions fell under Indian control by late 1941. These personal advances not only were transferable to jobs in white communities but also gave Native

Americans a "new self-confidence because of the assurance of the faith of others in their ability to work and direct the work of others."[44]

While the CCC-ID furnished desperately needed physical improvements to reservations and supplied some financial security among Indians, land ownership remained a serious problem. By 1933, Indians controlled only forty-nine million acres of the two hundred fifty million acres they owned in 1880, a loss that resulted from the conversion of Native American holdings into public lands, the abrogation of treaty provisions, and bureau revisions in its power to lease and sell tribal property. The historic pattern of Indian allotments being sold to white speculators accounted for much of the loss of Indian lands.[45]

Years of poverty and destitution motivated individuals to sell their allotments. When asked what became of his property, one young Chippewa simply replied: "Someone talked me into selling." With the cash, he added, "I got me a car. And I got some liquor. I smashed up the car. Now all I got is the pants I stand up in."[46] Often paid less than fair market value, the cash transaction usually represented more money than the allottee had ever held. Unaware of basic investment opportunities or simple budgeting skills, and with little or no regular income, the paltry profits vanished quickly and many Indians found themselves both poor and landless. One observer in 1935 estimated that one hundred thousand Indians were without land holdings, a figure representing slightly less than one-third of the Native American population.[47]

Those who retained their land, especially those who resided on reservations in the Great Plains, generally failed to produce harvests sufficient for subsistence. Agricultural skills and farm equipment eluded Indians. In addition, there existed little arable land. Individual allotments remained small in an environment that required extensive acreage for primitive farming. Since the 1880s, the federal government realized that a minimum of four hundred acres was necessary for successful, family-oriented farming in the Great Plains; as late as 1935, agricultural experts working for the federal government added that "a 160-tract is, of course, pathetically inadequate to support a family." Indian farmers in the region typically owned far less.[48]

The Indian Reorganization Act addressed Native American agricultural concerns and promised the acquisition of land for Indian ownership. It authorized Washington to purchase lands adjacent to reservations and to cede those territories to tribal councils. The Bureau of Indian Affairs also received permission to restore certain lands to tribal ownership that had earlier been reclaimed by the federal government. Under these provisions, millions of acres were returned to Indian control. The Shoshone and Arapaho, for example, together gained

1,250,000 acres for joint ownership in April 1940. An additional 1,200,000 acres were acquired for Native Americans at a cost of six million dollars as a result of John Collier tapping into provisions for land distribution through the Resettlement Administration.[49]

To make the land productive and profitable for Indians, the IRA established a revolving credit fund of ten million dollars. Under its provisions, the government was allowed to issue large loans to tribal councils from which individual Indians could borrow money to purchase tools, equipment, seed, and other necessities for productive farming. A long-term repayment schedule at three percent interest induced many Indians to seek tribal loans. By 1940, half of the allocated credit had been issued.[50] Field agents from the Department of Agriculture offered personal advice to Indian farmers, reservation day schools gave instruction in food preservation, and activities of the CCC-ID extended irrigation systems to embrace more Indian lands. With money available, personal oversight by farm agents, support through the developing educational system, land reclamation, and the acquisition of additional acreage, reservation-based agriculture realized a noticeable and positive redirection prior to World War II.

Cattle and sheep ranching also benefited under Collier's administration of the BIA. Acreage gains physically extended the range for grazing; however, much of that land required improvements. Collier and the Soil Conservation Service (SCS), a division of the Department of Agriculture, combined funds to implement erosion control efforts, irrigation projects, and the sowing of grassland. Although the money originated with the SCS, the work itself was performed by the CCC-ID. Through the revolving loan fund, tribal councils and individual ranchers borrowed nine hundred thousand dollars for the purchase of additional cattle. The Rosebud Sioux Reservation alone received three hundred head of cattle and a fifteen percent increase in grazing land; this, noted tribal chairman Antoine Roubideaux, generated a rebirth of the reservation's ranching industry and brought more money into the hands of Sioux ranchers before World War II.[51]

Among Navajo ranchers, the problem was not one of insufficient herds but an overabundant supply of cattle and sheep. Excessive grazing carried the potential for financial ruin as underfed cattle and sheep brought lower market prices. The commissioner's response to the Navajo predicament was stock reduction, combined with the purchase of additional lands, reseeding, irrigation, and the construction of wells. Although the size of herds would decline, livestock would be of a higher quality and net greater profits at market.

Many Navajos failed to comprehend the logic of stock reduction. Traditionally, individual wealth within the tribe was determined, in part, by the size of one's herd. Stock reduction threatened the basis of Indian status in the community and potentially undermined the structure of Navajo society itself. Economically, it made little sense to many Navajos that greater profits would result from fewer sheep or cattle. For those who did understand Collier's plan, charges of paternalism echoed across the reservation. Their denunciation of the plan and the BIA was aimed at Collier's interference in tribal self-determination, the overarching goal of the Indian Reorganization Act. Despite Indian objections, Collier implemented the program and only later received a muted concurrence from the Navajo Tribal Council—an acquiescence grudgingly given following President Roosevelt's direct appeal to tribal members. In a personal letter to the Navajo Council, the president indicated the program was absolutely essential to protect tribal lands. The numerical reduction of sheep, goats, cattle, and horses would permit the growth of larger grasslands and, as a result, allow herds to fatten and bring higher market prices. Roosevelt acknowledged the short-term sacrifice among Navajo ranchers but promised long-term benefits.[52]

Stock reduction garnered the effects the BIA intended. Twenty-five percent of the Navajo herds were reduced, which, when coupled with additional acreage and land development, drove cattle values upward. The net price per head leaped $6.50. Sheep reductions encouraged a similar pattern. Although the Navajo owned one hundred twenty thousand fewer sheep in 1941 than they had in 1935, wool production increased from two million pounds annually to three million pounds. On a national level between 1933 and 1939, the number of Native Americans owning cattle actually doubled, principally the product of the revolving loan fund. The number of steer was raised from 167,373 to 267,551. Income earned from the cattle industry alone jumped from $263,000 to $3,125,000 annually.[53] Certainly the entire nation fared much better economically in 1939 than in 1933; however, Native American finances and their prospects of further advances never before appeared so bright and were a direct result of changes brought by Collier's leadership.

On the eve of World War II, Native Americans could point to numerous positive alterations to their living standards—changes accomplished under the Indian New Deal. Acreage under Indian ownership was considerably greater, lands were more capable of sustaining agricultural pursuits, and profits from ranching and farming witnessed dramatic growth. Forest fires on reservations were less frequent, transportation across tribal lands improved, insects became less troublesome, and water was substantially more available. The physical conservation of Native American lands proved a prominent feature of the Indian New Deal; the redevelopment of Indian land, soil, water, and vegetation received significant investment in the years just before World War II.

Critics have argued correctly that much of the economic prosperity Indians gained prior to and during World War II proved artificial, initially sustained by federally funded programs and, later, by the industrial demands of modern warfare. Nonetheless, the immediate flow of cash into Indian hands and the concurrent development of job skills were lifesavers for a minority drowning in poverty and destitution. Reared on the Rosebud Sioux Reservation, Benjamin Reifel recalled years later that before the IRA "we had the most sickening poverty that one could imagine." Many Indians survived by eating their horses. "Impoverishment was everywhere." On the Qualla Cherokee Reservation in western North Carolina, a federal census-taker in 1930 described the Cherokee dwellings as being "worse than filthy; no furnishings, and not fit for a hog pen—garbage knee deep about the house; offensive odors" commonplace. "Flies in droves; sanitation uncared for." "Webster," the official added, "does not list words that will describe this place. . . . I don't see how they live and they are not living, but just existing." Philleo Nash, who worked as an anthropologist among Indians in the 1930s and was appointed commissioner of Indian Affairs in 1961, agreed that reservation living conditions were deplorable before implementation of the IRA and Collier's supplemental programs for reform. Policy redirection, along with active involvement and direct aid given by the BIA under Collier, reversed those conditions throughout the 1930s and in the early war years. It was imperative that something be done. According to Nash, many Indians viewed the reform effort of the 1930s "like the old man who approached death. He said the alternative to getting old is much worse. The tribes were dying in 1932." The IRA, Nash said, saved American Indians from probable extinction.[54]

During Collier's administration, nearly eighty thousand Indian men secured employment and job training through the CCC-ID. Thousands of Native Americans gained employment in the Bureau of Indian Affairs itself, an opportunity historically closed to them. With tribal economies bolstered by the IRA and its secondary programs, the average annual income for Indians nationally in 1939 sat at $576, a figure three times higher than just six years earlier.

In the decade before World War II, health-care facilities and services experienced remarkable expansion, and educational programs not only served more children and adults but also proved more relevant to the Indians' actual needs. Noted one observer, "by and large, an increased devotion to the *idea* of education resulted" from the IRA and the reformist spirit that swirled around Indian reservations in the pre–World War II years. Benjamin Reifel echoed the sentiment. Speaking in 1986, he credited the IRA's educational program with an increased desire among Indians for academic and vocational training; "we now have more young men and women in universities and colleges" than before the IRA. "When I was in college in 1928," he continued, "I could count the number of Indian students . . . on the fingers of your hand."[55]

Between 1933 and 1940, reservations underwent a face-lift and, on the eve of World War II, held the potential for further tribal progress. Although substantial improvements in reservation life and a redirection in federal Indian policy appeared haphazard, settling onto some reservations while completely bypassing others, the work of reform, planned, organized, and instituted under John Collier's direction, raised Indians' expectations of survival and self-determination. Certainly the IRA was not intended by the commissioner to have assimilationist-oriented goals. He was not an assimilationist. Nonetheless, "if Indians acquired economic knowledge through their own tribal businesses and acquired political savvy in IRA tribal councils, they would be able to relate better to mainstream society."[56] Armed with job skills, work experience, and, in some cases, administrative and supervisory experience, those who desired movement into mainstream society found it much easier to make the transition. With a sound educational foundation, better health, and fewer worries for families remaining on the reservation, more Indians would make the move to off-reservation employment and residency. Concurrently, the IRA's emphasis on tribal redevelopment, its protection of traditional values, and its intention to allow Indians the right of self-government carried the promise of a revitalized and semi-independent community in which Indians could choose continued residency. Oliver LaFarge credited Collier's Indian Reorganization Act and his supplemental reform programs with altering the course of Native American survival. "Despite much backfiring and waste motion," he said, "the program does move forward primarily because the leaders in the Indian Office and in Congress really care." LaFarge, however, added that improvements in Indian welfare were at best tenuous; "it could be upset by anything from the results of another election to trouble in the silver bloc."[57]

As the decade of the thirties drew to a close, the nation's heavy industries commenced conversion to war-related manufacturing. Passage of the Selective Service and Training Act in September 1940, the registration and drafting of men into military service that soon followed, congressional authorization of the Lend-Lease Act the following March, and the formation of the Office of Civilian Defense at about the same time, all pointed to America's collision course with another war in Europe. Reluctantly, Americans concluded by mid-1941 that the United States' participation was inevitable. The positive changes in the lives of so many Indians—as individuals and as tribal communities—impressed upon Native Americans a sense of inclusion with the general population and a sense of national identity. The Indian Reorganization Act failed to solve numerous problems; in fact, it often increased tension between Indians and the federal government and constantly served as the cause for argument and debate. In spite of this, a redirection in Indian affairs was clearly visible. In 1941, Native Americans could scan the preceding one hundred years and find no better example of a sustained and sincere reformist spirit than that which had occurred over the previous decade. As the United States marshaled its energies and resources for war, and soon thereafter directly entered the holocaust, American Indians were situated in a position not originally intended by John Collier; they stood at the proverbial crossroads. In possession of skills, experiences, and knowledge gained under Collier's programs, many Indians recognized an enhanced opportunity for assimilation with white society through wartime service in the armed forces or on the home front. Others believed the commissioner's work breathed a renewed life into more traditional tribal structures and values and encouraged a continuation of a separate Indian identity and existence apart from mainstream American life. In either case, Worl War II would determine the Indians' direction.

Two

Nazi Propaganda
among American Indians

From its inception the Indian Reorganization Act (IRA) provoked fiery criticism from numerous quarters within the American population. Most opponents perceived Collier's program as a reversal of federal Indian policy from the goal of eventual assimilation of Indians into mainstream society to one of reinvigorated tribalism and an Indian identity separate and apart from the general population. The IRA, it was argued, contradicted fundamental values housed in the Dawes Severalty Act and in reform activities over the preceding fifty years. It appeared to counter the melting pot theory to which Americans gave verbal credence, although Jim Crow and Social Darwinism remained supreme in practice. Nazi Germany, however, believed something far more sinister was afoot.

Hitler's propagandists purveyed the warning that President Roosevelt's New Deal in fact heralded the advent of communism in the United States. More specifically, Nazis pointed to the Indian Reorganization Act as one of the most visibly communist-oriented programs of the FDR agenda. Emphasized as evidence was the act's promotion of traditional communal values and community structures as well as tribal ownership of property. The IRA's provisions clearly pointed to a concerted effort by the Roosevelt administration to instill communism first within American Indian communities and later into the broader society nationwide. To combat the obvious bend to the extreme political left, the German propaganda ministry midway through the decade initiated an effort to lure American Indians into a favorable view of Nazism. Hitler understood that should war ever erupt between Germany and the United States, full American national unity would be impossible to achieve if anticommunist, anti-New Deal propaganda commanded a firm base in the States.

Nazi propagandists linked the communist path to which FDR ostensibly committed America with the "Jewish world plot" and racism. Hitler's view of nationhood rested not only on a foundation of economic and military greatness but also on the "racial cohesion of the people."[1] Although American Indians comprised an inferior race in the eyes of Nazi ideological purists, they nonetheless had been victimized by world Jewry. American Jews, for personal financial gain, contended Nazis, shattered the racial cohesion of Native Americans by exploiting divisions among Indians and destroying native cultures. As Germany had pledged an offensive to combat the Jewish world menace, Nazis could not permit further exploitation of Indians by Jewish-controlled America. Propagandists proclaimed that German culture and Nazi ideology would rid the globe of Jewish domination.

This principle of Nazi ideology had first been applied to Japan. In *Mein Kampf* Hitler repeatedly stressed the innate inferiority of the Japanese people. He speculated that should Germany withdraw its resources, technology, and investments from Japan, that nation's economic and cultural advancement would collapse, returning Japan to an inferior state. The Japanese, Hitler asserted, were "culture-bearing" rather than "culture-creating" people. As long as Japan imitated German values and characteristics, Jewish and communist advances in Asia would be checked, prosperity would continue, and national development would proceed.[2] In a similar manner, propagandists suggested American Indians needed to align themselves with Nazism in order to counter communist enslavement and to prevent Jewish exploitation as directed by Roosevelt, Frances Perkins, Bernard Baruch, Henry Morgenthau, and the "pinko, Jew-loving" John Collier.[3] Anti-Semitism was portrayed as a crusade to halt the victimization of Indians by a Jewish-controlled American government responsible for the historic genocidal posture of federal Indian policies.

To disseminate the message, Germany employed a growing broadcast network to reach American Indians directly; however, the propaganda ministry soon discovered that few Indians owned radios capable of receiving such long-distance transmissions. To smooth that particular wrinkle in the ministry's plan, radio messages were received and circulated by pro-Nazi organizations within the United States that cultivated ties with Indian communities.[4]

From the German perspective, the single most important hurdle to be leaped in recruiting American Indians to Nazism was the issue of race. To conceal the full implication of Nazi racial doctrine, propagandists veiled their ideology with the inclusion of Native Americans as Aryans. In 1938 Berlin granted citizenship and Aryan status to the grandson of a Sioux woman and a German immigrant to the United States. Officials soon afterward extended the recognition to embrace all Sioux Indians. Berlin claimed that the personality and traditional military character of the Sioux clearly resembled those features found among true

Germans. The explanation advanced the idea that a lost tribe of Germanic people had wandered into the New World in the distant past and bred themselves into the native population, thus building a link to German ancestry.[5]

It was hoped that identification of Native Americans as Aryans would encourage the reception of Nazi ideology by a larger Indian audience. For those members of tribal groups not directly issued title to the preferred racial classification, propagandists pointed to the literary works of German novelists such as Karl May, who, in the late nineteenth century, asserted the notion that Indians could adopt and bear German culture—a concept similar to Hitler's view of Japanese society. The inference suggested the elevation of Indians in the German racial hierarchy.

May's works, which contributed to Hitler's racial awareness, featured the Germanic heroism of Old Shatterhand, a "superhuman, Teutonic figure" who displayed a richness of wisdom, noble virtues, and Christian ethics. In all of Shatterhand's adventures in the American West, the German frontiersman proved invincible because of those traits, along with his highly developed wilderness skills and his inherent German superiority.[6] In his 1897 volume *Christmas in the Wild West*, May's character blasted the environmentally destructive behavior of white Americans on the frontier and pointedly assailed Westerners for the "destruction and degeneration of the Indian nation." Old Shatterhand condemned Americans as European outcasts, morally bankrupt scoundrels bent on the ruination of anything or anyone in their path toward land and wealth.[7]

Christmas in the Wild West nestled itself well into Nazi propaganda. Old Shatterhand's trusted Indian companion was Winnetou who possessed an Aryan persona. His face appeared "almost Roman," his personality peaceful yet strong and determined. Winnetou displayed remarkable intelligence, and his bearing and mannerisms showed refinement. He was the "noble savage" of European construction. May's principal Indian character demonstrated that, with proper training, the nobility or "Germaness" of a Native American could emerge. Winnetou played the role of the "thoroughly Teutonized Indian sidekick."[8] May's publications seemingly proved that although Indians were not Aryan by birth, they certainly were capable of bearing German culture and, once prepared, they would be capable of halting the destruction and exploitation directed by Jewish-controlled America.

Karl May's novels were both logical and natural elements in Nazi propaganda. May was Adolf Hitler's favorite author, and much of the Führer's racist ideology was influenced by the writer. Moreover, May was widely known throughout Europe. His books were translated into twenty languages, bought by more than thirty million people, and read by an estimated three hundred million individuals. "To generations of Europeans," wrote one historian, "he was Germany's James Fenimore Cooper—'the greatest writer since Homer.'" The journal *Der Spiegel* afforded May an influence "greater than that of any other author between Johann Wolfgang von Goethe and Thomas Mann."[9] For most Europeans, May's publications framed their basic understanding of the American West and American Indians, and, once included into Hitler's propagandist tract, the Nazi racist ideology and Nazi activities among Indians seemed logical to most Germans. Berlin's amplification of those supposed Germanic traits and the Indians' ability to become "Teutonized" was intended to circumvent the racial exclusiveness of Nazism.

Adventure stories penned by May, however, served as only one source of the fascination Germans had for American Indians. As the historian Thomas A. Britten points out in his recent study of Indian participation in World War I, "the German people held a long-standing affinity for Native Americans, one that stretched back to the nineteenth century" and to earlier years. Britten attributed this interest primarily to the numerous "Wild West" shows, which traveled throughout Europe from the 1880s to the days immediately preceding the Great War. "Mock battles" were staged, war dances were performed, and occasionally Indian villages were erected "complete with tepees and campfires."[10] As important, yet ignored by Britten, letters from German immigrants in the American West traversed the Atlantic to families back home and frequently exaggerated Indian living arrangements, behaviors, and values. These colorful descriptions intrigued the parents, brothers, and sisters who remained in Germany, and families in turn read their letters from the New World with enthusiasm to friends and neighbors.

Through May's works, traveling shows, and letters from America several generations of Germans came to adopt a curious perception of Indians—savage yet adaptable to a state of nobility, racial inferiors yet distant racial comrades. Thomas Britten points to one German who, after World War I, explained his countrymen's interest in Native Americans by stating that "the Indian is closer to the German than to any other European. This may be due to our stronger leaning for that which is close to nature." He added that the Indian "is model and brother for us during our boyhood; among the dreams and longings of those years he remains one of our most cherished recollections."[11]

For many Germans, the most striking feature of the Indian character was his fighting ability. Karl May claimed that warriors "could throw a tomahawk and cut off the tip of an outstretched finger at a hundred paces."[12] Common descriptions of Indian warrior skills highlighted the Native American's ability at stalking the enemy, his devotion to cause and determination to win, his extreme bravery under fire, his uncanny sense of direction, and his stealth in eluding larger forces. The Indian warrior was patient, opportunistic, and in possession of a "sixth sense" in battle. In the eyes of Germans, these Indian traits closely matched their own and were given credence through captivity narratives in which German immigrants, held by Indian tribes, were eventually adopted by their captors and joined raids against white settlements. A natural warrior kinship seemed to exist between German captives and the Indians. Equally important to Germans was the perceived similarity between the traditional military structure of German society and tribal warrior societies among native cultures.

German affinity for Native Americans, then, was long-standing and obviously quite deep. When American politicians, department heads, and bureau officers in the 1930s glanced at German propaganda campaigns among Indians, the Nazi effort seemed misguided and perhaps ludicrous. But when viewed against a broader sweep of time and examined in its proper context, the decision made by Joseph Goebbel's propaganda ministry to spread the Nazi message to American Indians appears logical and in concert with the German understanding of Native Americans for over one hundred years. A continuity with the past was actually maintained.

Not recognizing Germany's perspective or the historical framework in which propagandists operated, few Americans fully appreciated Nazi efforts to sway Indian pre-war loyalty. Among those who did were John Collier and a small but aware group of scholars. "By no stretch of the imagination" could Indians be considered Aryan, responded the anthropologist Ales Hrdlicka of the Smithsonian Institution.[13] Historical evidence denied any such categorization. And Collier, the historian Jere Franco points out, responded in "a more heated, sarcastic" tone when he railed that "previously the Mormons had been denominating the Indians as 'The Lost Tribe of Israel'" and now "Hitler is kidnapping them."[14] Collier warned Indians that Hitler planned to deal with them as he dealt with Jews. Indians, he insisted, "are not Aryans. Hitler's plan dooms them to eternal servitude if they do not resist the slavemaster and to total extinction if they do resist the slavemaster." "Freedom," he continued, "is the passion of the Indians, and there can be no doubt in the side the Indian will take in a struggle which involves us all."[15]

Nazis posited two distinct positions in conflict between the American and German attitudes toward the Indian: the United States historically relegated Indians to extinction through warfare or federal Indian policies, but Germany admitted some Indians to full Aryan status and viewed all Native Americans as potential bearers of German culture. For centuries Indians suffered under the hands of the United States government, victimized by an unrelenting tide of white migration that usurped title to land and attempted to destroy native cultures. Indians had been decimated physically and culturally. "How could the American Indians think of bearing arms for their exploiters" if the United States and Germany one day waged war on one another? inquired one Nazi propagandist.[16] But the assignment of Aryan status for some Indians and cultural inclusion for most others appeared ridiculous to Native Americans themselves. Race remained a centerpiece of Nazi ideology, and acceptance of Indians who bore German culture still denoted a position of inferiority within the Nazi world-view. As a result, Berlin-directed propaganda spawned little favorable sentiment among Native Americans.

The failure of Berlin-based propaganda among Indians also resulted from its lack of any accurate understanding of Native American cultures and history. German knowledge of American Indians consisted of outdated, misunderstood, and misrepresented information generated by authors of popular fiction and frequently incorporated as factual material in articles printed in the European press. As late as 1941, a grossly inaccurate portrait of contemporary Indian life in the United States appeared in the fascist Madrid newspaper *El Alcazar*. The article, "Yankees and Yankeeland," meshed some fact with an abundance of stereotyped images that not only belied the historic and contemporary scenes but also blurred the two time periods. Described was a North American continent filled with innumerable tribes; yet the article cited a total native population of fifty thousand Indians. At no point did Native American numbers dip to such a low figure. An estimate in 1890 placed the Indian population at two hundred and forty-four thousand, the lowest recorded count. By the time of the article's publication, Native Americans had grown significantly and numbered nearly four hundred thousand.[17]

The article further described contemporary American Indians as wanderers and herd followers. Portrayed was a characteristic that at best identified a minute fraction of the continent's native groupings a century earlier. Moreover, the author contended that in "Indian Territory," presumably Oklahoma, tribes such as the Arapaho, Osage, and Apache lived unsubdued by whites. Wholesale murder of Native Americans and armed clashes between Indians and whites framed the everyday pattern of life in the area, the writer insisted. When an Indian "makes a false move," whites arm themselves and "shoot them in the street, if they do not hang them with the popular legal formula of the lynching law."[18] Although this article and others of similar bent were principally intended for European consumption, translations appeared inside the United

States and were channeled to Indian readers by domestic pro-Nazi organizations that believed Indians would recognize some basic truths in the writings.

"Yankees and Yankeeland" represented the imagery of Native Americans prevalent in European society. Much of the literature consumed in Germany for more than one hundred years highlighted man's taming the North American environment and conquering native peoples, as evidenced by the works of Karl May. Writers occasionally condemned white America's wastefulness of resources, their ruination of land and water, and the inability of frontier residents to maintain family bonds because of their migratory tendencies and general lawlessness. Most important for Nazi propaganda were stories detailing Indian-white conflicts.[19] The majority of European-produced "dime novels" were written by individuals who had neither visited the United States nor researched their subjects. Rather, they built their literature from popular and distorted images shrouded with Social Darwinism and *volkish* thought. The romance of the American West pervaded European cultures so completely that the frontier's "passing," along with all the stereotyped trappings of the region's history, seldom registered in the European consciousness. In this climate of thought, German propaganda against America's mistreatment of Indians and the current status of Indian-white relations achieved some credibility within Europe and tended to deflect partially Germany's own mistreatment of Jews prior to 1940.[20]

As a tool to elicit Indian support for the Nazi program, such articles actually proved counter-productive. Although Native Americans and whites agreed that Indians had been badly mistreated, "Yankees and Yankeeland" clearly revealed German misunderstanding of the United States in general, and American Indians in particular. With such far-fetched portraits sanctioned by Berlin under the veil of authenticity, Indians questioned the validity of Nazi arguments on other matters as well.

It would appear that Nazi propaganda efforts relative to American Indians were self-defeating; however, within the ministry's circle was a collection of highly competent individuals armed with the talents and knowledge to make propaganda among Native Americans more effective. Throughout the 1930s, thousands of Germans visited the United States; among them was the anthropologist Dr. Colin Ross. In 1934 and again in 1936 Ross traveled across the western states and frequently toured Indian reservations. The motive for these anthropological tours by Germans, wrote one recent scholar, was to learn Indian languages so that battlefield radio communication using Indian operators would be compromised should the United States and Germany again go to war. This particular concern stemmed from Germany's discovery that American combat forces in World War I had, on occasion, used Choctaw

Indians to transmit battlefield communications in their unique language.[21] Whether or not this specific mission applied to Ross is unclear. More likely at this date, however, was Germany's desire to secure information for use in the heated propaganda wars between the Roosevelt administration and Nazi Germany. Shortly after his return home in early 1937, Ross published "Der Balkan Amerikas."[22]

In the article, Ross summarized the goals of America's federal Indian policy over the preceding one hundred years. The United States, he said, first attempted extermination of the native population. Unable to accomplish the goal, Washington adopted an assimilationist strategy under the Dawes Severalty Act of 1887 to accomplish what violence could not complete—the elimination of a minority race in the United States. The act, Ross contended, had little chance for success from its very inception. How could the melting of Indians into white society truly be effected within a nation so hinged on racism as America? he wondered. The alleged new policy direction bound in the Indian Reorganization Act, he claimed, concealed the preference of federal authorities for direct subjugation and isolation of native peoples that would, eventually, result in the disappearance of Native Americans. Rather than revitalize traditional Indian cultures and communities, the IRA would actually retain poverty and the absence of economic growth on reservations. The continuation of staggeringly high death rates caused by malnutrition, disease, and suicide would ultimately gain what the earlier policies of warfare and assimilation proved incapable of accomplishing. Tribal self-determination and cultural pluralism were mere illusions to trick Indians into remaining on reservations, instead of moving them toward inclusion within white society. The Indians' only hope, Ross maintained, was the creation of a "red state," a section of land assigned to Indians for the development of a separate nation within a nation, one apart from federal control or interference.[23]

Ross's condemnation of poor living conditions on reservations, the failure of previous Indian policies, and the IRA's alleged redirection created a foundation for more effective propaganda activity. Although "Der Balkan Amerikas" seems to have received little direct exposure among Native Americans, the article was read by the German-American Bund, which cultivated ties with Indian organizations and summarized its theme in broadsides to Indian communities. The obvious difference between Ross's work and the portrait of Indian affairs disseminated throughout Europe by Nazi mouthpieces, such as *El Alcazar*, was one of relative accuracy. Ross surveyed concrete government programs of the past and those more recently commissioned by John Collier, and his argument closely mirrored one side of the debate posited by many white Americans and Indians themselves. A measure of credibility emerged in this line of Nazi propaganda. Collier, Secretary of the Interior Harold Ickes, and the body of reformers across the United States certainly recognized a potential threat in Colin Ross, especially in 1937, as numerous reservations continued to debate the merits and faults of the IRA. Pricked by Ross's attack, Collier ordered government agencies to track Ross and all other "crude propaganda" activities among American Indians. Close surveillance continued until the United States entered World War II in December 1941.[24]

Adding a sense of greater urgency to Collier was Ross's publication of two books by the end of 1937, *Unser Amerika (Our America)* and *Amerikas Shicksalsstunde (America's Hour of Destiny)*. Neither specifically addressed American Indians, but they did detail German contributions to American national development and predicted "the future arrival of a German Thomas Paine" who would awaken and unite Germany's "racial comrades" inside the United States (presumably Native Americans). As Nazi Germany's power expanded throughout Europe, Americans of German ancestry would link arms with German nationals at home to create a transatlantic union under the Nazi banner. With selected Indians officially identified as Aryan and others recognized as potential culture-bearers, Ross's message implied a concerted effort by Nazis to win the hearts and minds of Native Americans.[25]

Over the following months, Collier and his office concentrated on tribal revitalization through the IRA and other programs such as land reclamation, education reform, health services, and CCC-ID projects. Certainly, such intense effort would directly benefit Indian reservations and more quickly draw Native American communities closer to the status he personally envisioned, but Collier also believed Nazi activities among Indians would be silenced as BIA work materially improved reservation living standards and validated the integrity of a reversed federal Indian policy.

When Collier arrived at his office on December 2, 1938, he was jolted by an unexpected letter in the morning mail from Colin Ross himself. He read that Ross was currently in Baltimore and had been there for several days. Collier knew that a substantial Indian population resided in Maryland, lured to the cities by rising employment opportunities in the expanding defense industries. Ross commended the commissioner for the apparent redirection in Indian affairs and requested a personal interview with Collier to learn more of the plan for tribal revitalization before continuing his own travels through the United States. He informed Collier of his intention to film reservation conditions, which he expected had improved significantly since his last visit to America. A visual record, he assured Collier, would provide Germans with a "true picture of America today."[26]

This worried the commissioner. Collier understood the power of film in molding popular attitudes. A skillful writer and film crew could create a distorted image of reservation life and construct an effective propaganda message to both the German people and to American Indians. Reservation conditions had indeed undergone substantial positive change since Ross's earlier visit, but much work remained. Deepening Collier's concern was his awareness that Ms. Leni Riefenstahl, creator of the German propaganda masterpiece "Triumph of the Will," had a film crew in Los Angeles. The commissioner instantly assumed a direct and sinister connection between Ross and Riefenstahl.[27]

A flurry of anticipation filled the Office of Indian Affairs. Collier agreed to a meeting in Washington, primarily to determine Ross's true intentions. As if he needed a reminder, Secretary Ickes warned Collier that Ross belonged to the Nazi Party and therefore the commissioner should "be governed accordingly."[28]

The formal meeting, held two weeks later, served only to introduce the men to one another, each being guarded in his conversation. The next day, Ross proceeded westward on his journey. Collier, having had his IRA maligned by the German's pen one year earlier, refused to permit a second attack. The Indian Bureau forwarded memos to superintendents throughout the Southwest to alert them of Ross's impending visit and his plan to film reservations for probable propaganda use. Collier clearly warned each superintendent that Ross had a "direct relationship with the propaganda organization of the Nazis in Germany" and should take care to avoid casting any unfavorable image of Indian life, and he added one more directive. The State Department, Collier wrote, possessed no photograph of Dr. Ross. Superintendents were to make every conceivable, yet discreet, effort to secure one. He suggested placing Ross in a group shot with a number of Indians under the pretext of making a tribal memento, or perhaps one showing him sight-seeing for publication in the bureau's monthly journal *Indians at Work*.[29]

The precautions taken by Collier sufficed. Colin Ross failed to compile any film among Indians conducive to Nazi propaganda. The Office of Indian Affairs scored a victory, and Ross made no more trips to the United States. His only product from this tour was one minor article published in late 1939, "Amerika Greift nach der Weltmacht" (America Reaches for World Power). At no point in the writing did Ross mention the Indian communities he visited, but he did proclaim the United States ripe for social and racial revolution.[30]

Excerpts from Ross's writings were printed in Bundist literature distributed to American Indians, but little support for Nazi Germany resulted. Older Indians who held personal memories of days long lost occasionally echoed Nazi condemnation of the IRA and previous federal policies, not in preference for Hitler's regime but in opposition to any government or policy other than that of tribal choice. Some younger Indians teetered in their sentiments, unsure of how to respond to the Nazi message. To these uncertain few, the economic and social progress of Indians in white America seemed too slow, pinned to the discretion of congressional appropriations and not beneficial to all Indians. One Oklahoma Cherokee, Willis Mizer, said his neighbor's frustrations with the unhurried pace and inconsistency of Collier's IRA unplugged his ears to Nazi arguments. While repairing his fence one day, the neighbor broke his steady cadence of hammering with a smashing blow to the fence post and then turned to Mizer. "He [give] the Hitler salute," Mizer recalled, "and said that's the kind of government we ought to have." Then, in a tone frustrated by impoverishment and saddled with unrealized opportunity, he said Roosevelt's New Deal and Collier's programs "were poor pieces of machinery." Mizer confessed that occasionally he had to agree with his neighbor's sentiments, particularly when viewed against the apparent economic progress being made in Germany.[31]

Although it appeared that the majority of Native Americans gave scant attention to Germany's message, enough Nazi propaganda continued to filter among Indians to warrant Collier's verbal response. He conceded that slavery and extinction historically framed federal Indian policies. The world knew the indignities to which the United States subjected Native Americans in the past. But, he contended, "today that story is no more than a sad page from our history." The Office of Indian Affairs, he reminded his listeners, hoped to correct those injustices of an earlier time. The New Deal, the IRA, and the many supplemental programs emanating from Washington provided tangible evidence of redirected government policy, especially in medical care, educational services, and both tribal and personal economics. The government's commitment to redress the misdirection of previous generations was clearly visible, Collier insisted. His message acknowledged what many Indians themselves said in their rejection of Nazi propaganda. "My grandparents," said one Indian, "fought against the white man. In many respects we have been badly treated. In this land which once was ours, we are poor. Many people treat us as outcasts and inferiors." But, like Collier, he added that the redirection in federal policies and programs promised change. "Our conditions have slowly improved," he said. "The reservation schools are good," he continued, and "we are trained for trades and farming. The government defends our rights. We know that under Nazism we should have no rights at all. We are not Aryans."[32] Collier's reservation renewal efforts eroded the very foundation on which Nazi propagandists hoped to operate. New Deal and IRA programs restored the integrity of Indian cultures and improved the social and economic conditions that Germany intended to exploit.

World War II and the American Indian

While Berlin-based propaganda activities certainly proved worrisome for Collier, he found the work of domestic, pro-Nazi organizations far more troubling and potentially more corruptive of Indian loyalty for the United States. Literature disseminated by the Silver Shirt Legion, the German-American Bund, and the James True Associates all held one advantage over Berlin's propaganda—these Nazi proponents were all Americans themselves and, consequently, knew the fears and hopes that motivated the general population. Their ties with American society and culture were obviously far more intimate and interwoven with the very fabric of American life, and their understanding of the nation's history and contemporary patterns was much more realistic. Most importantly, the men and women who comprised the membership of these right-wing organizations had a personal stake in the country's future.

Of the Nazi ideological tenets trumpeted by American sympathizers, perhaps none was sounded more forcefully and often as the warning against the perceived worldwide communist menace. Although public hysteria of red infiltration dissipated in the early 1920s as the infamous Palmer Raids lost popular support, the actual fear of communism in America did not totally disappear; it had only retreated to the dark and dusty out-of-the-way closets of the nation's consciousness. Instead, rapid national economic growth commanded America's attention. There seemed to be few perils to prosperity, and communism was not one of them. But the Great Depression changed that view, and to many Americans FDR's New Deal opened the closet door for communism's reemergence. Arguing that Roosevelt's program was actually communism packaged neatly under the wrappings of relief, recovery, and reform, America's pro-Nazi organizations peeled apart the layers of each New Deal agency and policy.

In the Indian Reorganization Act they believed they found the most visible evidence of communism's new port of entry into American society. Rather than promote the perceived American tradition of "from many nations, one people" by melding Indians into the capitalist and democratic general population, pro-Nazis insisted that the IRA purposely contradicted assimilation in favor of a communal social structure. What better way to challenge the IRA than to have Indians speak for themselves? pro-Nazis asked. They did not have far to look in finding vocal opponents among Native Americans.

Elwood A. Towner, a Hoopa from the Siletz Reservation in Pendleton, Oregon, traveled along the West Coast states following passage of the IRA in a personal campaign to smear the Roosevelt administration and Collier's Indian New Deal. He had been reared under the assimilationist programs of the Bureau of Indian Affairs and, as a successful practicing attorney, offered himself as a model for Indian youth to emulate. Fearful that the IRA might "return Indians to the blanket" and stall assimilationist trends, Towner came to believe that both the act and bureau officials hoped to instill communism among Native Americans. Nazism, he assumed, provided the only competent alternative.[33]

Towner's personal crusade to discredit FDR, Collier, and the IRA quickly attracted the attention of Frederick G. Collett, founder of Indians of California. A former Congregational minister who had conducted missionary work among California's native population from 1910 to 1932, Collett created the organization in part to solicit money from Indians with which to "advance Indian claims" against the federal government. In his bid to represent California Indians, in 1934 Collett filed suit against the United States for treaty violations and collected fees from every Indian who wished his representation. Although the United States Circuit Court of Claims did agree to a twelve-million-dollar settlement, the money was to be held in trust with the Department of the Interior and dispersed at the secretary's discretion. This arrangement angered Collett, who had promised Indians cash payments, but Collett himself infuriated Collier and the Office of Indian Affairs by his fee collection, which countered authorized procedures.[34] Moreover, Collett continued his fundraising efforts, and by 1938 he had amassed $181,000 and nearly seventeen thousand members statewide.[35]

Unknown to most contributors was Collett's affiliation with the German-American Bund. Instead of using the collected funds to litigate on behalf of Native American claims, Collett channeled the money into the Bund's congressional lobbying activities, organization programs, and expense accounts. He encouraged Indians to attend monthly meetings in Los Angeles ("coincidentally" located at Bund headquarters) where they were exposed to vehement attacks against the current state of Indian affairs created by the Jewish-inspired communist menace in the United States. Collett did oppose the direction of federal Indian policy, seeing in the IRA communist leanings, and he repeatedly echoed the position of longtime critics of federal Indian policy that the Bureau of Indian Affairs itself should be abolished once and for all. Without the federal guardianship found in the BIA, Indians would be able to find their way into the American mainstream. Without the IRA's push for traditional, communal tribal society, Indians would be able to break free of communist entrapment and atheism. He and other Bund speakers incessantly championed Nazi tenets and called on Indians to enlist themselves into American pro-Nazi organizations. As the Bund itself accepted membership only from persons of direct German ancestry, Collett encouraged Indians to support the Silver Shirt Legion and even provided its commander, William Dudley Pelley, with a mailing list of California Indians.[36]

In 1939 Collett invited Elwood Towner to speak before a branch of the Indians of California, located in Eureka. Dressed in traditional Indian attire and sporting a Nazi armband, Towner appeared before a collection of fifty Indian men on 8 July. Identifying himself as Red Cloud, he traced the impact of American Jews, or "chuck-na-gin" (the "children of Satan" and "gold worshippers"), on federal Indian policy. In the United States, he argued, "Indians and gentile Christians" must fight "the forces of evil—the reds, pinks, and Jews" in the Roosevelt administration. "All those running the government," Towner ranted, "are Jews," including the president himself whose real name is "Rosenfelt." Furthermore, he continued, many FDR appointees allied themselves with the American Civil Liberties Union, which "is a branch of the Communist Party."[37]

He then focused his commentary on the Indian Reorganization Act, which, he reminded his audience, promised Indian self-determination. Creators of the act pointed to its simplicity and the Indians' right to veto the plan should it not address their peculiar circumstances. However, he continued, the policy actually proved too complicated, and those tribes that accepted it were duped by the communists in Washington. The IRA held out the "beautiful promises" housed in Marxian philosophy. Its only significant impact, Towner argued, was a negative one—tribal fragmentation caused by the debate over IRA ratification. Once the "Wheeler-Howard Act was signed by that dirty, stinking Jew in the White House, 254 treaties were automatically destroyed," releasing Washington from its obligations to Native Americans. The scrapped assimilationist path insured continued poverty for American Indians. "The Wheeler-Howard Act," Towner maintained, "is communism working in the Indian Service. Communism is Judaism."[38]

To halt the Jewish-directed communist threat to Native Americans, "Indians must join hands with other super-patriotic organizations," Towner insisted. "The Silver Shirts propose justice" for American Indians, and William Dudley Pelley vowed the placement of an Indian in the Cabinet once a Silver Shirt revolution succeeded. Towner further emphasized Pelley's pledge to make the Bureau of Indian Affairs one comprised solely of Native Americans, once "all the Jews were eliminated." "American Indians," he stated, "must not be afraid of Naziism [sic]." Following his tirade, Towner distributed Nazi literature published by both the Bund and the Silver Shirts.[39]

Towner's charges seemed too fantastic for the audience. Not only did the Eureka spectators dismiss him, but Indians throughout the region held "little re-gard for him" because of the "sentiments he expressed."[40] Similarly, fewer Indi-ans attended Bund meetings in Los Angeles, as the Nazi message became sharper and more vocal. While some Indians challenged a possible communist inclination in the IRA and denounced the anti-assimilationist bent of Collier's original vision, most Native Americans actually realized greater opportunities for assimilation as an inadvertent result of IRA programs. Moreover, individuals such as Towner did not truly represent the values, experiences or expectations of the larger Indian population. As for the Bund, by its own admission Indian membership was not accepted. How could such an organization have the Indi-ans' interest in its heart? The proverbial jury was still out regarding Indians of California.

There was, however, one organization that did gather considerable support from Native Americans because it was a union exclusively for Indians. Estab-lished in Washington, D.C., on June 8, 1934, just ten days prior to the final pas-sage of the Wheeler-Howard Act, the American Indian Federation (AIF) created a national base, although the overwhelming majority of its 3,500 hundred members belonged to southern tribes. Founded on ideals expressed the previ-ous decade by the Indian leader Carlos Montezuma, the AIF adamantly op-posed any "return to the blanket." Montezuma, a Yavapai Apache who earned a medical degree and built a career as a respected physician in Chicago, believed that the success and extent of inclusion with white society he attained demon-strated the opportunities available to Indians in the United States. Full citizen-ship, a sound education received in integrated public schools, and a conscious, concerted effort to adopt the values of white society all permitted the Indians assimilation with the general population. The primary obstacle for Indians, he argued, was the continued guardianship exercised by the Bureau of Indian Af-fairs. Efforts to reform Indian policy and to make the BIA more responsive to Indians "only meant the strengthening, not the diminishing, of bureaucratic control in the lives of American Indians." This perspective framed the AIF's philosophical structure, observed historian Laurence Hauptman. In Mon-tezuma's words, "No amount of reorganization of the Indian Bureau will abol-ish the Indian Bureau"; reform and reorganization would only enlarge federal supervision and control over Native Americans. Montezuma's goal was to de-stroy the very institution and mindset that "enshakled" Indians.[41] Based on his views, then, the AIF's most radical tenet advocated the abolition of the Bureau of Indian Affairs "with its un-American principles of slavery, greed and oppres-sion." Promoted was a vision in which Native Americans would "take their place beside all other people in this land of opportunity."[42] Staunch proponents of assimilation, the AIF called for an end to federal guardianship and opposed the IRA, which, members believed, retarded the inclusion of Indians into mainstream society.

The federation's organizers included Joseph Bruner, a Creek from Sapulpa, Oklahoma, who was heavily invested in oil and real estate development, and O. K. Chandler, who held a personal grudge against John Collier and the Indian Bureau. Aiding in the founding of the AIF was Frederick Collett.[43] From its outset, the American Indian Federation held firm to conservative and assimilationist directions, but it also originated in the spirit of a vendetta with a visible pro-Nazi inclination.

Federation members championed pure capitalist tenets and adherence to the melting pot ideal. While Nazi theories of race were unquestionably in conflict with ideas of racial amalgamation through assimilation, AIF organizers rallied behind the Nazi attack against communism, which members believed was the soul of Roosevelt's New Deal legislation. Collier's program for tribal revitalization, the Federation argued, impeded Indian progress toward complete and final assimilation and self-improvement by the communist direction sanctioned by the IRA. Those "vicious communist features" housed in the new federal Indian policy, the group asserted, attracted Communist Party propaganda and exploitation. Unfortunately for Collier, this particular allegation received partial confirmation from FBI agents. On Montana reservations, Communist Party literature appeared in sufficient quantities to warrant federal investigation.[44] Publicity surrounding Party activities in Montana validated AIF contentions and rewarded the organization with additional members. Moreover, Communist Party work on the upper Plains reservations convinced many members to listen more intently to anticommunist harangues from pro-Nazi sympathizers. As one AIF supporter commented, the apparent path toward "communal bliss" crystallized Federation skepticism of the Roosevelt administration and the Indian Bureau and created an opening for Nazi propaganda.[45]

While the Federation was not a Nazi organization inside the United States, as early as July 1936 the AIF did show clear signs of Nazi influence. Observers at that year's Federation convention in Salt Lake City, including Floyd LaRouche, a bureau employee stationed at the Carson Indian Agency in Stewart, Nevada, reported a definite "preoccupation with anti-communism, anti-Jewish, anti-Administration propaganda" that paralleled "the activities of fascist organizations" elsewhere in the United States and in Europe.[46] The convention attracted a small audience; there were only thirty to forty listeners for the dozens of speeches delivered. LaRouche informed Collier that few speakers addressed Indian issues directly, but in those that did, the perceived communist leanings of the commissioner and the IRA were the principal topics. More than anything, said LaRouche, the convention resembled an "anti-Communist drive." During the course of the convention, the AIF supplied attendees with literature that openly connected the Federation to a "strong anti-Semitic and pro-Fascist philosophy." Among the articles distributed was "Communism with the Mask Off," originally delivered as a speech by Joseph Goebbels at the Nuremburg rally in September 1935.[47] Informed of the pro-Nazi trappings found at the Salt Lake City AIF Convention, coupled with the AIF's outspoken denunciation of the IRA, John Collier's interest was not only piqued, he also felt warned.

Most irritating and worrisome for the commissioner was Alice Lee Jemison. A New York Seneca, Jemison affiliated herself with the AIF at its founding and soon emerged as its sharpest and most vehement critic of Collier, the IRA, and the entire Roosevelt administration. Wrote one of her supporters, she was a "cultured woman . . . and a skillful speaker and writer" whose talents benefited the AIF and the broader anti-New Deal coalition.[48] Jemison undeniably proved herself adept with both the spoken word and the pen, but during the 1930s her own conflicting statements regarding her personal life brought into question her truthfulness and cast doubt upon her motivations for attacking the Roosevelt administration. According to one historian, Jemison identified herself as a Seneca Indian, but she occasionally referred to herself as Cherokee. In 1928, at age twenty-six, she left her husband Verne Jemison. Ten years later she claimed marriage to a Washington, D.C., man, but in 1940 she once again named Verne Jemison as her husband. Moreover, Alice Jemison's work history included brief stints at a Buffalo law office and numerous other short-term positions. She authored several stinging newspaper articles severely critical of the Bureau of Indian Affairs and served as personal secretary to a former Seneca Council president. Once elected as secretary for the American Indian Federation, Jemison claimed to represent the Seneca Nation in an official capacity, although the Seneca Council "did not authorize Jemison to represent them" at congressional hearings.[49] Jemison's apparent lack of candor regarding her personal life, her seemingly unstable work history, and a spurious standing with the Seneca Tribal Council created extreme concern in the halls of the Indian Bureau, especially as she commanded an increasingly visible and active presence in the crusade against Collier and the IRA—a position made all the more troubling for the commissioner as she publicly linked herself with pro-Nazi organizations within the United States.

Laurence Hauptman has countered that assessment, arguing Jemison's private life was "one of hardships, against almost insurmountable difficulties."

Ever-present poverty plagued her life, halted her education, and forced her into a "variety of jobs from the age of twelve onward: nursemaid, housekeeper, door-to-door salesperson, factory worker, store clerk, farmer, peddler, theater usher, dressmaker, practical nurse, beautician, operator of a confectionery store, as well as secretary." Saddled with the responsibility of rearing two children without a husband, life frequently seemed desperate. As for her tribal identity, Jemison's mother was Seneca, but her father was Cherokee. This, argues Hauptman, explained her claim to Cherokee identity, although he notes Seneca society was matrilineal and "consequently Jemison was legally an enrolled Seneca." Moreover, Jemison served as a "girl Friday" to Seneca President Ray Jimerson, conducted legal research for the tribe, and "on at least two occasions, she was nominated by the Seneca Tribal Council for positions in the Indian service." Clearly, Hauptman stresses, Jemison did, in fact, represent the Seneca people.[50]

The two conflicting portraits of her personal life and role in tribal affairs resemble the Indian Bureau's initial curiosity and concern over Jemison—a curiosity and concern that, for many in the bureau, was soon resolved. In the autumn of 1937, Jemison and her two small children took residency in Washington, where she became the unpaid representative for Federation president, Joseph Bruner.[51] In that capacity, Jemison played the role of BIA watchdog and the AIF spokesperson in the nation's capital. Almost immediately, her presence received bureau attention.

Less the reporter and more the barking, sniping critic, Jemison's verbal assaults on the IRA, Collier, and the entire bureau resounded throughout the halls of the Department of the Interior. Her scathing attacks unremittingly alleged a communist intent behind federal Indian policy, with the underlying principle of the IRA being the abolition of land allotments for common ownership and to "have the Indians live in a state of communal bliss"—an experiment in communism, she insisted. The act required Native Americans to set aside assimilation for continued tribal poverty and strict government supervision, she thundered. Moreover, she tied the originators and enforcers of the IRA to the American Civil Liberties Union, "a commie front" organization.[52]

John Collier, Jemison said, hoped "to exploit the Indian" by keeping him "in his primitive state . . . as wards" and as "poor savages." She concurred with Bruner's assessment that "the fundamental ideas of the Commissioner's plan or program are Communistic . . . and had their origins in . . . the American Civil Liberties Union," which had consistently defended Communists and extreme liberal positions since its founding.[53]

Jemison cited the IRA's education reform program as specific, undeniable evidence in support of her accusations. Clear in its design was the educational philosophy of John Dewey who, she reminded her listeners, had himself belonged to the ACLU. Dewey, she claimed, "is recognized as an educational guide" in the Soviet Union, and "his influence has been manifest in the reorganization of the educational system in Soviet Russia."[54] In part, Jemison was correct; Collier and his education director Willard Beatty did adhere to the Dewey philosophy and did incorporate a similar system of schooling into the IRA. What she failed to realize was that Dewey's vision of education had been widely accepted and practiced throughout the United States since the 1890s and was premised on the view that a practical, relevant, hands-on approach to education for the masses was necessary for democracy's survival in America.

She further revealed that Willard Beatty also aligned himself with Dr. George Counts, Professor of Education at Columbia University, who in the summer of 1935 served as an instructor at the University of Moscow. He also had recently authored *The Soviet Challenge to America* and translated *New Russia's Primer* into English. Of the two works, Jemison contended the latter carried the greater threat to Native Americans. The primer, she argued, attempted to demonstrate the superiority of the Soviet Union over the United States and pointed to the book's introduction, where it was written that "anyone who had read the book can never believe in the capitalist system." Jemison ascribed the phrase to the hand of Counts rather than to the original Soviet author. That statement, she added, proved Counts to be "completely in sympathy with the communist program of Soviet Russia." In her view, personal ties between Counts and Beatty implicated the education director as a communist.[55]

Jemison's indictment of Beatty, however, rested on more than his mere personal connection with Counts. As education director for the BIA, Beatty endorsed the use of the translated *New Russia's Primer* for use at the Cherokee Indian School in western North Carolina, and in Jemison's mind this action verified the director's communist leaning.[56] He insisted the text served as a necessary tool for greater insight into the Soviet educational system and the larger Soviet culture, not to indoctrinate Indians into the merits of communism but to broaden student awareness of the surrounding world, which was, he believed, the purpose of education.

Even John Collier did not escape Jemison's wrath. The commissioner rubber-stamped the adoption of *New Russia Primer*. In her appearance before the Dies Committee on Un-American Activities on November 21, 1938, Jemison provided as evidence Collier's signed letter of authorization. That his statement of approval contained the condition the work be used as "collateral reading in a course on industrial geography" failed to dissuade Jemison from her allegation that he, too, was fostering communism among the Cherokee Indians.[57]

Without much debate, it can be argued effectively that Jemison's political stance against Collier, the bureau, and the Roosevelt administration in general stemmed from conservative leanings developed throughout her early life. As a product of western New York attitudes, Jemison distrusted "Washington-directed policies" and feared a "dominant, omnipotent government." She, like many Americans, saw FDR's New Deal as "financial boondoggle, communist-inspired and anti-Christian." As a champion of Montezuma's perspective, Jemison extended his view of Indian Bureau reform to national, non-Indian reform programs. She was convinced, as was much of the broader population, that Roosevelt's efforts to provide relief, recovery, and reform ultimately tightened Washington's tentacles around most every facet of individual life and was, therefore, un-American.[58]

Initially, it seems Alice Lee Jemison did not seek out Nazi affiliated organizations for support in her attacks on the IRA and the Indian Bureau, but her incessant verbal assault certainly echoed Nazi rantings. As early as 1936 she attracted the eyes and ears of fascist sympathizers in the United States, and they, in turn, unquestionably discovered an amenable colleague in her. Did Jemison take membership in any of the pro-Nazi organizations that littered the nation before World War II? No, she did not. Did she fully promote Nazi doctrine? Although the evidence remains somewhat clouded, it is unlikely that Jemison was a complete admirer of Nazism, particularly its emphasis on racial superiority. More realistic is that once direct communication between Jemison and pro-Nazi groups commenced, each used the other to advance their respective goals. In short, Jemison "danced with the Devil" to extend her anti-Indian New Deal tirades to larger audiences.

Among the organizations with which she publicly aligned herself was the Silver Shirt Legion, an Asheville, North Carolina-based band of Nazi sympathizers guided by William Dudley Pelley. A vicious and unrestrained critic of FDR and the New Deal, Pelley expanded his forays against the administration to include attacks on the Indian Reorganization Act. He condemned federal Indian policy for its imprisonment of Indians on their reservations and its dramatic turn from assimilation. The IRA "deprived them of their property," he argued, in a concerted effort by Roosevelt to "instill communism among Indian tribes." So convinced was he of FDR's antidemocratic purpose, Pelley charged the administration with the overt manipulation of Indians toward a communist posture so that "they would be natural allies of the Red in case of a revolutionary show-down."[59]

The curiously similar message spewed by both Pelley and Jemison led Collier to suspect an alliance between the two, a union seemingly confirmed in August

1936 when Jemison spoke at the American National Conference in Asheville. Alongside Jemison on the speaker's platform sat Pelley, the pro-Nazi James True, and several Bundists. Following the numerous and lengthy public harangues by the various guests, Nazi literature was distributed to the audience, some of which was distributed by Indians wearing Nazi armbands.[60] Equally troubling to Collier was the presence of Bundists and other pro-Nazi representatives at the American Indian Federation Conference in Salt Lake City that same year.

The following March, Pelley's monthly publication *The New Liberation* (with copies distributed in Germany) contained an article titled "Silver Shirts Propose Justice to the American Indian." The writer charged Collier and the Bureau of Indian Affairs with "conspiracy to unlawfully use the monies of the United States and to publish unauthorized propaganda among the Indians." It specifically accused Collier of allocating bureau funds for the indoctrination of communism among Native Americans, and the author pledged Silver Shirt financing to the AIF for its anti-IRA campaign. Soon afterwards, Pelley received Frederick Collett's written support, along with that of the Indians of California and the German-American Bund. Collett promised his personal assistance in the development and presentation of arguments on behalf of the American Indian Federation challenge to the communist menace emanating from the White House and the Department of the Interior. With the Silver Shirt Legion picking up the federation banner and funding some of its activities, and both the AIF and legion backed by West Coast pro-Nazi organizations, Collier and the FBI quickly became convinced that a serious bond existed among all these groups and individuals.[61]

If any doubts lingered, they dissipated by late 1937. In an effort to reduce unemployment, improve transportation through Appalachia, and stimulate the economy, the Department of the Interior announced plans to construct the Blue Ridge Parkway through the North Carolina mountains. When it was revealed that the project required a one-thousand-foot right-of-way thirteen miles in length through the Cherokee Reservation, the AIF and Silver Shirts rose in defiance. Their immediate complaint concerned the loss of individual land ownership and family displacement among the Cherokees. Once again, they argued, communist New Deal programs hoped to corrupt the Indians' assimilationist direction.

Washington's rebuttal stressed economic benefits to the region. The program first promised jobs with good wages to the region's unemployed, white and Indian alike. Second, the highway would ultimately stimulate tourism in the Carolina mountains, which carried the potential for business development throughout the area. Moreover, the parkway was part of the government's larger endeavor to improve transportation nationwide with road construction, airport construction, and completion of the East Coast's intracoastal waterway. And, Washington pointed out, should war ever erupt between the United States and Germany, America's coastal communities and shipping lanes would likely be targeted by Hitler's navy. Inland transport of vital military goods would be served by highways such as the Blue Ridge project.

Pelley's paranoia and fascist rebuttal continued into 1939 when the Silver Shirts printed and distributed among Cherokees a pamphlet titled "Indians Aren't Red!" Pelley alleged the highway program to be nothing more than a communist plot initiated by FDR with the Indian Bureau's endorsement. The IRA, he argued, simply promoted communism among Native Americans, and a parkway through the Cherokee Reservation would allow passing motorists a positive image of communism in action. The Blue Ridge Parkway, then, would become "the backbone of the entire plot to Sovietize these Indians into a model community for indoctrinating touring America with Communism."[62]

Collier believed few Indians read the article, but many Cherokees were aware of its contents. Congressman Zebulon Weaver of Asheville retorted that Pelley's brochure and AIF operations in the region disturbed the peacefulness of the local Cherokees. He added that "Indians Aren't Red!" had even found readership in Berlin, with much of its message incorporated into Nazi propaganda tracts. Those German documents, Weaver continued, resurfaced in Pelley's own camp for distribution to the Cherokees.[63] Clearly, Silver Shirt activities and those of the AIF exhibited a close relationship, and both proved quite involved with North Carolina Indians.

Since the establishment of the Silver Shirt Legion in 1933, Washington considered Pelley a serious menace to New Deal programs in the Southeast. In 1935 he was slapped with a fine by a North Carolina court for printing and distributing false literature, and in 1939 his files were seized by local lawmen as evidence in a similar charge. From the moment he organized the Silver Shirts, Pelley was tailed and investigated constantly by the Federal Bureau of Investigation. Even after Pearl Harbor, Pelley remained virulent in his pro-fascist posturing and in 1942 was convicted of sedition. Without question, his ties to Alice Lee Jemison and the American Indian Federation, along with his propaganda activity among Indians and obvious direct channel to Goebbels's ministry, shaped an image of Pelley as a potentially sinister force against the Indian Bureau.

Equally threatening to the bureau was James True, a one-time respected New Orleans journalist who, in the middle 1930s, emerged as a rabid anticommunist, Roosevelt antagonist, and cofounder of the isolationist union America First. His political and social views found ready acceptance in the German-American Bund, the Silver Shirt Legion, and other right-wing groups such as the Christian Mobilizers of New York and the Militant Christian Patriots. Like Pelley, True cultivated contacts with the Fichte Bund in Hamburg, Germany, for which he wrote and distributed articles, and in 1936 he founded his own pro-Nazi organization, the James True Associates, which pledged the destruction of Jewish controlled politics and institutions within the United States. Moreover, he promised to halt communist expansion in America and singled out the Roosevelt administration as its chief architect.[64]

True's organization went beyond mere verbal and symbolic threats. In "covering the nation with the fiery swastika," True advocated violence to achieve the association's goals and prominently displayed on his office desk in Washington a weapon he termed "kike killer." Patented, the instrument was a spiked ax handle and notched with finger grips.[65] In the spring of 1936 the associates planned a pogrom against Jewish populations in selected American cities and discussed the forced overthrow of the Roosevelt administration—a revolution to include the assassination of President Roosevelt. Funded through contributions his own organization raised, and supplemented with money donated by the Silver Shirts, the German-American Bund, and the American Nationalist Confederation, True's followers commenced the purchase of weapons. In Seattle alone his representatives expected to buy one hundred rifles, three hundred handguns, and several thousand rounds of ammunition for the planned September massacre. Although the watchful eyes of the FBI collapsed the attempted purchase in Seattle, agents reported his success in other, smaller cities.[66]

With his plans uncovered by FBI agents in Washington State and his organization under intense surveillance, True scuttled the scheduled pogrom. Undaunted, the James True Associates availed themselves to all pro-Nazi groups and promised to secure "peashooters" in "any quantity at a right price." Washington instantly identified True as "one of the most vicious Nazi pamphleteers" in the United States, made even worse by his extreme commitment to violence and his "direct contact with the Nazi propaganda office in Germany and Nazi agents in this country."[67]

As the pogrom folded, True's "pattern of a putsch" aimed itself at the Bureau of Indian Affairs. Aware of anti-administration diatribes emanating from the AIF and cognizant of the federation's developing connection with the Silver Shirts, True sought inroads with the Indian organization during the Asheville conference in August. He had sat next to Alice Lee Jemison on the speaker's platform and heard her rifle the accusation that the "Office of Indian Affairs is

. . . the most dangerous, Christ-mocking, Communist-aiding, subversive and seditious organization in the Nation." Her malevolent attack, the depth of her anger, and the philosophy she espoused seemed to mirror his own. While listening to her speech, True decided to cultivate a close relationship with Jemison. In the weeks that followed, True's monthly publication "Industrial Control Report" solicited donations from subscribers expressly for the purpose of providing financial support for Jemison's work in Washington. Because the FBI's ever-watchful eyes now followed his every movement, True code-named the Seneca "Pocohantas" and used the Bund's AIF liaison Henry D. Allen as his personal messenger to Jemison.[68]

In a special circular to his membership in October 1937, True credited Jemison and the AIF with the most visible opposition to the "communist phases of the New Deal." She "worked tirelessly" in the Indian struggle, he wrote, and had "bombarded members of Congress with evidence and charges of maladministration, sedition, communism, and atheism." Moreover, Jemison was largely responsible for uncovering the "misuse of public funds by the Commissioner of Indian Affairs." At the moment, he confided to his readers, Jemison's personal finances were spent, and AIF operating funds were insufficient for her continued support. From his readers and all association members True requested additional monetary aid for Jemison as a reward for her "indefatigable and loyal work for Americanism."[69]

Without doubt True's motives for aiding Jemison were partly self-serving. The seemingly large membership of the AIF and its growing prominence as an anticommunist, anti-Roosevelt organization led him to conclude wrongly that the AIF was representative of the general Indian population. Through her and the AIF, True believed his message would reach more deeply into Native American communities from coast to coast and net the associates more supporters, if not an actual increase in its membership roster. A nationally broad base, contributing funds to the associates, was required for the eventual revolution against Jewish, communist-controlled America to succeed. American Indians certainly appeared to be natural participants in that struggle. Supplying financial aid to Jemison, he hoped, would enable her to travel to reservations regionally, and perhaps nationally, and spread the fascist perspective.

As True expected, envelopes from association members soon arrived on his desk, each containing whatever money the contributor could afford. With the donations transferred to "Pocohantas," Alice Lee Jemison toured much of the Great Plains during the summer of 1938 in an old Chevrolet she purchased in Philadelphia.[70] In her addresses to Indians, she repeatedly chastised the Roosevelt administration and the Office of Indian Affairs arguing that "only one form of living is provided [for] in the Wheeler-Howard Act, and that is communal living with all property, real and personal, held in common." Indians who opposed the IRA, she claimed, had been "starved" and "coerced" into giving their assent. As True assumed she would do, Jemison's attacks implied the soundness of Nazi ideology, and in some public statements she echoed his vision of a time not too far in the future when extermination of all Jews and communists would be complete.[71]

By late 1938, the flow of cash from James True to Jemison through Henry Allen forced the Justice Department to connect the Seneca Indian directly to the German-American Bund. Known to the FBI as a "Nazi agent" and active member of the Bund, Allen based his operations in southern California. Collier was very much aware that Allen served as the personal representative for Pablo Delgado, the leader of the outlawed Mexican Gold Shirts, and disseminated Nazi propaganda among the Yaqui Indians in Mexico. Allen had also smuggled weapons northward across the border and helped organize in the United States the American White Guardsmen, a Gold Shirt branch.[72] Given that activity, Collier was sure that Henry Allen posed a potentially serious threat to the Office of Indian Affairs. More convincing for the commissioner, however, was his discovery that Allen spent the entire evening at Jemison's home while on a short overnight visit to Washington in 1937. But Jemison's Great Plains tour provided the conclusive evidence Washington desired. In her travels through Oklahoma, she was joined by Allen, and together they conducted fundraising campaigns and held speaking engagements among reservation Indians.[73]

Before meeting Jemison in Oklahoma, Allen visited Fritz Kuhn in Chicago. Forever loyal to Adolf Hitler and the Third Reich, Kuhn served as president of the German-American Bund and was planning a national rally for its twenty-five thousand members that summer. Allen summarized AIF opposition to the Roosevelt administration and highlighted the anti-Semitic, anticommunist, and anti-New Deal harangues issued by Jemison and others within the Indian organization. He then suggested Kuhn address Indian-related issues at the Bund's forthcoming convention. Kuhn agreed. The Aryan status afforded to Native Americans by Berlin warranted Bundist amplification, and the prevalence of communist and Jewish designs in the Indian Reorganization Act demanded the Bund's immediate attention. Since both the Bund and American Indians faced the same enemy, cooperation between the two groups was logical and necessary.[74]

As promised, Kuhn delivered a biting speech at the Bund rally that year and called on American Indians to unite fully with the Nazi program for the United States. Following the example set by other fascist rallies across the nation, Kuhn secured several Indians to address the assemblage. A Cherokee who identified himself as "Chief New Moon" announced his spirited complicity with Nazi activities in America and openly referred to himself as a "full fledged Nazi" warrior against communism. New Moon encouraged Indians across the country to unite, champion Bundist goals, and defy the Indian Bureau's current policies. Other Native American speakers repeated New Moon's warnings of a Jewish-directed conspiracy to destroy capitalism and democracy in the United States and bring atheistic communism to the nation. Similar to fascist-oriented conventions at Salt Lake City, Asheville, and other communities, Native Americans dressed in traditional tribal attire, and sporting Nazi armbands, distributed literature prepared by Berlin and American-based fascist organizations.[75]

The following spring, Kuhn added to the foundation laid by Allen and Jemison in the Bund's April 1939 edition of *Deutscher Weckruf Und Beobachter and the Friendly American,* a published collection of pro-Nazi writings. In his article "Our Indian Wards and their Guardian," Kuhn blasted Collier and Ickes as enemies of all Indians and proponents of communism's expansion throughout America. He traced the exploitative nature of federal Indian policy to date and warned Native Americans that the IRA was intended to prevent assimilation. Sounding much like Alice Lee Jemison, Kuhn further stated that "Indian wards of a Christian Nation are being forced into a program of anti-Christian Communism." The Indians' only recourse rested with massive, total opposition to federal policies. Such a move would best be accomplished with the aid of the German-American Bund.[76]

That the Bund commanded a rather large national audience and received frequent media attention in itself proved worrisome for the Roosevelt administration. That Jemison cultivated ties to the Bund through Henry Allen seriously troubled Collier. Now that the Bund openly proclaimed a common bond with the AIF and Indians nationwide, the commissioner was alarmed.[77]

The pro-Nazi sentiments of Jemison and other members of the AIF inadvertently snagged a North Dakota congressman. In April 1939, at the same time Kuhn published *Deutscher Weckruf Und Beobachter and the Friendly American,* the AIF proposed a means for increasing its own membership and gaining a congressional financial allotment for the settlement of outstanding Indian claims against the United States. The plan suggested the collection of one dollar from each federation member and the same amount for each deceased relative or ancestor. In return, the AIF promised lobbying efforts for a federal grant of three thousand dollars "for each living Indian who paid his contribution and $3,000 in the name of each dead relative or ancestor." Touted as a method for ending Native American reliance on congressional appropriations, lobbyists convinced Representative Usher L. Burdick of North Dakota to introduce the measure in Congress. Framed and presented as House Resolution 5921 on April 20, the bill sent tremors throughout the Indian Bureau.[78]

By the end of the decade, there existed considerable opposition in Congress to the Indian Reorganization Act. Its original co-author, Burton K. Wheeler himself, was among those who now called for its repeal. The myriad of programs and projects the IRA funded had, by 1939, proved quite expensive. With a European war almost certain in the near future, many Americans believed it increasingly important to shift appropriations from domestic civilian programs to defense spending. Moreover, prior champions of the IRA now held the opinion that Collier's plan in fact returned Indians to the blanket rather than made them more prepared for eventual assimilation with mainstream society. Throughout Congress, as the decade drew to a close, voices grew louder for ending the IRA, settling outstanding Indian claims, and bringing Indians into the larger population. Burdick viewed the AIF "three for one" plan as one answer to the rising congressional tide.

Unknown to the North Dakota congressman and to most of the 4,664 Indian contributors, the German-American Bund and the James True Associates shared responsibility with the AIF in the creation of the bill. True's organization principally campaigned among West Coast Indians, while Allen's zone centered on prior connections made in Oklahoma.[79] Not able to prove conclusively that a portion of the expected federal windfall would filter into Bund, True and AIF coffers, Collier and the Interior Department assumed a financial bonanza to be likely if the bill received congressional endorsement. At the very least, passage of the legislation would enhance the image of pro-Nazi organizations among Native Americans.

Both Collier and Secretary Ickes labeled the proposal a "scheme" and a "racket" commissioned by Nazi sympathizers. In April 1939, Collier publicly linked the AIF-backed bill with subversive sponsors and called the federation a "front" for Nazi activities in the United States. He then set aside his emotional condemnation for a more constrained legal and economic perspective. Collier reminded Indians that federal law only permitted tribes, not individual Indians, to make claims against the United States. Under that provision, Burdick's bill would most surely meet defeat. Additionally, the total outlay of grants would exceed ten billion dollars, a figure that could not be accommodated given the current dual economic crises of national defense and continued depression.[80] Recognizing the soundness of Collier's financial and legal statement, most Indians withdrew their original contribution. On April 28, Secretary Ickes asked Congressman Burdick to scrap H.R. 5921. Once Burdick himself understood the financial implications and was presented with information regarding the AIF's ties to Nazi-related unions, he honored Ickes's request and removed the bill from the House docket.[81]

As the flames of war were lit in Europe in September of 1939, Collier felt assured that no Berlin-based program was able "to sway Indians in general toward the adoption of the principles of Nazism." Joseph Goebbels's propaganda ministry in Germany had failed in its bid to carve direct inroads into Native American communities; the effort made by Colin Ross was compromised by the Indian Bureau, the allocation of Aryan status to Native Americans seemed laughable to Indians themselves, and much of the Nazi literature prepared by the ministry and its branch units proved out of touch with the realities of Indian history and cultures. Nonetheless, Collier continued to warn Indians of the potential influence of homegrown pro-fascist organizations such as the Silver Shirt Legion, the James True Associates, and the German-American Bund. Rather than being "fantastic, ludicrous, half insane, [and] negligible," as many Americans viewed domestic pro-Nazi activities to be, they were instead quite pervasive and in many instances persuasive. Their attention to Indian-related issues and the complicity of AIF members, such as Alice Lee Jemison, demanded a vigilant watch. Norway had ignored fascist activities, Collier reminded Indians, as had Holland, Belgium, and France. Ludicrous and fantastic? "They don't say it any more, and England and her dependencies don't say it any more," he added. "Fifth-column activity," said Collier, "singled out the Indians" and "actively courted" them in a bid to subvert national unity.[82]

Just before war erupted in Europe, the American Indian Federation moved to soften its severe verbal blasts against the administration and to distance itself from "fifth-column" organizations. To many members, the federation had devolved into a Nazi mouthpiece rather than pressing the pro-assimilationist agenda on which the organization was founded. By the late 1930s, the AIF no longer appeared the union it originally purported itself to be.

Moreover, political and military currents on the other side of the Atlantic heated anti-Nazi sentiment within the United States. Hitler's absorption of the Sudetenland into the Third Reich and later his annexation of the remainder of Czechoslovakia heightened expectations for war and compelled Roosevelt to concentrate more of the nation's energies on defense preparation. The last thing the AIF needed in the developing crisis was to cast in the public's mind the appearance of complicity with fascism. At the very least, such a perception would possibly block white America's receptivity to Indian assimilation; at its worst, such a view would foster the perspective of Indians as un-American and enemies of the United States.

Indian leaders themselves, such as Oliver LaFarge, condemned the AIF's pro-Nazi elements, and Jesse Cornplanter, a New York Seneca from the Tonowanda Reservation, openly denounced the federation specifically because of Jemison's activities. Cornplanter argued that since his own reservation rejected the IRA by tribal vote, Jemison no longer possessed any legitimate tribal authority to represent Seneca opposition to the policy. For the Senecas the issue was resolved, and Jemison's continued posturing against the IRA was unnecessary. Unless the AIF censured her fascist tirades and banished all Nazi presence in the federation, he said, both she and the organization must be considered "enemies of the United States" and "fifth columnists."[83]

Given the mounting tide of opposition to Nazi connections from AIF members themselves, the federation took steps to clean up its image. In mid 1939 AIF president Joseph Bruner announced, "We resent and we most vehemently deny that there is any relation between the American Indian Federation and any group objectionable to a loyal, patriotic citizen." To add credence to Bruner's posturing, the AIF encouraged Alice Lee Jemison to resign from the AIF, which she did in July.[84] Bruner did not repudiate his earlier criticism of FDR, Collier, the Indian Bureau, or the IRA, nor did he apologize for having advanced AIF arguments through pro-Nazi channels. He unquestionably continued to see in the IRA the seeds of communism in the United States, and he remained fiercely convinced of the necessity of Indian assimilation into mainstream society. Still, the AIF's public separation from anything remotely construed as fascist was essential for the organization's survival in late 1939, and its members openly pledged loyalty for the United States and cooperation with America's mobilization of resources and manpower.

John Collier sounded a note of relief in letters he wrote to the Joint Army-Navy Selective Service Committee and to Secretary Ickes in mid-1940. Although there is "evidence that subversive agents have been at work among certain groups of these Indians," he said, most Native Americans rebuffed pro-Nazi propaganda. "In practically every case" where Hitler's minions attempted to construct inroads, affinity for Nazi ideology had been "disavowed by the vast majority of Indians," whom Native American leaders and organizations "claimed to represent."[85]

In 1940 Collier conceded that Nazi propaganda never scored widespread support among Indians, and Indian alliance with fascist organizations had been minimal. In the months that followed Bruner's proclamation and Jemison's resignation from the AIF, Collier understood clearly that Indian loyalty for the United States was real and was never threatened on any large scale. The magnitude of Native American support for defense mobilization in 1940 provided sufficient evidence. Hindsight generally presents a clearer picture of reality, and this proved true for the commissioner.

Was John Collier wrong for having been so concerned about German propaganda efforts and Nazi fifth-column activities among Native Americans? When placed into the broader setting of the 1930s, the commissioner's fears are understandable. Economic depression strangled nations globally and fostered a myriad of political and social responses to the crisis. Fascism not only gripped Italy and Germany but also had vocal adherents in Great Britain and other European countries. Concurrently, communism garnered numerous followers on the continent. In the United States fascist organizations such as the German-American Bund flourished, extremists such as Father Coughlin and Louisiana's Huey Long spewed their anti-Semitic and rabidly fascist rantings across the radio, and paramilitary units such as the Silver Shirt Legion prepared for revolution. At the other end of the political spectrum, the Communist Party of America experienced a sizable growth in membership, especially following President Roosevelt's diplomatic recognition of the Soviet Union in 1933. Roosevelt's New Deal itself diverged sharply from preceding federal policies by accepting a measure of responsibility for the welfare of business and the general population and by actively using its authority to protect life, liberty, and property. An effective response to the Great Depression was required; American solutions, however, were quite diverse.

The same diversity rang true on Indian reservations. Collier offered the Indian Reorganization Act as his answer to the economic, political, and social crises found among Native Americans, but the IRA failed to gain the unanimous support he expected. The act received attacks from many quarters, most vocally from Indians who trumpeted assimilation. To those Indians and to whites who opposed anything which, even innocently, smacked of communism, the IRA proved ripe for an attack on the Roosevelt administration. Nazis in Germany and their sympathizers within the United States, therefore, believed a natural alliance with anti-IRA Indians existed, and their intense work to propagate Nazi ideology during the turmoil of the 1930s seemed to contain a serious threat to the Indian Bureau. In this context, then, Collier's acute concern for Nazi propaganda among Indians was not so much paranoid as it was a response to visible developments in both national and global settings. Not until Washington commenced full-scale defense preparation in 1940 did Collier realize Indian acceptance of Nazism to be less threatening than he first imagined it to be.

Three

American Indians Enlist

An early snowstorm blanketed northeastern Arizona in the autumn of 1940. Amidst the gray sky and falling snow, small groups of men appeared on the horizon. Few in number at first glance but increasingly more numerous, individuals soon could be seen in all directions converging on a single building in the isolated community of Fort Defiance. Slowly, yet deliberately, these Navajos formed a line at the building's entrance. They had traveled miles from their homes despite the inclement weather and bitter cold to comply with the Selective Service Act recently passed by Congress. Without regard for the weather, a line remained most of the day until each man registered for the military draft. Many Navajos held handguns and rifles brought with them on the assumption that registration meant immediate induction.[1]

Scenes similar to this occurred across the United States for the remainder of that season and throughout the following year. By November 1941, nearly forty-two thousand Native Americans, aged twenty-one to thirty-five, had fulfilled their registration requirement. This number represented almost two-thirds of all eligible Indian males. Not only did Indians comply with draft registration, many voluntarily enlisted in the armed forces rather than wait for induction orders. Of the 4,500 Indians in service one week before Pearl Harbor, more than sixty percent had enlisted.[2]

Japan's aerial assault on Hawaii only accelerated Native American enlistment. From reservations in every corner of the United States, from every remote patch of Indian farmland nationwide, and from burgeoning Indian subcommunities found along urban streets, thousands of young men made their way to military induction centers, where they stood alongside other Americans volunteering for service in the armed forces. In the immediate wake of the Pearl Harbor catastrophe, the induction of the native population into the armed forces doubled from almost twenty percent to forty percent of the twenty-five thousand Indians who actually served during the course of World War II. More than one hundred Ojibwa men from the Lac Court Oreilles Reservation in

Wisconsin, with a population of only 1,700, were in uniform by mid-1943. At the same time, forty percent of all able-bodied Crows were in service. Two thousand Sioux Indians enlisted in the various military branches. Twenty-two men from the Sioux Little Eagle community, with a total population of only three hundred, were in service in early 1942; of these, only two had been drafted. It was also reported in the news media that not one single Jicarilla Apache had sought deferment from the draft, and *Indians at Work* boasted that in the length of one single day, 16 February 1942, 2,693 Navajos complied with selective service registration requirements. One observer noted that "if the entire population enlisted in the same proportion as Indians, there would be no need for selective service."[3]

Indian compliance with draft registration appeared so positive over the first fifteen months following passage of the Selective Service Act that Commissioner of Indian Affairs John Collier claimed nearly one hundred percent cooperation among Native American men. He proudly announced that the total number of Indians inducted reflected about one-third of those eligible, a percentage rate exceeding that of any other race in the United States.[4]

In a seemingly convoluted manner, the Indians' patriotic response manifested itself further through their frequent condemnation of conscription. More than one tribe opposed the draft by demanding that everyone fight, not just those who enlisted or who were randomly chosen by the selective service process. "Since when has it been necessary to conscript the Sioux as fighters?" asked one Indian on the Rosebud Reservation. Refusing to wait for induction orders, he and eight friends reported to the nearest Army recruitment center and offered themselves for service.[5]

The enthusiasm for war was not confined only to young men. Kitus Tecumseh, a descendent of the Shawnee warrior who had attempted a pan-Indian union against white incursions into the Ohio River Valley more than one hundred years earlier, had himself served on a submarine chaser in World War I. Although wounded in combat and left partly disabled, Tecumseh tried to enlist at the Cedar Rapids (Iowa) Naval Recruitment Station. Bravado proved common among the young Indian men who sought enlistment. Joe Big Son, a twenty-seven-year-old Blackfoot, promised listeners, "I'll scalp the Japs if I get near one" and use the trophies to "decorate the town of Arlee after the war is over." Big Son traveled to Washington, where he enlisted in the army at Fort Lewis.[6]

Collier cheered the Indians' zeal. He recognized Indian registration and enlistment as both an individual decision and one supported by the broader tribal community, and he fully believed that their willing participation in the nation's defense effort reflected positively on the BIA and his controversial reforms.

While young men made their way into the armed forces, reservations commenced the conversion of boarding schools into military infirmaries. Scrap metal collection quickly became community-wide functions, women organized airplane-spotting units and armed themselves in home-defense teams, and war bond purchases soon surpassed the public's conception of Indian financial capabilities.[7] Indeed, entire tribes marshaled their energies and resources in preparation of America's entry into the war overseas, just as individual men signed their names or made their marks on registration and enlistment papers. The patriotic fervor that clearly enveloped American Indians mirrored the rousing clamor exuding from the larger, general population and signaled the Indians' voluntary involvement in the coming war.

The apparent totality of Indian support impressed Collier, the Indian Bureau, Washington officials, and the general public, but still the commissioner openly worried that many eligible Indian men would inadvertently clash with officials of draft registration. Collier was very much aware of World War I precedents. In that earlier war, only Native Americans who were citizens fell under selective service requirements. In applying draft registration and compulsory military service to those Native Americans, Commissioner of Indian Affairs Cato Sells confronted the reality that many potential Indian registrants lived on rather remote, isolated patches of land. Simply informing those individuals of draft registration proved most difficult. In addition, their ability to speak English was at best quite limited and prevented the induction of men who otherwise qualified for service. Equally troubling for the commissioner, few Indians comprehended the draft process itself, and this generated widespread confusion and concern. Perhaps the greatest problem Sells faced, however, was the issue of citizenship. Indians who appeared before draft boards frequently were "unsure if they were citizens" and consequently liable for compulsory service. To the peculiar issues that swirled around Indian registrants, Commissioner Sells applied some unusual solutions. The Bureau of Indian Affairs shepherded draft boards to distant reservations "rather than forcing Indians to present themselves before the regular draft boards as whites did." Sells also committed his office to a concerted effort to educate Native Americans on the Selective Service Act, relying on reservation superintendents to lay the foundation of understanding and supplementing that instruction with visits from BIA and Selective Service officials as needed. As for the matter of citizenship, the commissioner informed reservation-based draft boards that "if there is any doubt whatever in your mind to the status of the individual, or his clear liability to the draft, resolve it in favor of non-citizenship."[8]

Collier confronted essentially the same problems in 1940 that challenged

Sells in 1917, despite overall improvements garnered by the Indian Reorganization Act. On larger reservations, such as the Navajo Reservation that crossed Arizona and New Mexico, few good roads existed, and many Indians lived in areas without any transportation network whatsoever. This directly contributed to inefficient postal delivery that resulted in many Navajo men not receiving their notification to register with the draft or to report to induction centers. As an added complication, Indians occasionally relocated across state boundaries and seldom thought to leave forwarding addresses. Faced with this potential nightmare, the commissioner created a "special police force" to make contact with isolated or relocated Indians and inform them of selective service requirements or induction orders. Still, Collier did not anticipate much success even with this endeavor; too little money was available with which to fund the unit, and manpower proved limited as men left for military service or found higher paying positions in defense industries. Through no fault of their own, the commissioner expected many Indians to run afoul of the Selective Service System.[9] Where practical, Collier resurrected Sells's strategy for the registration of Indians on reservations themselves.

Impressive as Indian draft registration and induction was, the rate of Native American enlistment would have been much higher had Indian health and literacy levels been greater. Regardless of medical and educational gains made in the previous decade, one-third of all Indians who sought enlistment were rejected for military service. Even those who were overweight were turned away by army recruiters. "Don't want to run," said one rejected Indian, "want to fight." Although this particular example was publicized repeatedly in the press and was often attributed to individuals from several different tribes, the underlying message remained clear—many Native Americans were physically unfit for service in the armed forces.[10]

Tribes continued to be plagued with greater than normal mortality rates along with higher levels of infectious disease and malnutrition. Nationally, rejections for military service by December 1943 totaled 38 percent for white recruits and almost 58 percent for African Americans. Collier was unquestionably pleased that the Indians' rejection rate closely resembled that of white recruits.[11] The picture, however, was fundamentally flawed. Individual states with large Indian populations, particularly those states of the Southwest and upper Great Plains, frequently had higher rates of rejection than states with smaller native populations. Within Arizona alone, only 27 percent of whites were kept from military service, while Indians and African Americans encountered rates of 45 percent and 46 percent, respectively.[12] On larger reservations, Indian communities were often widely dispersed, and individual families often lived in remote and inaccessible areas far removed from modern health services, public sanitation, and health education programs centrally located on reservations under the umbrella of IRA reform. Across the Southwest, there was a greater frequency of self-imposed community isolation from modern America, founded on a general suspicion or fear of white encroachment into traditional tribal structures and the potentially corruptive influence of white values and culture on community standards. Such an attitude pervaded numerous Indian communities, even at the expense of tribal health.

Poverty, too, played a critical role in the poor health of Native Americans. Low income certainly precluded the search for medical service and the purchase of prescription drugs; it also prevented many Indians from providing their families with the clothing and quality food necessary for good health. Typically, the more remote the community and individual family, the fewer were the prospects for earning wages sufficient to pay for health care. Among those who had access to medical care and health education, many of the very problems condemned in the Meriam Report of 1928 persisted on the eve of World War II. Singularly chastised by Meriam's investigators was the habit practiced by many physicians of giving only a quick, cursory glance at one eye in trachoma examinations; yet, it was trachoma that tripped Arizona Indians at military induction centers. Eleven percent of all Arizona Indian rejections turned on this one particular medical condition. Equally prominent were problems of the ears, nose, and throat, which together caused another eleven percent of all Arizona Indian rejections. Pulmonary, cardiovascular, and musculo-skeletal problems were each responsible for another fifteen percent of all Indian rejections in the state.[13] The majority of health problems that most affected Arizona's male native population were made worse by the general absence of adequate medical care facilities on Indian reservations, the relative isolation in which many communities and families lived, and continued improper diagnostic procedures at many medical centers. Given the "conditions under which the Indians have been living and the lack of funds for carrying on an adequate program among them," said Congressman Francis Case of South Dakota, "it is not surprising if the Indians do show a large number of rejectees for physical reasons."[14]

Health conditions, however, proved to be only half the reason for the high rejection rate of Arizona's Indians for military service. Standardized tests given at induction centers examined the educational and mental competency of new recruits. While only twelve percent of Arizona's white males and twenty-three percent of African Americans fell below the armed forces' minimal standard, almost forty-nine percent of the native population failed to pass the mandated exam.[15] As in the arena of physical health, Indians of Arizona suffered a slightly higher rate of educational and mental "deficiency" than did Native Americans living in most other states. Again, this was largely the product of tribal and individual isolation from white society. Limited contact with the general population reduced the likelihood that Native Americans would understand the glaring truisms, much less the subtle nuances, of white society necessary to scoring well on standardized tests prepared by white academic institutions. Except for the most acculturated Indians, the failure of Indian Service educational programs and systems precluded success in meeting the intellectual standards set by the armed forces. Conditions were slightly better on Indian reservations that were more compact physically and surrounded more completely by white society.

In May of 1941, Secretary of War Henry Stimson demanded a full investigation into the "abnormal rejection rate of Indians." The Indian Bureau responded to Stimson's expressed concern by pointing to what it believed to be several critical dissimilarities between Indian and white societies and cultures. First, medical examiners at induction centers had little or no prior association with the native population. Physicians, therefore, often mistook the Indians' "stoicism, reticence, and shyness" as "indications of mental deficiency," said Collier. Second, for many Indians the trip to nearby cities where induction centers were located proved to be their "first view, of a large city built by white men." Said one Selective Service Board member who served the Navajo, "It was fairly common for some Navaho [sic] men to wander carelessly about Phoenix, 'lost', and unmindful of any schedule they had to meet at the Induction Station."[16] Their late arrival for medical and educational testing suggested their inability to understand and obey simple orders or to comprehend the importance of their presence at the induction site. Finally, Collier admitted that the revamped education programs developed under the Indian Reorganization Act and other federal agencies had not been fully available to many Indians, especially in those regions where the native population was more dispersed. Both Collier and the War Department recommended that medical doctors and test administrators at induction centers grant leniency and be more understanding of the background from which American Indians came before stamping their forms "Rejected for Military Service."[17]

The rather high rate of rejection for military service among Indians frustrated many of those Native Americans who offered themselves to the armed forces. John Collier worried that a backlash effect might result, one that might dampen Indian enthusiasm for the nation's war effort. His concern seemed justified when some Native Americans charged the Selective Service System with racism. In the Southwest, Indians increasingly feared "not that the Navajos will be selected for service, but rather that they will be discriminated against by local boards, and will not be accepted." It appeared to many Indians that the rate of rejection turned not so much on physical, educational, or mental deficiencies but on an obvious preference for white recruits.[18] Such a perspective seemed warranted when placed into the broader context of Indian-white relations: both Arizona and New Mexico still refused the extension of suffrage to Indians, and standardized tests at induction, by design, reflected the knowledge, values, and experiences common to most whites. Jim-Crow-styled racial segregation was enforced in many small cities in the Southwest and in the Great Plains states, and occasionally recruiters openly demonstrated their prejudice toward Native Americans. Little wonder that some Indians viewed the "abnormal rejection rate" to be but part of a larger pattern of racism against American Indians.

The charge of racism was not new. As Thomas Britten recounts in his recent study *American Indians and World War I*, many Navajo men in 1917 believed that once drafted "they would be placed in the front lines to save the lives of white soldiers."[19] Interestingly, Navajo perceptions of racism had altered slightly between the two wars, from a fear of inclusion to one of noninclusion. What remained the same was the Indians' belief that the Selective Service continued preferential treatment for white recruits, and in 1941 the perception of racism revealed a fundamental distrust among Indians for the federal government in spite of Collier's reform efforts.

Collier and Selective Service personnel assured Native Americans that racism was not the underlying cause for so many Indians being turned away from the armed forces. He reminded them that Indian recruits served with white inductees and currently held commissions in all branches of the military. Throughout 1941, the bureau's publication *Indians at Work* printed written and visual examples of Indian service in the armed forces, evaluated the progressive reforms on reservations intended to enhance health care and education, and praised tribal commitment to the nation's defense preparations. Collier insisted that racial discrimination carried no weight in the registration or enlistment of Indians for military service, and in the periodical and in public addresses the commissioner informed Indians that he had persuaded Selective Service physicians and test administrators to consider cultural differences when evaluating Indian recruits. He also informed Indians that he had personally convinced Selective Service officials to be lenient with those persons who registered late with the draft.[20] Collier's often repeated assurance and his personal visits to many of the reservations quieted much of the emotionally charged concerns expressed by Indians.

A fundamental problem remained that excluded thousands of Indians from military service; more than a few Indian males did not possess the military's most essential requirement—the ability to speak English. The Indian Bureau confronted the same issue during World War I and was aware that the problem persisted on the eve of World War II, but noted Indian anthropologist and proponent of the Indian New Deal, Oliver LaFarge, was among the first observers to address the matter directly in 1940. In November of that year, LaFarge dispatched a letter to Commissioner Collier in which he identified three categories of Native Americans. He termed the first group "legal Indians." The label referred to those persons who contained such a distant biological connection to Indian ancestry that they barely qualified as tribal members. Over the years, these individuals aligned themselves with the native population only when it was financially beneficial to do so. "Legal Indians," he wrote, generally expected an active role in tribal affairs when land deals arose that might generate themselves some monetary reward. Residing within the structure of white society and identified as whites in their daily living patterns, these "Indians" encountered few obstacles and entered the armed forces with ease.[21]

"Acculturated Indians" identified LaFarge's second division among Native Americans. Whether full-blooded Indians or mixed with white parentage, persons of this category typically dwelled within the Indian community, participated in tribal ceremonies, and functioned daily as a contributing member of the reservation. Programs that emerged specifically from the IRA, and opportunities afforded by the larger New Deal, advanced their personal economic growth and afforded them an improved educational foundation and level of health that guaranteed their acceptance for military service. "Acculturated Indians," LaFarge added, faced only the most minimal hurdles in adapting themselves to service in white units.[22]

LaFarge labeled the third, and final, group as "primitive Indians." For these individuals, a total absence of English language capabilities proved commonplace. Isolation from white society, whether self-imposed or not, and their strict maintenance of traditional tribal values and customs made their induction into white military units tantamount to culture shock and guaranteed failure. This particular category most troubled LaFarge. Within the "primitive Indian" grouping, the traditional warrior spirit prevailed in its most emotional form and served as the impetus for enlistment in the armed forces. Rejection of these men for military service, he contended, only perpetuated their isolation and promised to retard the development of governmental programs among them once Washington's finances permitted the effort.[23] Two-thirds of the eligible native male population found avenues into America's armed forces; unless a path was discovered that would permit "primitive Indian" participation in the nation's war effort, the United States would not utilize fully her manpower resources at the point in time that men were most in need.

J. C. Morgan, chairman of the Navajo Tribal Council and former vice president of the American Indian Federation, concurred with LaFarge's assessment. Having challenged Collier earlier on tribal economic matters, Morgan bypassed the commissioner and presented Secretary of the Interior Ickes a plan to accomplish the induction of "primitive Indians." He suggested that the unacculturated Navajos be sworn into the army and trained as a single, separate unit on the Navajo Reservation. Accustomed to the environment and in constant association with others of similar experiences, values, and capabilities, "primitive Indians" would more quickly learn the skills necessary for later assignment to white units. Morgan and LaFarge believed the prospect of increased Native American inclusion in the armed forces, through the creation of "one or more all-Indian training units," symbolized the elevated identity to which most Indians aspired—an identity as respected and contributing members of American society.[24]

Without hesitation, LaFarge supported Morgan's proposal. This alternative would strengthen the manpower reserves of the armed forces, and it would also raise the level of acculturation among those Indians most in need. If the segregated effort fell short of performance expectations, then a semi-trained unit would exist for national defense within the territorial boundaries of the United States. A trained, domestic force would prove essential should any Axis power invade American soil, a prospect that in 1941 was deemed quite possible by astute observers. The two men presented their concept to selected members of Congress, the War Department, and reservation superintendents.

The superintendent of the Navajo Reservation voiced his opinion that the disqualification of Indians because of the language barrier was counterproductive. Indians who freely offered themselves for military service would be committed to learn English as rapidly as possible in order to be transferred to white combat units. Unlike those Indians who actively opposed draft registration and induction in other areas of the nation, the Navajos, he wrote in his letter to Collier, did not wish to avoid military service. Their rejection for service on the language issue seemed inexcusable when minimal English skills could be acquired with relative ease in the proper setting. Already, Superintendent Fryer added, the sentiment had emerged among Indians that "the Government is fooling us again." The campaign gathered momentum, and in the spring of 1941 Collier and the Indian Bureau were convinced that all-Indian training units were feasible.[25]

Morgan's plan was not without its critics, some of whom contended that talk of an all-Indian training unit was itself cloaked in racism. Rather than an integrationist approach to Indian-white relations, racial segregation was being touted as the preferred course. Jim Crow, they argued, manifested itself as fully among the Indians of the Southwest as it did among African Americans of the Old Confederacy. More moderate critics saw reservation-based training to be an impediment to acculturation and assimilation. Total immersion into white culture offered the quickest method for learning the ways of the white world. Interestingly, common to both perspectives was the essential premise that Indians and whites should blend with one another. This represented the central value present among assimilationist reformers who framed the Dawes Severalty Act of 1887, who championed integration within the armed forces long before and during World War I, and who more recently challenged Collier's vision of cultural pluralism.[26] In short, complete inclusion of "primitive Indians" underscored their preference that Native Americans as a distinct race would one day truly vanish and meld into the dominant society.

Some advocates of all-Indian training units promoted the program's political dimensions, although their supporting arguments sounded rather dubious at best and forced many Indians to scratch their heads in wonder. An all-Indian unit, these proponents said, might be used in parades and formal ceremonies of state to impress foreign dignitaries. Public display would illuminate the diversity of America's population and the nation's commitment to racial inclusion and equality. It would further exhibit Washington's successful effort in redirecting federal Indian policy and the movement of Indians into the broader society. The continent-wide visibility of such a unit would also demonstrate America's respect and honor for Indian willingness to participate in national defense.[27] These advocates were oblivious to the possibility that the very act of displaying an all-Indian unit in public, patriotic gatherings might be construed as further evidence of America's continuing policy of racial segregation.

Collier preferred total integration of Indians with white forces, in concert with established War Department policy, but he consented to Morgan's request with the stipulation that only "primitive Indians" be segregated and only for the duration of a short, preparatory training course. Once language skills improved and Indians gained an acceptable hold on military discipline, Native American transfers to white units would begin. The process, he said, must be completed with speed. The commissioner hoped to avert any accusation of racial segregation for purposes other than short-term training.[28]

Despite the appearance of a workable solution for enlisting "primitive Indians" and fully using Native American manpower, staunch opposition arose in the higher echelons of the armed forces. In spring 1941, Assistant Chief of Staff General William E. Shedd flatly rejected any consideration of an all-Indian training unit. Shedd stated categorically that Indians should serve with, and as, white recruits in both training and combat. Segregation of Native Americans compromised military structure. The armed forces already consisted of two racial divisions, black and white; further division required additional expenses and carried with it a potential breakdown in the "coordinated and cooperative effort" among the segregated units. "Utter confusion" in administrative services, he added, would result.[29]

Left unspoken, but certainly another point for consideration, was the army's standard policy of building unit cohesion in training and then placing that unit as a gelled team in an overseas duty post. An all-Indian training unit carried the potential breakdown of this established system, and as replacements it would be unlikely that formerly "primitive Indians" would be able to blend into the unit's existing camaraderie.[30]

The War Department nonetheless agreed to "contemplate" the creation of an all-Indian training battalion at a later date.[31] The army's response was well understood: the issue would be filed, and there it would remain. But, from one perspective, there was a glimmer of light in the army's position. The military's insistence on racially combined training confirmed to Native Americans the nation's commitment to Indian inclusion with whites in the armed forces. As in World War I, American Indians would not face racial segregation and the dehumanizing imprint that forced separation creates; Selective Service regulations promised Indian induction as white recruits, but the army's choice not to institute Morgan's plan provided an additional guarantee for those least acculturated. Indians who preferred assimilation with the larger society believed the army's refusal to create separate training units actually hastened the process of acculturation and eventual blending into white society.

Morgan, LaFarge, and many others who trumpeted assimilation viewed the War Department's decision from a different angle. To them, total inclusion signaled a denial of the "primitive" Indians' opportunity to begin the acculturation process. If assimilation was, indeed, the goal of twentieth-century American Indians, then the refusal to form all-Indian training units proved the government's willingness for a rather large segment of Indians to fall short of the final end. Unable to secure the basic knowledge required for induction into the armed forces "primitive Indians" retreated to their homes, ever more suspicious of federal authority. On the eve of World War II and amidst the patriotic clamor rising on reservations, LaFarge's third category of Native Americans arrived at a cultural crossroads that most Indians encountered later in the decade. Rather than determine for themselves what course to pursue—the path toward greater acculturation and possible assimilation or the retention of traditional community life—external forces dictated which avenue they would follow, retrenchment into an ethnocentric posture.

The loss of "primitives" to the war effort troubled many Indians, but the overwhelming majority of Native Americans overtly demonstrated their loyalty for the United States by offering themselves to the armed forces. More than 4,500 Navajos, and most Pueblos and Apaches, registered for the draft during the first three months of conscription. Between September 1940 and March 1941, nearly one-half of all eligible Indian men at the Fort Peck Sioux-Assiniboine Reservation in Montana enlisted. By April, enlistment among all Indians was fifteen times greater than the number of draftees. By the end of December 1941, all but three of the Ojibwa's single men at Grand Portage Reservation in Minnesota joined the armed forces. Of the five hundred residents on the Mesquakie Sac-Fox Indian Reservation, nineteen men were in the armed forces shortly after Pearl Harbor. In a letter to the commissioner in spring 1942, Mae Williamson, a Blackfoot, informed Collier that one hundred young men had already enlisted in the armed forces, among them were her husband's five brothers. "Thus it is throughout the tribe," she wrote. By the following March, six Indian families across Montana each had contributed five sons to the army and navy. Enlistment was viewed with so much respect and importance among Native Americans that following Pearl Harbor, Sioux Indians performed the Sun Dance—the first such ceremony in fifty years.[32]

The extent of patriotism among Native Americans was impressive. Their nearly one-hundred-percent compliance with draft registration, their rate of enlistment, and the extreme support given Indian inductees by tribal communities all surpassed the most optimistic expectations held by government administrators and the general public alike. John Collier himself was probably dazed by the apparent totality of Indian support for national defense, although it is doubtful he would have ever admitted a moment of surprise. In seeking an explanation for the spirit that pervaded Indians nationally, Collier looked to himself and to Indian Bureau programs. He assumed reservation improvements made under the IRA encouraged Indian patriotism. The redirection of federal Indian policy brought more than the physical redevelopment of tribally owned lands and herds. It provided much more than additional hospitals, clinics, schools, and professionally trained staffs to operate the facilities. Bureau endeavors gave reservation Indians far more than the skills required for off-reservation employment or the emergence of prosperous tribal economies. To the commissioner and his closest supporters, the IRA and other programs he sponsored in the 1930s proved to Native Americans a new commitment from Washington—from the American people—to treat Indians with fairness, equality, and respect.[33] Congressman John Coffee of Washington echoed Collier's sentiment. "After the injustices the Indian has suffered, he still is ready for an all-out defense of democracy, because only democracy can better his lot." American Indians, he added, "are fighting for America because America has made a conscientious effort to right old wrongs and improve the life of our Indians." Indians "have seen in recent years, particularly under the enlightened administration of Commissioner Collier, that democracy gradually corrects those injustices," Coffee added.[34]

While the Indian New Deal reinvigorated some tribal customs and promoted cultural pluralism, it concurrently increased and widened the opportunities for Indian movement into mainstream society. The most central feature of the IRA was the program's emphasis on self-determination, and this, Collier believed, was the ultimate reason for Indian patriotism and complicity with national defense. "Indians," he said, "have identified the struggle of democracies the world over with their own struggle of the last century." Native Americans historically fought for the right "to retain their cultural independence, the right to their native religions, and the right to local democracy." The current global conflict meshed well with Indian history; it was "a struggle against the totalitarian concept of a super-race dominating, absorbing, and reducing to serfdom the small minority group of a different culture." Wrote Richard Neuberger, "I have talked with many of our Indians, both in and out of the Army. They regard the war with hope. They believe it will lead to more opportunity and less inequalities for the people of China, India, South America, and the island nations."[35]

The commissioner believed Indians recognized a correlation between their own struggle for freedom and self-determination and the same aspiration held by Europeans and Asians who opposed Axis forces. Although the Indians' complete right of self-determination remained unfulfilled, "it may be that they see in a victory of the democracies a guarantee that they too shall be permitted to live their own lives," Collier wrote. The experience of the previous ten years proved the bureau's resolve to promote that end. America's involvement in the world war indicated the nation's adherence to the principle of freedom for all nationalities and races, he added.[36] For Collier, then, Indian participation in the war evidenced a loyalty to the United States founded on the recent redirection of federal Indian policy and the respect Washington now accorded native cultures.

The commissioner correctly identified one motivating force behind Indian participation in the war, but it was a limited and biased opinion. When Indians surveyed the years between Collier's appointment as commissioner and the advent of World War II, visible progress was certainly evident. Individual and tribal incomes had attained record levels by 1941. Job opportunities for Indians expanded both on and off reservations as a product of vocational training, practical education programs, and work experience gained through the Civilian Conservation Corps-Indian Division. Health care showed marked improvements, tribal land holdings increased, and stock values and agricultural productivity netted substantial profits. And, as Collier explained, Indian self-determination found some measure of legitimacy in tribal constitutions.

Equally important, however, was the broader perception of change that shadowed the 1930s. The spirit of Roosevelt's New Deal filtered across the United States, loosening its three-point promise of relief, recovery, and reform into states nationwide. While the Indian Reorganization Act encountered fierce opposition from many quarters, and rightly so, it nonetheless represented Washington's desire to recast Indian-white relations, reconstruct tribal communities, and allow Indians to chart their own paths. The federal government, in essence, confessed its mistakes of previous administrations and actively solicited input from Indians themselves. Although the IRA smacked of white dominance, continued federal paternalism, and required bureau approval of tribal constitutions, the feeling of impending change nonetheless pervaded reservations. The rhetoric emanating from Washington, the news media, and the general public as the United States entered World War II extended the shadows of reform into a perceived new world order. FDR's four freedoms—freedom from want, freedom from fear, freedom of speech, and freedom of religion—echoed into every corner of the globe and propagated the ideals of peace, equality, and humanity to all cultures and races once the Axis powers were defeated. The war was frequently described as a "peoples' war" and a war to "destroy evil." Presented was the image of a multicultural, multiracial, multi-religious force of rightness in a war to reshape the world into a democratic and egalitarian global society. Although so much of the message was propaganda prepared for popular consumption, the image was a heartfelt one for many people, including Native Americans.

Collier's explanation of Indian loyalty was most clearly evoked by the Navajo Tribal Council meeting at Window Rock, Arizona, in June 1940. Fully three months before the Selective Service Act passed through Congress, the council's attention focused on the existing threat to world peace rather than immediate tribal concerns. On June 3, the Navajos unanimously passed a resolution that stated the tribe's stance on the current international crisis. It warned all Indians on the reservation that un-American activities would be "dealt with severely" and swiftly. Pledging loyalty to the United States, the document declared that the Navajos "stand ready to aid and defend our Government and institutions against all subversives and armed conflict."[37] The key term in the statement was the single word "our." Not only did it refer to tribal government, society, and lands, it concurrently signified an understanding of Navajo inclusion with the United States. The resolution further stated that tribal members were devoted "to the system which recognizes minority rights and a way of life that has placed us among the greatest people of our race." Passed without dissent, the document confirmed the tribe's connection with the American system.[38]

As Collier surmised, Navajos realized the government's attempt to correct past wrongs. While the process utilized by Collier and the Bureau of Indian Affairs occasionally frustrated and infuriated the tribe, most members appreciated the overarching reformist programs of the 1930s and the specific efforts to revitalize tribal economics, education, health care, and culture. Clearly, much work remained, and many battles with Washington policymakers were expected, but for the first time Navajos believed their collective voice would be heard and would determine future relations with the federal government. Given such an assessment, the tribal council encouraged Navajo men to support fully America's war effort. The "threat of foreign invasion and the destruction of the great liberties and benefits which we enjoy on our Reservation" demanded Indian compliance with draft registration and military service. The United States deserved Indian loyalty.[39]

Similar notes sounded throughout 1940 and 1941. The Mission Indian Federation in southern California sent President Roosevelt "a message of loyalty and readiness to serve our great nation." They set aside for the duration of the crisis their ninety-year struggle to gain financial compensation for lands lost to white settlement. An Idaho rancher, speaking for his tribe, said, "we know victory will mean new hope for men and women who have no hope." America's involvement in the war, he added, would aid those people under Axis domination whose lives and rights were in jeopardy. He believed that the changes for Native Americans during the previous decade revealed a new, fresh attitude in Washington toward minorities and oppressed peoples. To the rancher, the United States' role in the war seemed to be an extension of that attitude globally.[40]

Indian participation, however, resulted from more than the sense of inclusion as Americans. Fear permeated Native American communities as it did non-Indian locales. By the autumn of 1941, Germany commanded western Europe, much of central and southern Europe, North Africa, and a portion of the Soviet Union. Hitler's *Luftwaffe* crossed the English Channel, leveled much of London, and threatened the extension of its air superiority over the British Isles. And, in the Pacific, Japan marched ever closer to American possessions. Conceivably, a direct movement on the United States or its territories was possible. By early December 1941, war was considered inevitable for the United States, and on December 7 the mangling carnage of modern war exploded in Hawaii. Three days later, Commissioner Collier gave Indians a personal motive for fighting the Axis powers. A Nazi victory, he warned, would reduce Native Americans to a state of slavery or extermination. "Don't think that killing off the whole Indian race would be anything new" for the Axis nations. "Germany right now is deliberately exterminating the Poles, who are about as numerous as the Indians," and, he added, "the same thing is happening to the Greeks right now. That is what we face if we lose the war."[41]

Collier's words created a foreboding atmosphere among Indians, especially so in the immediate wake of Pearl Harbor. A war in which a minority race was to be exterminated carried very real and vivid images and emotions among American Indians, and the irony of the commissioner's warning was not lost on Native Americans. Over the course of four centuries, Indians had been stripped of their lands and reduced to a population only a fraction of its original number, despite their determined and heroic resistance. Only fifty years earlier, the United States cavalry shredded Big Foot's band of Sioux at Wounded Knee. Many elderly Indians held personal recollections of tribal flight from army detachments and armed battles with white soldiers, and a few were children at the time of the Sand Creek Massacre. The horror of genocide once experienced would not be repeated. The European and Pacific wars now washed onto America's shores, and Indians, like other Americans, were determined to defend their lives, their homes, their land and their nation. Said one Navajo who enlisted in 1942, "I'm doing this for my people" and for "the many American people, also the unborn children which would be the generation to come."[42]

While the enlistment of many Indians reflected a concerted determination not to suffer humiliation and destruction by conquest again, the value of the land itself spurred many other Indians to join the armed forces. In contrast to the temporal and linear underpinnings of Christian religion and its fundamental premise that God's Word is universal, Indian spirituality was (and is) spatial. All life, knowledge, and truth are derived from the land, as is tribal identity. Although much of the Indians' land physically was not theirs any longer, said James Martin, an Oklahoma Osage, most Native Americans sensed it always would be.[43]

Protection of tribal land was necessary, and an armed defense was required to halt Axis conquest. When asked why he enlisted, Albert Smith, a Navajo code talker during the war, responded, "this conflict involved Mother Earth being dominated by foreign countries. It was our responsibility to defend her." Cozy Stanley Brown echoed Smith's sentiment: "My main reason for going to war was to protect my land and my people because the elderly people said that the earth was our mother. . . . the Navajo people get their blessings from the four sacred mountains, our mother the earth, father the sun and the air we breathe." After a moment for further reflection, Brown added, "There are Anglos and different Indian tribes living on the earth who have pride in it. That was my main reason for fighting in the war; also, I wanted to live on the earth in the future. . . . The Anglos say 'Democracy,' which means they have pride in the American flag. We Navajos respect things the same way they do."[44]

Undeniably, numerous other motivations led American Indians into service during World War II. Many tribes had contributed warriors as scouts to the United States Cavalry in the nineteenth century, while others allied themselves with either Americans or Europeans in eighteenth-century frontier wars. "Go and fight as your forefathers did . . . our Great White Father is calling us to help. We must go," Three Calves called to younger men on the Blackfoot Indian Reservation. As was true for Indian service in World War I, enlistment proved a combination of "pride of Indian heritage and race, and pride of being American." A long-standing tribal tradition of military alliance with the United States, therefore, encouraged tribal communities such as the Iroquois tribes and the Crow to enlist and support the war effort. Young men remembered stories told by their fathers who served in the Great War, recollections of visits to London, Paris, and through the French countryside. Without much thought given to the impending horrors of warfare, sons of World War I doughboys imagined their own travel to European cities and Asian islands.[45] Financial considerations also affected the decision of Indians. Those with skills insufficient for employment in defense industries found military pay quite attractive, especially for those men who resided on reservations that received limited federal aid during the 1930s or were bypassed by bureau-funded works projects. Moreover, the promise of specialized training transferable to civilian life following the war attracted others. Personal finances and the prospects for post-war employment played as important a role in World War II enlistment as it did twenty-five years later for Indian men who joined the armed forces during the Vietnam War, when fully fifty percent of Indian veterans reported "financial reasons" as their motivation for enlistment.[46] Additionally, the imprint of federal Indian-school training that historically stressed patriotism and an American identity led many young men along the course toward enlistment.

And, without question, a desire for vengeance spurred some Indians to go to war. On December 8, 1941, Barney Old Coyote Jr., a Crow, stood in the icy morning Montana wind waiting for the bus to carry him to Hardin High School. Friends at the bus stop spoke of the attack on Pearl Harbor the previous day and President Roosevelt's planned declaration of war against Japan only hours away. As the bus rumbled into view in the distance, Old Coyote wished his friends well and returned home. Filled with rage over the unprovoked assault and determined to avenge the lives of sailors and soldiers killed in Hawaii, he borrowed money from his older brother and traveled to Billings, seventy-five miles away, to enlist in the army. Being only seventeen years old, army recruiters rejected his application but said that with written parental permission, he would be reconsidered. Three days later, and in possession of his mother's reluctant consent, both Barney and his brother joined the army and, after training, saw combat in North Africa.[47]

American Indians enlisted for a myriad of reasons, but the press and government offices highlighted one unique motivation and ascribed to it the position of primacy. Pearl Harbor, it appeared to whites, ignited a latent "warrior tradition" that still simmered among Native Americans. Determined to capture honor and glory in combat as their ancestors had achieved, Indians readily volunteered their service to America's armed forces. As with most news stories and government reports, a strand of truth ran through published reports, and this particular line of thought was fundamentally valid. A warrior tradition certainly encouraged numerous Indians to enlist. Warrior societies had experienced a slow disintegration with each passing year since the cessation of Indian-white hostilities. In some Indian communities, ceremonies had vanished entirely. Combat duty, then, permitted Indians who historically maintained and valued warrior societies the opportunity to revitalize tribal culture and in the process gain personal prestige, respect, and honor in the manner of their ancestors.[48]

For the news media, however, the image of a renewed warrior spirit made good human-interest stories. Descriptions of Indian war dances and purification rituals dotted the pages of major newspapers from coast to coast. Reports of Indians carrying their rifles to draft registration and enlistment centers drew the curiosity of a national audience. When Kitus Tecumseh laid plans to form an Indian "scouting force" for combat, the *New York Times* publicized the story to demonstrate both the wartime cooperation of Native Americans and the prevalence of the warrior tradition.[49] Newspapers printed photographs of Indians with General Douglas MacArthur, stories of the Sioux Sun Dance ceremony, and the marriages of Indian servicemen to white women, but consistently larger space was devoted to the Indians' combat exploits.[50] The stories, without question, attracted the attention of readers, filled space in daily papers, and demonstrated the apparent unanimity of support for the war effort, even among America's most romanticized minority group. A revived warrior spirit connected white readers to the popular portrayals of American Indians found in dime novels, in comic books, and in film. The mystic Indian warrior of an earlier time in the context of modern war captured the imagination of readers and often put a twinkle in the eye and a slight grin on their faces. In short, such stories made good copy.

Equally important, coverage of Indians in combat, serving alongside white soldiers and sailors, presented readers with the impression that Native Americans were indeed considered part of the white mainstream and consequently ready for their final inclusion with the broader society. The appearance of equal treatment and equal opportunity suggested there was no longer need for reservations and direct federal aid. Stories of heroism under fire and self-sacrifice in combat implied the Indians' own sense of an American identity, an image the press hoped to instill in the general population. Given the angle provided by the news media, readers devoured stories of Indian warriors in the fight against Germany and Japan and indirectly found satisfaction that the "American Way" proved valid among the nation's minority groups.

For similar reasons, the federal government detailed the Indians' combat performance. Secretary of the Interior Harold Ickes praised one Omaha Indian, who, in 1943, landed "alone under heavy [enemy] fire" to mark the beaches at Licata, Sicily, for the infantry assault that followed. Ickes pointed to a Sioux commando who earned the respect of his unit after eliminating ten Germans in a single raid. Commissioner Collier commended Private First Class Albert

Wahweotten, a Potawatomi, who charged two hundred yards ahead of his own line to clear a German-occupied house. Armed with an M-1 rifle and a bazooka, Private Wahweotten fired a rocket at the enemy position from a distance of ten yards, then rushed the house, and captured twelve German soldiers. Collier also praised Lieutenant William Fredenberg, a Menominee, who flew an air assault against a German "marshaling yard." Credited to the lieutenant was the destruction of three locomotives. Despite heavy ground fire, Fredenberg remained at the scene strafing small gun emplacements until he spent all of his ammunition.[51]

The emphasis on the Indians' warrior tradition served the interests of the press and Washington agencies and was well received by the general public. But the warrior spirit more importantly served Native Americans. For those who invoked cultural tradition, a renewed Indian identity commanded precedence over the more prevalent, widely held assumption that Indians favored racial assimilation. It represented a conscious decision for Indians at the crossroads to follow the path toward cultural revitalization and an identity apart from whites. The warrior spirit once more instilled pride in the Indian heritage.

Indian enlistment in the nation's armed forces was not confined to a single explanation. Service in the army and navy was the product of numerous forces influencing the decision of Native American men. Common to all explanations was the belief that, for their service, Indians would receive something of personal value—inclusion by white society, a sense of self-worth, pride in a renewed warrior spirit and its link to Indian heritage, evidence of patriotism and loyalty for the United States, financial return, a contribution to the common welfare and salvation of human kind, or simply the defense of tribal lands. Perhaps that is, in itself, what made World War II so important for American Indians—their conscious, personal decision to enlist (or to accept compulsory service) represented a choice, an element of self-determination, that would directly influence their post-war lives. The same proved true of those who remained on the home front.

Four

Indian Draft Resistance: Questioning Identity

Indian support for America's war effort appeared all-pervasive. The overwhelming rate of Native American enlistment in the armed forces, the Indians' combat record in Europe and Asia, vivid displays of patriotism on reservations, and the Indians' voluntary movement into defense industries on the home front all validated such an assessment in the mind of John Collier, other Washington officials, and even the general public. In spite of appearances, however, America's romanticized minority proved fragmented in its reaction to the nation's mobilization as early as 1940. Underlying the image of unanimity was an Indian population comprised of many separate cultures and within each culture numerous individual tribes, each tribe with its own unique character, values, and experiences. Given the diversity among Native Americans, a current of Indian protest throughout the period of mobilization and war should not have surprised Washington. Like their white counterparts, religious values embedded within some tribal communities conflicted sharply with the nation's response to war. Similar to African Americans, racism separated some Indians from a complete union with America's wartime objectives. Although verbalized by a numerically small number of Indians, resistance underscored serious issues unresolved by recent changes in federal Indian policy, issues that encouraged a postwar reevaluation of the Indians' self identity.

With passage of the Selective Service Act in 1940, John Collier pricked his ears for whatever negative response Indians might offer. Little time elapsed before he first heard the faintest sound of consternation. Consistent with his prior response to Native American arguments regarding the Indian Reorganization Act, Collier assumed Indian draft resistance stemmed from a simple misunderstanding of the law. In a brief letter to one Selective Service official in Washington, Collier mildly wrote, "Were we dealing with slackers or professional troublemakers, I should feel differently and urge prompt, punitive measures, but the Indians on these reservations are not slackers. They are not radicals or agitators." "It is," he said, "a case of merely making them understand" the law's intention.[1] The commissioner believed opposition to the law was quite minimal, and once the concept of compulsory draft registration and military induction by lottery was explained sufficiently to Indians, resistance would vanish completely.

Collier thought Indian complaints hinged on their view of loyalty for the United States. Volunteerism clearly indicated patriotism; military service by lottery implied an unwillingness to serve. He was certain that such a perception formed the crux of Indian resistance to the draft. "There are," he said, "many patriotic Indians who find the Selective Service Act distasteful not because they object to military service, but because they consider it a reflection on their loyalty to their country."[2] Neither compulsory registration nor conscription questioned one's allegiance to the United States, he assured Indians.

The commissioner correctly identified this as one source of Indian draft resistance, but he overlooked more fundamental issues such as the retention of traditional religious values, particularly among less acculturated southwestern Indians. Zuni religion historically justified defensive warfare and only rarely condoned offensive combat. When an external force directly threatened the security or preservation of the family and tribe, a combative response was warranted, and for that reason Zuni Indians clearly maintained a warrior structure within their community. Most often, however, it served principally as a tribal police force. Once the tribe committed itself to war, religious leaders offered prayers for vindication, and the outcome of battle rested on divine response. Because spiritual intervention determined victory or defeat, the emotional envelope surrounding a warrior spirit and warrior exaltation that was found among other Indian cultures commanded no respect among the Zuni. Tied into religion, also, was the Zuni fear of white America's incursion into tribal culture. Throughout the century prior to World War II, Zuni Indians did adopt many of the physical trappings of white society, but they did so reluctantly. Termed "antagonistic acculturation" by anthropologist Peter Farb, the Zuni took as their own only those features of white culture that would protect them from dominance by white society itself. Particularly threatening to the Zuni, wrote Farb, was the corruptive imprint modern white technology and values would have on Zuni religion. For that reason, the Zuni strove to remain distant from white influences. Insulation could, in part, be accomplished by avoiding compulsory military service.[3]

Throughout 1940 and 1941, Zunis surveyed international developments and America's mobilization and concluded that the United States would certainly become involved in a war overseas. The Selective Service Act only confirmed that assessment. Zunis had complied with federal laws and Indian policies since the turn of the century, and they further fulfilled their obligations through the registration of more than two hundred young men between October, 1940 and January 1941. However, as American military preparedness increased and the prospect of war shifted from the realm of possibility to one of probability, Zuni elders increasingly questioned the nature of the coming conflict. Was it to be defensive or offensive?

In early January 1941 one tribal religious leader living in Gallup, New Mexico, received his induction notice. Although he had earlier registered for the draft, he now sensed America's role in the approaching war to be offensive in character. He saw no direct threat to the security and preservation of the nation or to Zuni tribal existence. True to his spiritual understanding, he filed an appeal for deferment as a conscientious objector, and on January 23 his request was granted. He was, the draft board stated, "entitled to the same consideration given ministers of other religions."[4]

With one deferment secured, the tribal council requested exemptions for all Zunis holding religious posts, and the Selective Service quickly and without argument granted the preferred classification to all who applied. Feeling confident with recent successes, the Zuni council then petitioned the federal government for a blanket deferment for all tribal members, claiming that every man belonged to some priesthood or performed a significant role in religious activities. On this request Washington balked. The Zuni council persisted by creating new religious offices and resurrecting those abandoned decades earlier. The effort netted deferments for some Zuni men, but a total reclassification never materialized. Once the United States actually entered the war, more Zuni Indians registered with the Selective Service, lost their appeals for deferment, and reluctantly entered the armed forces. By 1945, 213 Zunis had served in the American military, approximately ten percent of the eligible Zuni male population. Upon their return home, Zuni veterans received no hero's welcome and instead were viewed with suspicion for signs of corruptive white influence.[5]

Neighboring Hopi Indians employed a similar tactic, and did so for essentially the same religious reasons but with much less success than the Zunis. In late October 1940 the Hopi Reservation superintendent at Holbrook, Arizona, Seth Wilson, wired Commissioner Collier that fourteen tribal members claimed conscientious objector status for religious reasons. Collier suggested that those men follow appropriate channels, file appeals with the Selective Service System, and await the board's decision. He forwarded to Secretary Ickes a summation of the Hopis' arguments and tendered his opinion that the Indians would receive deferments.[6]

Within two weeks the board sent its reply. Eight of the men were informed their appeals had been carefully evaluated and that they were now deferred from induction. Appeals for the remaining six, however, were rejected. Wilson and members of the local draft board spent hours in consultation with the young men and their families and encouraged each to comply with compulsory military service. His effort failed. The Hopis vehemently denounced the board's decision and held steadfast to their religious-based opposition to military service, despite Washington's threats of prosecution for draft evasion.[7]

Members of the appeals board wrongly interpreted Hopi resistance to be the logical continuation of a recalcitrant Hopi opposition to federal authority. Within the Indian community were several individuals who fiercely challenged Washington's Indian policies and actively encouraged Hopi families to distance themselves from federal services such as government schools. These men had proven themselves impediments to the smooth implementation of government programs for many years. Such posturing at this particularly critical point in time cultivated an opinion among some Indian Bureau and Selective Service officials that these resistors were "hostile," disloyal, and potential subversives. Hopi draft evasion, then, appeared to be a political response to federal law rather than a religious position, as expressed by the Zunis.[8]

Contrary to Washington's perception, Hopi resistance stemmed from traditional tribal spirituality. Like their Zuni neighbors, these Hopis did not object to defensive warfare, only to offensive action, which American involvement would most likely be. Moreover, they, too, believed white influence was corruptive and destructive of traditional tribal values. Absorption of white values would be nearly impossible to prevent if inducted into military service; facing the greatest threat of corruption would be Hopi spirituality. John Collier recognized this to be one source of Hopi resistance and advised members of the bureau and the Selective Service System that opposition to the draft "grows out of a religious tradition even though it may not be a conscientious objection against warfare . . . in the way that the white men construe it."[9]

The threat of prosecution only made the Hopis more determined to resist. The six men fled into the surrounding hillside to avoid arrest. Superintendent Wilson, hoping to defuse rising tensions, solicited Collier's help. Wilson partially understood and concurred with the Hopis' stance. He informed the commissioner that even local whites urged extreme leniency in this particular case. Indeed, he added, all those who dealt with this situation held sympathy for the resistors.[10] Angering not only the Hopis but the superintendent as well, Collier dropped his earlier limited defense and refused to interfere with the Justice Department's prosecution of the Indians. Apprehended, tried, and convicted of draft evasion, each of the six Hopis was sentenced to a one-year prison term. Said one of the men, prison was a "cinch." Conditions there proved better than those found on the reservation, and he received pay while incarcerated.[11]

Two pointedly different worldviews were in direct conflict with one another. The Selective Service System failed to comprehend the extent of the Hopis' and Zunis' retention of traditional religious values and typically confused Indian arguments founded upon spirituality with political dissatisfaction. That assessment, along with the belief that draft evasion would only spread if not dealt with severely at this juncture, made federal prosecution seem the logical response to Selective Service officials. Although acculturation had swept across and enveloped much of the Indian population nationally, many Indians still held firm to traditional spirituality. Relinquishing one's religion normally marks the final separation from long-accepted cultural values. Based on traditional spirituality, draft evasion among those Hopis who championed cultural revitalization was itself a logical and natural response to the crisis of compulsory military service.

The commissioner's acquiescence to Hopi prosecution, in spite of the support given the six men by Wilson and the surrounding white community, illuminated clearly his desire for total Indian compliance with registration and induction orders. What better image to convey to the national population than an Indian minority, historically mistreated, now fully in concert with white American values and goals? Certainly, such a popularly viewed portrait would reward Collier with broader approval for his work as Indian Bureau commissioner. But his response, or lack of one, also revealed a significant flaw in his supposed understanding of Indian cultures and conditions. While in one breath Collier acknowledged the Indians' "religious tradition" as the center-pin in draft resistance, he himself did not grant the argument enough credence to warrant his intervention on behalf of the Hopis. By permitting federal prosecution, Collier provided tacit agreement that the Indians' religious opposition to the draft and to the approaching war served only as a means not to comply with compulsory military service. His behavior further contradicted his own promotion of traditional Indian spiritual renewal as trumpeted in the Indian Reorganization Act a few years earlier.

Collier's reticence in supporting the Hopis rested, in part, on an incident that occurred the previous summer. In August 1940, the annual Hopi Snake Dance was performed in Hotevilla, Arizona. Built into the tribal religion was a belief that at one time Indians and whites lived harmoniously together in an "underworld." However, a "Two Heart," or wicked soul, incited a split between the two groups and turned loose evil into the world. As punishment for the people's susceptibility to evil, the Great Spirit cast both races from this Garden of Eden into the outer world of wickedness. One day, Hopi religion taught, a white savior would destroy all evil "Two Hearts" and reunite the races. This "great white brother" would then lead the righteous back to the underworld from which they had been cast.[12]

During the festivities, Don Talayesva, the son of a former chief, detailed a vision he experienced. The "great white brother" would soon return, he said, and "Hopis and whites [will] be united as one people and live in peace and prosperity such as once existed in the underworld." What shocked reservation officials and BIA personnel was Talayesva's physical description of the "great white brother," one which showed the image of the redeemer in the face of Adolf Hitler—a man who reunified the German people, reinstilled national pride, and returned prosperity to his nation.[13] Disturbed by Talayesva's favorable portrait of Hitler, Collier discounted the vision as but another example of Nazi propaganda among Native Americans. When confronted with Hopi draft resistance in late autumn, most visibly manifested by the six men who were prosecuted, Collier mistakenly concluded that Nazism rather than traditional spirituality fused the core of draft resistance in that particular instance.

Spiritual-based opposition to compulsory military service eluded Collier's understanding, but so too did the issue of race as a reason for draft resistance. Despite much progress during the 1930s, a portion of white society maintained a racist perspective toward American Indians. Federal law prohibited the racial segregation of Indians from whites in military units, as African Americans faced, but Indians nonetheless feared discrimination from Selective Service officials. The pervasive idea among the Navajos was "not that the Navajo will be selected for service, but rather that they will be discriminated against by local boards and will not be accepted for service."[14] Collier interpreted the comment as evidence of the Indians' simple misunderstanding of the Selective Service process, and he assured the Navajos that race would not prevent the induction of any Indian. For the Navajos, the commissioner's statement held true, but race did ensnare many other Indians.

In August 1941, Collier and the secretary of the Interior both received letters from the superintendent of the Flathead Indian Reservation in Montana, who accused the navy's recruitment officer with refusing to enlist one Warren Gardipe. Although the Flathead possessed qualifications sought by the navy, his Indian identity precluded his acceptance, said the superintendent. A Works Progress Administration staff member, who had accompanied Gardipe that morning and witnessed the rejection, corroborated the story. Both Ickes and Collier forwarded their concerns to Secretary of the Navy Frank Knox. By October, the Department of the Navy removed the recruiting officer from his post and openly solicited Indian enlistment. By that time, however, Warren Gardipe had enlisted in the army and was stationed in Hawaii.[15]

Indians in the navy often complained that they seldom received promotions. Seaman Second Class Franklin Gritts was one of many cases. A graduate of the University of Oklahoma, Gritts resided in Farragut, Idaho, where he worked as a teacher for four years prior to his enlistment in late 1942. With a college degree in hand and perhaps inspired by Indian officers in other branches, Gritts applied for the navy's Officer Candidate School in October 1943. Within one week, Lieutenant E. A. Van Diest at Camp Waldron informed the seaman that the navy rejected his application. According to Van Diest, Gritts was denied admission because of his Indian identity.[16]

Protests from Gritts, Gardipe, and other Indians supplied the commissioner with examples of racism in the navy, but Collier ascribed the actions of recruiters and administrators to simple misunderstanding of the racial status of Native Americans in the armed forces. He pointed to the Marine Corps' open solicitation of Indian recruits as proof of a nonracist policy in the armed forces. Equally important, Collier added, the army held the largest number of Indians in uniform, and in both services Native Americans served with, and as, white personnel as proscribed by federal law. To the commissioner, then, a failure to communicate effectively the racial identification of Indians in the military accounted for the navy's apparent racism. Again, Collier's simplistic response to Indian grievances underscored his superficial understanding and grasp of problems faced by American Indians.

Perhaps more serious than the attitudes and behaviors among some navy personnel was the intensity of racism directed by a single state agency in Virginia. There, State Registrar for Vital Statistics Walter Ashby Plecker proved to be the Indians' chief antagonist. The product of post-Civil War white society, Plecker breathed the fire of the stereotyped southern racist. He believed "racial contamination" would destroy the nation if blacks and whites mingled with one another socially or sexually; the same would occur if whites and Indians failed to remain apart.[17]

But on the eve of America's entry into World War II, Plecker faced a public who, both nationally and statewide, increasingly viewed Indians as higher in racial status than African Americans. In some quarters of society, not only were Indians given elevated status, they were quickly becoming accepted as whites in the community. In the nation's armed forces, Native Americans were fully included as white recruits. Attempting to quell arguments that Indians should be considered and treated as whites, the Vital Statistics Office in Virginia bluntly stated that "no native-born Virginians claiming to be Indians . . . are unmixed with Negro blood."[18] With this single brief declaration, the registrar officially relegated Indians to an African American racial identity to prevent "contamination" of the white race.

Plecker assumed the role of self-appointed expert on Indian ethnicity, although he lacked professional training and admittedly based his credentials squarely on his limited reading in the field. The registrar's powerful position in government along with his sweeping political influence in state politics drew some lower-level officials into his orbit and easily convinced similar-minded racists of his credibility. But Plecker needed indisputable, factual evidence to mute counterarguments from potential political adversaries and those who might seek legislative redress on behalf of the native population in Virginia.

Much of the supporting documentation he amassed derived from old federal census records, marriage forms, birth and death certificates, and, in Plecker's terms, other "reliable" sources. Plecker uncovered written accusations made by a few white citizens in the mid-nineteenth century of Indian intermarriage with African Americans, particularly among the Pamunkey, Chickahominey, Gingaskin and Nottoway tribes—the principal claimants of Indian identity since the early 1800s. If true, the allegation would certainly build a biological link between some blacks and tidewater Indians, but it would certainly not sustain Plecker's blanket contention that all persons in the state claiming an Indian identity were actually African American. Corroborative anthropological evidence was needed to validate those century-old accusations. Plecker did not reveal the spurious source of the alleged racial intermingling, but the accusation in fact originated in an 1840 petition to the state assembly that requested the termination of the Pamunkey-Mattaponi Reservation in the tidewater region. The document's author, one T. W. S. Gregory, hoped to secure Indian land holdings for his own personal ownership, a move that would have been easily accomplished if an African American racial identity had been affixed to local Indians. The state, however, denied Gregory's petition and confirmed the integrity of the reservation.[19]

Aware that the Gregory Petition was by itself a weak plank in his developing argument, Plecker turned to academia for a sturdier base of support. Scholars, he argued, proved cohabitation and intermarriage between Indians and blacks in Virginia. In both an 1894 bulletin from the Bureau of American Ethnology and a 1913 publication, *The Free Negro in Virginia, 1619–1865,* Virginia's Indian population was described as heavily mixed with the Negro race, and the Pamunkeys specifically were said to have "not a little" biological tie with the black community of the state. Plecker further pointed to more recently published material, particularly E. Franklin Frazier's 1939 work *The Negro Family in the United States.* "The Pamunkey Tribe of Indians in Virginia," Frazier wrote, "is typical of those communities of mixed-bloods which, having originated in the association between Indians and Negroes, gradually lost their Indian character."[20] Frazier's observation gave the Gregory Petition a measure of credibility. He added that the Indian "blood has so largely mingled with that of the Negro race as to have obliterated all striking features of Indian extraction" and concluded his polemic with the assertion that Indian identification as African American seemed logical because "the tribe [Pamunkey] has been almost absorbed by the local negroes [sic]."[21] Again, empirical evidence proved nonexistent, but the mere fact that scholars of sound reputation drew such a conclusion sufficed for Plecker and his cadre of state officials.

Claiming a biological connection between Indians and African Americans through their mutual association, and actually taking action to define Indians as blacks by law, were two entirely different matters. To accomplish the second objective, Plecker informed the federal census bureau that in the nineteenth century Virginia's native race fell under the classification "free persons of color" or " free Negroes" in census records, blurring whatever racial distinction that might have existed earlier. While the Gregory Petition sank to defeat in the state assembly in 1840, Virginia legislators nonetheless agreed soon afterward that Indians and freed blacks in the state had developed such an intimate relationship that racial mixing inevitably brought the two races into a single identity. Because the bureau shifted Indians to a separate listing later in the century, Plecker insisted, federal records contained an inaccuracy in desperate need of correction. Wielding the collected scholarly evidence, he announced forcefully that "we have their pedigree back," and the census bureau should act in accordance with the findings of the State Office of Vital Statistics.[22]

Although the Census Bureau ignored Plecker's argument, the registrar succeeded in reducing the total Indian population count in Virginia records. The Fifteenth Census of the United States, taken in 1930, listed 779 Native Americans statewide, a figure equal to one-tenth of one percent of Virginia's total population. Ten years later, the Sixteenth Census cited only 198 Indians in the state, a drop of nearly seventy-five percent. Counties that historically contained the bulk of Virginia's natives found themselves officially without an Indian population at all in the 1940 count.[23]

Some emigration from Virginia unquestionably occurred, especially as employment opportunities mushroomed in defense industries late in the 1930s. Nevertheless, this alone could not explain such a tremendous depopulation of Native Americans in the state when viewed against rising employment demands within the tidewater region itself during the same years. The Norfolk Naval Yard and the Hampton Roads areas were among the fastest developing defense sectors in the United States. Such a pronounced decline in numbers could only be attributed to the impact of Plecker's assault and influence over Virginia census recorders.

John Collier seemed oblivious to the registrar's crusade against Indian identification with white society prior to America's declaration of war against Japan and Germany. Indian protests from tidewater communities landed on the desks of lesser officials in the Indian Bureau and were uniformly returned to Virginia authorities for resolution. In all likelihood, Collier mistakenly believed Plecker's influence was considerably less than Indian complaints suggested.

The commissioner assumed that tidewater Indians were recognized as a separate race in Virginia. Tribal goals on reservations statewide focused on the revitalization of Indian identity and culture by the late 1930s and in Collier's view clearly reflected national trends under the Indian Reorganization Act. What he failed to understand was that the effort in Virginia was not so much a desire to renew traditional native culture in the name of pluralism as it was a concerted defensive struggle to halt Plecker's spirited campaign to assign Virginia Indians to an African American racial classification. With Plecker a formidable roadblock to Indian assimilation, and with most Native Americans adamantly opposed to racial classification with African Americans, Indians began vigorously to pursue recognition as a third racial group, separate from both whites and blacks. [24]

Walter Ashby Plecker's drive for non-contamination of the white race and efforts to reassign Indians to a black racial status was by no means peculiar in 1940, although the method and depth of the attack was most extreme in Virginia. The Houma of Mississippi and the Tunica of Louisiana faced racism daily, so much so that a large proportion of these Indians were "anxious to move to Houston, Texas, where they [would] be free of racial discrimination and . . . have a better chance" of achieving a more satisfactory living environment.[25] In Robeson County, North Carolina, a three-tier system of racial segregation existed, separating whites, Indians, and blacks in all public facilities. Each race had its own water fountains, restrooms, schools, and theater seating, with separate movie house entrances. Without question, Jim Crow segregation remained alive and well throughout the South and frequently extended its embrace to Native Americans. The principal difference between Virginia and other states of the Old Confederacy was that there was no one in authority like Plecker, who forced a Negro classification onto Indians. Certainly, states across the South discriminated against Indians, as did the residents and governments of states in other regions, but the discrimination was directed toward them as Indians rather than as African American. With a separate identity as Native American, Indians in those states moved into white circles and entered the military as white inductees.

Passage of the Selective Service Act in September 1940 intensified the Indians' opposition to Plecker and demanded an immediate resolution to the issue of racial classification. As the armed forces swelled with new recruits, tidewater Indians were horrified to discover they were listed as "colored" registrants and therefore to be inducted into all-black army units.[26] Prescribed by federal law, Native Americans were to be listed and inducted as white recruits, while African American inductees would train and serve in racially segregated military units. Many Virginia natives desired full assimilation with white America; to a person, tidewater Indians wished to avoid the discriminatory laws and practices that African Americans endured daily. Blocking the path toward Indian identity and recognition as white for military purposes was Plecker's earlier determination that "no native-born Virginians claiming to be Indians . . . are unmixed with Negro blood."

Protesting their unexpected classification as African American, the Chickahominies hurried a letter to Secretary Harold Ickes. Tribal leaders categorically denied any previous intermarriage with blacks and added that tribal members never even associated socially with persons of that race. In visible contrast with military service during the Great War, they reminded the secretary that "the other time our boys registered [in World War I] they registered as Indians and went with the white." "Now," wrote tribal chief J. L. Adams, "it seems as if they want to send us with the colored." The letter to Ickes ended with an ominous note: "We don't mind our boys going if they can be sent right and not with the colored."[27]

Ickes asked General Lewis B. Hershey, national director of Selective Service, to investigate the confused situation in Virginia, and in so doing he expressed his belief that the Chickahominies possessed a definite Indian heritage apart from both whites and blacks.[28] But the tempo of mobilization forced Hershey's attention to more pressing matters. The war in Europe was in its second year, the *Luftwaffe* mercilessly blasted London and other sites in England each day, the flow of child refugees into the United States increased monthly, and the American campaign "Bundles for Britain" consumed much of the public's energy. Washington officials sensed imminent peril to the continued peace and safety of the United States. President Roosevelt called on Congress to approve the Lend-Lease Act and convinced the general public that Great Britain was

America's current line of defense against Hitler's plan for global domination. At the same time, Secretary of State Cordell Hull searched for any workable agreement with Japan to prevent hostilities in the Pacific. Each Gallup Poll survey showed more Americans were certain war would inevitably come to America. In these anxious days, national mobilization of resources, industry, and manpower commanded priority. Hershey's task was to construct a military force for the United States capable of waging total war in possibly two theaters of operation concurrently. As for Native Americans, Hershey believed the issue of Indian racial classification for military service had already been decided in the Selective Service Act. Little wonder he decided to forward the Chickahominey protest to another office.

Hershey returned the matter to Virginia and directly ordered Virginia Selective Service director Colonel Mills F. Neal to resolve the question of Chickahominey identity. Neal, in turn, issued a memorandum to all local draft boards in the state ordering them to delay induction of those persons claiming an Indian identity until a final decision could be made by his office. In his own mind, Neal believed the Selective Service held no authority to determine the racial identity of any registrant. All persons in Virginia who could give evidence to support an Indian ancestry should be ordered to white training facilities.[29] In search of guidance, Neal solicited the opinion of the War Department itself. Unknown to the colonel, similar questions of Indian racial classification had surfaced in other East Coast states, and the War Department was about to forward a directive to all draft boards.

On March 3, 1941, the War Department ordered local boards to determine the "ethnic origin" of all registrants. Not only would physical appearance be used as a determinant, so would any reports of an Indian's personal association with African Americans, regardless of the nature and extent of that relationship.[30] In effect, Virginia's native population would be registered and inducted according to personal prejudices of local boards.

The War Department's directive enraged Colonel Neal. Local boards were "without lawful authority" to consider race, creed, or color in the registration and induction process. He highlighted Selective Service Regulations, Paragraph 326, to support his position. Draft boards will have completed their assignment, the paragraph read in part, "when it determines that a man, without regard for his race, creed or color, is Class 1-A or some other class." This specific phrase, he insisted, proved that racial identification remained outside the boards' responsibility.[31]

That April, in a bid to circumvent the War Department directive and local board prejudices, Neal intervened on behalf of seven Virginia Indians who refused induction as black recruits. Neal ordered their reclassification as "Indian mix" and sent them to the white training facility at Fort Meade, Maryland. Upon their arrival at camp, the Indians' folders were rejected by the commanding officer and referred back to the local board for reclassification as black inductees.[32] Throughout the summer and autumn of 1941, Neal and his staff sluggishly worked to formulate a policy that would eliminate the confusion in Virginia, but Japan's attack on Pearl Harbor brought the period of debate to an immediate close.

In a bid to finalize the issue of Indian racial identification and expedite the flow of manpower to the nation's armed forces, the War Department issued Memo 336 on January 7, 1942. The memo called attention to the department's earlier decision that "members of the Indian race will be inducted as white trainees." It added, however, that should doubts arise as to a registrant's "Indianness," local boards were empowered to "delay . . . induction of persons registered as 'Indian' pending the proper determination of classification (White or Colored)." The ruling granted an investigation period not to exceed sixty days.[33]

Memo 336 affirmed the War Department's position that any "ascertainable Negro blood" warranted listing as a black registrant. Furthermore, investigators were to consider "whether their [Indians'] associates are Negro and whether they are treated as Whites in the social patterns of their community and State."[34] With a national emergency now facing the United States and rapid mobilization required, Memo 336 emerged as the department's final response to the question of Indian racial identity in Virginia. Rather than resolve the question for tidewater Indians, the ruling actually fueled Native American draft resistance in the state. The War Department simply sidestepped the fundamental issue for expediency and allowed Walter Ashby Plecker's influence to continue unimpeded.

In late January 1942, the National Selective Service Headquarters proclaimed February 16 as another day of draft registration. An estimated 220,000 men were expected to comply with the latest call, and no reclassifications would be permitted unless there existed "circumstances over which the registrant had no control." As anticipated, Virginia's Indians filed their names and awaited induction orders, which, for members of the Eastern and Western Chickahominies, arrived in early summer. To their surprise, Chickahominey inductees received an African American identification and were sent to a training camp for blacks. Once there, the group of one dozen Western Chickahominies refused to leave their assigned barracks until reclassification as white inductees was granted. Eastern Chickahominies responded just as adamantly, but added that only armed force would dislodge them from their barracks. Determined to avoid violence, the United States Army chose to negotiate a peaceful resolution by permitting the protest to work its way through proper channels.[35]

Chickahominey chief O. Oliver Adkins forwarded two tribal letters of protest, one to the War Department and the other to Governor Colgate Darden of Virginia. Adkins pointed to the state's 1893 recognition of the Chickahominies as a tribal unit, confirming Virginia's acceptance of Indian identity for the Chickahominies. In that year, he wrote, "a tribal school and a church were built and financed by the Indian people" — a school and church strictly "for the Tribe alone." Financial difficulties forced the closure of the school from 1905 to 1920, but the facility reopened with state funding. During the interim, Chickahominies received an invitation from neighboring black schools, but the tribe refused to enroll its children there. Moreover, Adkins stressed, to stem allegations of racial mixing, the Chickahominies forbade the intermarriage of tribal members with African Americans. "We did not want to be classified as Negro people," he said. The tribe's self-imposed isolation from the black community, Adkins insisted, eliminated all contentions that the Chickahominies could be identified with the black race under the provisions of Memo 336.[36]

Chief Adkins then broadened his protest to a more general rebuttal of army race classification. "Indians," he contended, "are not trying to avoid the draft or serving in the United States Army." Tribal members opposed only one issue, racial classification as African American. "What have we to fight for?" he asked. "For the individuals who deny us our Birth Rights . . . and [who] classify us to a creed that we do not belong, to which we may be mistreated as Negroes? My people are American Indians of the State of Virginia." "They will not go as Colored or as Negroes," he thundered. Adkins's letter accused the state registrar and his supporters of usurping the Indians' right to vote, to obtain higher education, and to live in peace alongside white Americans — privileges also denied to African Americans. The curtailment of civil rights and now the attempt to induct Indians into black military units all proved Plecker's commitment to link Native Americans in Virginia to the non-white listing in a biracial state structure. "The White people have their place, the Negro have [sic] his place but the Virginia Indian has no place or voice in the Government," he continued, and Adkins assured both Darden and the War Department that mass protest and refusal to serve would continue until reclassification as Indian was granted.[37] Adkins's letter, applauded by the Chickahominey tribal council, gave notice that Virginia Indians had, in fact, moved beyond a desire to be listed simply as white registrants to a demand that they be recognized as a third race in a presently biracial state—one separate and apart from both whites and blacks.

Governor Darden replied with a garbled and patronizing letter wrapped in the vagueness of political rhetoric, but he promised that his office would study the problem carefully. Action from Darden's office never came. In Washington, the War Department sat on the Indians' protest until September 18, at which time the chief's letter was forwarded to the Military Personnel Division for action. Whether that office or the Chickahominies' local board ordered a reversal of racial classification remains unclear. Nonetheless, the western band gained recognition as Indians while Eastern Chickahominies were listed as "nationality unknown" and allowed to serve with white troops.[38] Given the determined and unified opposition to an African American identity and the very real threat of violent confrontation, the army's action constituted a practical means for diffusing the conflict.

But the possibility of violence alone did not force a change in racial identity. Government documents and affidavits collected by Indians from whites and African Americans confirmed Adkins's argument that the Chickahominies historically "restrained" relations with the black community. Local boards were provided evidence that the marriage of an Indian and an African American had always resulted in the expulsion of the Indian from tribal rolls, often from the community itself. Indeed, tribal Chickahominies showed signs of intermarriage, but that had been entirely with whites. By 1940, tribal concerns centered on the "reinforcement" of bloodlines by attracting Indian immigrants from outside Virginia. So intolerant of blacks were the Chickahominies that on several occasions attempts were made to buy out African American farmers and property owners living on, or adjacent to, Indian lands. Moreover, the Indians also banned the presence of black physicians and ministers on the reservation, even at the expense and well-being of the tribe.[39]

Nearly fifty years after the Chickahominies' battle for racial reclassification, Professor Helen Rountree of Old Dominion University suggested that the Indians' success rested more squarely on the written testimonies of tidewater whites who perceived tribal members to be Indians rather than African American and who pressed their influence in Washington. This, along with a strong, determined tribal leadership, which held "good contacts in Washington," aided the Indians' position significantly.[40] White neighbors did substantiate Chickahominey arguments with signed affidavits, and there were certainly "contacts" in federal departments who held nothing less than disgust for Walter Ashby Plecker and who would consequently challenge his position on Indian identity.

Overlooked in Professor Rountree's assessment is the tribe's own initiation of resistance and its intention to fight Washington's ruling regardless of white support. The Adkins letter effectively countered Memo 336 provisions point by point, and the Indians' forceful, threatening stance at army training centers added the dimension of potential domestic violence at the very moment when the United States government needed a unanimous spirit of wartime cooperation. Rather than be passive victims of government rulings or the puppets of liberal whites, the Chickahominies themselves defied Washington and Richmond to reestablish a separate Indian identity. Without question, voices of sympathetic whites contributed weight to the Chickahominey argument and helped tip the scale in the Indians' favor. Ultimately, however, resistance was directed by Indians for their own benefit, and reclassification was won as a direct result of their own effort.

Although Memo 336 attempted to resolve the issue of Indian race classification in Virginia, it instead generated further confusion, dissent, and varying interpretations among local draft boards. A required, extensive investigation into the ethnic background of each registrant claiming Indian identity forced local officials to sift through mounds of affidavits, school records, and government documents such as marriage, birth, and death certificates. The depth of work necessary for each case presented boards with a backlog of appeals. By autumn 1942, in an effort to meet induction quotas and circumvent the investigative quagmire, King William County set aside one day to register as Indian all who claimed the racial listing. The Upper Mattaponi Indians were inducted without question of ethnicity.[41] Because of Chickahominey reclassification and the nightmarish responsibility placed on local boards to determine ethnicity, it proved much easier and quicker to assign an Indian identity to registrants when appeals were filed. The inadvertent result was the emergence of national population figures that contradicted themselves. Listed in selective service files as Indians but in the federal census as "Negroes," Virginia's Native Americans held dual identity and, consequently, now had a potential legal foundation from which to nullify Plecker's pre-war gains.

The apparent change in local board behavior arrived too late for one tidewater Indian. Oliver Fortune, a Pamunkey, dutifully answered the February 16, 1942 call for draft registration. Rather than wait for his induction notice, Fortune volunteered for service in the United States Army the following month and soon afterward was issued orders for basic training. As he closely read his orders, Fortune noticed that he had been assigned to the Negro Military Training Center. Determined not to be listed as an African American, the Pamunkey pursued the only course he believed open to him — noncompliance. As one of his attorneys later commented, "Evidently Fortune was classified as a Negro by his draft board and either [he, Fortune] did not know it or did not make a complaint until his induction order was issued." Noncompliance brought Fortune a federal charge of refusal to serve. That his objection to service was "because of an error in racial classification of which he had not complained in court heretofore" mattered little. The Pamunkey's trial date, set for October 30 in Richmond, appeared to both Walter Ashby Plecker and his detractors as the final, authoritative determinant in the battle over Indian racial identity in Virginia.[42]

The Pamunkey Tribe solicited help from Congressman Dave E. Satterfield Jr., the district's congressional representative. Satterfield approached the Commissioner of Indian Affairs with the expectation that the BIA would intercede on behalf of Virginia's Indians, and Oliver Fortune specifically. John Collier replied that "without in any way speaking disparagingly of Negroes, I do feel that something should be done" for Fortune; however, he added that "unfortunately it is not a decision which I can or have any authority to make."[43]

Collier commanded no direct authority over draft boards, but as commissioner of Indian Affairs he was in a position to sustain the Indian identity of Pamunkeys, Chickahominies, and other Virginia tribes. Such a move on his part probably would have quelled the disturbances in the Old Dominion. Not only was Collier approached by Satterfield, but Plecker himself mailed to the commissioner copies of documents that he believed proved an African American lineage to those claiming Indian identity. He urged the BIA to act in accordance with the evidence. Sensing his entrapment between two explosive forces, Collier remained true to form and sidestepped the issue by remanding the matter back to Virginia for settlement.[44] To Indians, Collier's refusal to inject bureau opinion smacked of collusion with Plecker.

The Pamunkey Tribal Council continued its protest on behalf of Fortune, even without Collier's support. In a letter to Governor Darden in July 1942, the council expressed "distress and alarm" that tribal members were classified as black inductees. "This action," the letter read, "simply blots out our Tribe, our race, our descent, and places us as negroes [sic]." The council charted tribal history from the early 1600s and conclusively documented themselves in Virginia law as a legal, reservation Indian tribe. Why, they wondered, were there only two identifiable races now? "If the government says he is not white, therefore he is a negro [sic], are we to be blotted out?" the letter asked. The Indians responded to their own rhetorical question: "This would be an act of death to us—death to what we so value in life, our Indian heritage, race, descent, and tribe."[45]

Lloyd G. Carr, Harrison Fellow at the University of Pennsylvania and legal resident of Virginia, rose in defense of Fortune and the Pamunkey tribe. In the late 1930s Carr lived among the Pamunkey while studying traditional medical cures and became "impressed to find that the Powhatan Indian spirit is strong and vigorous, that the tribal laws are cherished and upheld today." In his letter to Darden, Carr insisted these Indians "are holding tenaciously to their fine tradition, culture, and honor. To have this spirit, this fire, muffed out by an intolerable and prejudiced man as W. A. Plecker is inconceivable and should not come to pass."[46] Like a growing number of white Virginians, Carr realized the registrar's influence over local draft boards. Had Fortune's Caroline County board not been so responsive to Plecker, he would not have had to resist induction. He challenged Governor Darden to protect "the identity of the American Indians" within Virginia. Carr expected that the scientific evidence he forwarded to Darden, both his own research and that of other published scholars, would convince the governor of the racial identity of tidewater natives.[47] As with the Chickahominey request for intervention, Governor Darden waffled. His failure to take a definitive stand compelled many state residents to assume he either supported Plecker's point of view or was intimidated by the registrar's political influence.

On October 30, Oliver Fortune appeared before the court. The prosecution revealed documents proving his prior enrollment in a segregated, black school and that one of his parents and one grandparent were listed as "colored" residents. Moreover, prosecutors argued, the Pamunkey Tribe belonged to a larger body of Indians comprised of several different tribal groupings. A significant number of anthropologists and ethnologists believed the combined tribes, normally referred to as the Rappahannocks, had intermarried with freed blacks in the years immediately following the Civil War, although the prosecution admitted that scholars possessed no verifying documentation. The state further provided the testimony of some neighboring whites who contended that the Pamunkeys maintained close ties with the African American community.[48]

Fortune's defense refuted any biological connection with African Americans and insisted that his few associations with blacks occurred from necessity only. Official state documents, attorneys argued, recorded individuals as either white or "colored." That Fortune's mother was not white did not imply she was African American. And neither attendance at black educational institutions nor general association with African Americans affected racial identity, the defense countered. In fact, state documents themselves forced Fortune to attend the all-black Virginia State College for Negroes. A designation as "colored" on official forms blocked the Pamunkey's admission to traditionally white institutions.

The same listing barred Pamunkeys, like Fortune, from white medical facilities and other public services. Personal association with African Americans, the defense continued, resulted not from his own choice but from state mandates.[49]

Regarding the alleged post–Civil War intermingling of Indians and African Americans, Fortune's attorneys contended tidewater natives were "induced" by Republicans of the era "to assign themselves to the status of 'colored people.'" Native Americans were told that acceptance of the "colored" listing would net them voting rights and other opportunities freed blacks were to gain during Reconstruction. To attain those benefits, Indians "resigned themselves to the situation." Fortune's racial identity, then, was the product of external political and social necessities, not biology.[50]

It mattered little that Fortune's attorneys aired a logical, coherent, and conclusive argument; the defense found it impossible to hurdle the simplest, basic provision of Memo 336. By necessity or choice, Fortune had, indeed, associated with African Americans. The Selective Service Court had no recourse but to rule against Oliver Fortune. The Pamunkey immediately filed an appeal, and a second hearing was scheduled for January 12, 1943.

In the meantime, tribal chief Otho S. Nelson solicited intervention directly from the White House. President Roosevelt's secretary referred the request to General Hershey, who in turn ordered Virginia authorities to handle the issue. Once again, the loop back to state officials was made with nothing to show for the effort. After waging the same arguments presented in the first hearing, Fortune lost his case a second time and was sentenced to two years in the federal reformatory in Petersburg.[51]

Walter Ashby Plecker seized upon the court's ruling to stall further Indian attempts at securing a separate racial identity. The registrar issued a circular statewide that listed "county by county, all of the surnames of people of 'suspicious' origin supposedly trying to 'pass' as 'white.'" The document, mailed to all medical doctors, school administrators, clerks of court, and local draft boards, explained the "threat" these purported Indians posed to the racial well-being of the state of Virginia. In the circular, Plecker vented his rage that individuals, such as Fortune, would resort to litigation in their bid to avoid service with African Americans and to merge with the white race.[52]

Plecker's continued suppression of the state's native population finally brought the intervention of Frank Speck, professor of anthropology at the University of Pennsylvania and perhaps the foremost authority on Virginia Indians. His thirty years of scholarly work among the Pamunkeys and other tidewater tribes lent credibility to his counterattack against the registrar.[53] Through the news media and public lectures, Professor Speck condemned Plecker's mean-spirited and purposeful misuse of scholarly sources, among them John Garland Pollard's 1894 article "The Pamunkey Indians." Plecker habitually quoted Pollard's statement that there existed "not a little" Negro blood among the Pamunkeys. Speck recognized the phrase as being out of context and turned the quotation against the registrar. Indeed, Pollard had written that Pamunkey ancestry included non-Indians, but the passage actually read "there has been considerable intermixture of white blood in the tribe, and not a little of that of the Negro." This in no way implied a predominant Negro line, or even a heavy mixture, Speck argued. Plecker failed to mention the biological connection of this particular tribe to the white race. Using the registrar's line of reasoning, Speck suggested it only seemed logical that if those Pamunkeys who intermarried with African Americans were to be cited as black in racial listings, the children of Indian-white intercourse would be considered white. Speck showed that Pollard's article was quick to add that "the laws of the tribe now," in 1894, "strictly prohibit marriage to persons of African descent." In fact, Pollard continued, the "Laws of the Pamunkey Indian Town," dated February 18, 1886, contained as the first principle that "No member of the Pamunkey Tribe shall intermarry with anyy [sic] Nation except the White or Indian under penalty of forfeiting their rights in Town."[54]

Speck stood firm in his contention that since 1886 the Pamunkeys consciously sought total racial segregation from African Americans. Their laws and tribal actions, such as barring the employment of black teachers at the local community school, attested to the Indians' goals of either assimilation or a separate identity. Even Pollard concluded that the Pamunkeys appeared more Indian than black, and he foresaw possible movement of the tribe toward total assimilation with white society.[55]

Speck whittled and chipped away at Plecker's racist posturing against tidewater Indians, reaching larger audiences as his articles crept into newspapers across the state. Point by point he removed the planks from the registrar's platform and forged in the public mind the image of a state official hell-bent on the obliteration of an ethnic group's identity. Plecker's views "[are] framed maliciously in unnecessary animosity," he wrote. No other explanation, he argued, could account for the registrar's notion of a black identity for the Pamunkeys, a position that conflicted with documented evidence, the "infrequency of marriage with non-Indians, and . . . [the] expulsion and expatriation of those who violate the tradition against inter-association or marriage with Negroes." Speck encouraged all tidewater natives, regardless of tribal affiliation, to fight draft classification as African Americans, but not in a manner conducive to violence.

Armed confrontations, he warned, would only alienate white society at large and government officials in particular.[56]

Press coverage of Speck's vehement tirade against Plecker continued throughout the war years and increasingly aroused public sympathy for Virginia Indians, especially when Plecker responded that "these mongrels" should not "escape from the negro [sic] race." To a growing number of Virginians, Plecker waged a battle over race similar to that of Adolf Hitler. Said one state resident, "We rave about Mr. Hitler's treatment of the Jews in the countries he has overrun, and overlook the way we have treated the Indians." "How can we expect Brotherhood or peace," she asked, "if we are going to discriminate against a group in our own state just because they are small in number?"[57]

John Collier's silence finally broke in March 1943 as public sentiment in Virginia grew more vocal and letters to his office became more numerous. Early in the month Collier received in the mail a note of protest from one Mrs. Ruth Rogers of Norfolk who decried Plecker's insistence that she was black rather than Indian. She had personally experienced the registrar's accusatory finger when she attempted to gain service at white public institutions, but she was also incensed over draft classification that snagged friends and family members. Mrs. Rogers lodged complaints with the Office of Vital Statistics and in one letter to Plecker announced her intention to contact Collier. Confronted with Speck's popular challenge to his position, the increased frequency of draft board nonconformance with Memo 336, and a public in greater sympathy for tidewater Indians, Plecker fired a letter to the commissioner. He insisted Mrs. Rogers should be listed as black, and he added that "all so-called Indians in Virginia are negroes [sic]." Aware that the registrar had in no way tempered his perspective or his comments, Collier openly rebuked Plecker and stated that the registrar's position was "intolerable."[58]

By late summer 1943, Plecker's stranglehold on government agencies loosened. The publicity given Speck and other scholars allowed state and local officials to recognize the fallacy of the registrar's arguments, and his weakening position assured them that any effort by Plecker to choke funding would face legislative wrath. More important for Indians facing the military service was the long awaited response from Collier. Local draft boards interpreted his denunciation of the registrar to be final recognition of Indian identity in Virginia, and, armed with the inference and desirous of remedying the investigative muddle, boards readily listed Indian recruits as whites and ordered them to the appropriate training facilities.

As for Oliver Fortune, Professor Speck convinced Petersburg attorney Charles

Edgar Gilliam to review the Pamunkey's case and sentence.[59] Gilliam recognized that Fortune's association with African Americans and his official "colored" listing on state documents trapped the Pamunkey under Memo 336 provisions. However, he offered a resolution that he believed might remove Fortune from the Petersburg Reformatory. He suggested Fortune request reclassification as a conscientious objector and seek parole or discharge on the condition he perform nonmilitary, nonracially classed work. Admittedly, this response evaded the real issue, but it at least would free Fortune from his incarceration. Speck concurred. In mid-August 1943, Oliver Fortune left prison and entered a co program in a local hospital.[60]

By the end of World War II, eighteen Pamunkeys and dozens of other Virginia Indians had served in white units of the armed forces. This, along with Plecker's retirement on May 15, 1946, heightened Indian expectations for a redirection in state government attitudes regarding Native American racial status and listings. To their dismay, the registrar's replacement committed himself to sustaining Plecker's policy. Dismay quickly turned to disgust with publication of *The Gold Star Honor Roll of Virginians in the Second World War*. Prepared by the Virginia World War II History Commission, the document listed all state residents who were killed in action and who later died from wounds suffered in combat. Only one Indian was cited in the rather lengthy list. Tribes found the names of their lost sons identified as African American.[61]

Both the honor roll and the apparent continuation of Plecker's influence in the Office of Vital Statistics proved that little change resulted from the Indians' struggle during World War II. Rather than "simple misunderstanding" of the selective service process, as Collier earlier claimed, racism in the southeastern United States snared Indians and formed the parameters of Indian draft resistance.

The obvious setback embittered tidewater natives and in the postwar years prompted greater self-imposed isolation from the non-Indian world. Virginia Indians felt compelled to redefine themselves as Native Americans. Tribal revitalization was deemed the only viable solution. By 1950, through their own lobbying efforts, tidewater Indians gained increased recognition of their native identity. The Seventeenth Census of the United States cited 1,056 Indians in the state, a substantial increase over the 1940 listing.[62] Not a product of Indian migration into Virginia, the figure represented instead a forceful new attitude, or spirit, among the native inhabitants to carve their own place in society—apart from whites and blacks.

Five

The Limits of Indian Sovereignty

In the arid southwestern corner of Arizona dwelled a small band of Papago Indians. Numbering approximately one hundred, this community in the Hickiwan District firmly held to traditional values that dictated daily existence—a lifestyle exercised by their fathers and their fathers before them. Modern America surrounded the town, but twentieth-century realities seldom penetrated tribal defenses. "They were the last of the Papagos to hold on to the ceremonial doings," said Peter Blaine, tribal council chairman in the early 1940s. On the eve of World War II, "they still played the real old Papago games. . . . Some of their women up there still tattooed their chins." Hickiwan was, indeed, among the most isolated of Indian communities inside the United States. Although Blaine was himself a Papago, he, too, was a stranger among the community's residents. Said Blaine, they "didn't know there was any other kind of people. . . . Some of these people never saw a white man during their whole lives. They had no knowledge of the outside world. . . . Some didn't even know there was a reservation."[1]

The Hickiwan Papagos certainly maintained a remote existence and fiercely guarded traditional values and community structures, but Blaine's observations were not totally accurate. Villagers were very much aware of a world outside their own immediate circle. While more traditional clothing proved commonplace, manufactured garments from the East found their way into the community, and men of the tribe occasionally ventured into nearby towns. Papago tribal leaders also understood that a nation, the United States, enveloped their own community, and many were quite cognizant of America's territorial claims. This latter point was the source of conflict between Washington and Hickiwan residents. The Papagos' self-declared autonomy from the United States had been long-standing and rested upon the tribe's denunciation of the Gadsden Purchase. They viewed themselves as a people who resided outside the territorial boundaries of both the United States government and the state of Arizona.[2]

Their conviction persisted well into the spring of 1940 and visibly manifested itself when eighty-year-old Chief Pia Machita refused the Arizona Livestock Sanitation Board's entry into Indian lands. Shortly afterward, he instructed tribal members not to answer questions asked by federal census takers. Five separate and lengthy meetings with Indian agents from neighboring Papago villages were held before Machita relented; and his capitulation only followed government assurance that the census in no way threatened tribal autonomy.[3] That assurance, however, proved short-lived. In September, Congress passed the Selective Training and Service Act and announced October 1 as a national day of registration.

As chairman of the intertribal Papago Council, Peter Blaine personally visited Machita's community to explain the recently enacted legislation and to encourage young men of draft age to comply with the law. Years later, Blaine recalled the Indians' response: "Why does the Army want our young boys?" Machita asked. When informed of the war in Europe and that it might descend on the United States, Machita queried, "Are they going to draft our young boys into the war?" Blaine assured the chief that the Papago men would not be compelled to serve in America's armed forces. "Your young people here never had schooling and they're too young. They can't take a young man that never went to school." "He has to be able to understand the white man to get drafted," Blaine said to Machita.[4]

Registration day passed without much activity in the Hickiwan District, nor was there much thought given to draft registration until tribal elders received notice from the Indian Bureau several days later that eligible Papago men from the village had failed to register with the Selective Service. This was not news to Pia Machita. Blaine's explanation of draft registration suggested to the chief that his men did not have to comply with the act since they were uneducated and would, therefore, not have to serve. But, more important, in the final week of September, Machita informed the young men of the tribe that congressional acts were not applicable to them and that registration was not compulsory for the Papagos. Machita responded to the communiqué's strong recommendation that all eligible men register by stating that it was not so much a failure to comply with the law as much as it was a complete rejection of the act. Again, he insisted the United States commanded no legitimate authority over the Papagos.[5]

Federal officials hurried to Hickiwan with the hope of quickly resolving the issue; the problem, they thought, was simply one of misunderstanding the law and the Papagos' status within the United States. Machita maintained his defiant stance, despite a three-hour conference in which Washington's representatives explained the purpose of registration and the penalties for evasion. Still, he gave no ground. Frustrated, the government's agents informed the chief that he would face federal criminal charges of "inciting resistance to draft registration" unless he instructed tribal members to comply with the Selective Service Act, and those men who continued to ignore federal law would be charged with draft evasion. October 16 was set as the deadline for Papago compliance; thereafter, Machita and other resistors would be arrested and prosecuted. Machita remained unfazed by the warning, and the government's threat went unheeded.[6]

As promised, the Justice Department dispatched to the village on the appointed day Deputy Marshall Henry Smith, a Papago Reservation Indian police officer, and a half-dozen deputized Indians. Machita was rustled from bed as the agents arrived in the village, and he greeted them at the door of his home. The officers carried arrest warrants for Machita and twenty other men, and they ordered the chief to step outside his house. The presence of federally designated agents in the community stirred residents, filling some with curiosity and others with immediate anger. Forty tribal members quickly surrounded the officers. When Smith announced his intention to arrest the chief and all those men who resisted draft registration, the Papago assured the officers that there would be no such arrests made. A standoff ensued. In an effort to intimidate the gathered tribal members and insure the successful completion of his mission, Smith invoked the authority of the United States government. Hearing that, and determined not to have Machita arrested, the gathered Indians assaulted the agents, disarmed them, and chased them down the road toward Tucson.[7]

In the months that followed, Blaine and Indian Bureau representatives met with Machita and encouraged him to have his young men register for the draft. Compliance, however, would in itself suggest Papago submission to federal authority over the tribe. Machita held firm to his conviction that his tribe was not part of the United States and therefore federal law was not applicable to his community. Reports filtered throughout the region that Machita fled into the surrounding countryside to avoid arrest, but contrary to the rumors the chief continued his daily routines until his arrest in spring 1941. Although a story sifted through the news media that Machita and his tribe battled arresting agents and hoisted a Mexican flag atop a mast in a hostile and defiant gesture toward the United States, "there was no fighting" and no symbolic posturing.[8]

Pia Machita and another chief, Leandro, were tried and convicted for inciting tribal members to resist the Selective Service Act, and both men were incarcerated at Terminal Island, California. Neither man served his full sentence. Machita was released early from prison soon after his daughter lost an arm in an accident. Needed by his family, federal authorities conceded his presence at home was essential to family survival.[9] Public sympathy also worked toward Machita's early release. There seemed to be something romantic, almost noble, in one elderly man's battle to preserve his people's traditions, values, customs, and independence. The popular image of a man, wrinkled and stooped by the passage of so many years, long silvery hair draped loosely over his bowed shoulders, a worn and tattered coat that swallowed his curved figure and baggy pants, and one feeble hand that clasped the other as he boarded the train for prison, altogether fashioned a public sentiment resentful of his imprisonment. Sympathizers wondered if his freedom, and that of his tribe, were anything less than the same freedom that the world's democracies now struggled to preserve. To Washington, however, the successful prosecution of Pia Machita supplied evidence of federal authority over the Papagos and the tribe's membership with the United States.

Resistance in the Hickiwan District countered the response given by neighboring Papago tribes. Nearly ninety percent of all eligible men on the broader reservation freely complied with draft registration and military induction in 1940 and 1941. What separated the Hickiwan Papagos from others in the Southwest was the extreme isolation in which Pia Machita's people lived. Virtually unacculturated and untouched by any federal program to the eve of World War II, they steadfastly held to their presumption of independence and retained an identity apart from all others. The commissioner of Indian Affairs' belief that Native American draft resistance stemmed from "simple misunderstanding of the law" showed itself to be as erroneous in the Papago case as it had for the Indians of tidewater Virginia. In the Southeast, Collier could not comprehend the uncertain racial status that trapped Indians and affected social identity; in the Southwest, he failed to understand the impact of long-term isolation on Indian national identity.

For reasons similar to those given by the Papagos, the Seminole Indians of Florida also objected to compulsory registration and military service. Over the span of many generations, the Seminoles lived quietly near the Everglades and eked out a living through self-sufficient farming. Their minimal contact with white society was generally limited to service as hunting guides and as sellers of crafts to tourists. White movement into Florida after the Great War had pushed the Indian population ever closer to life in the swamps. Although the Bureau of Indian Affairs established two reservations for the Seminoles in the late 1920s, the Indians received scant attention from Washington and even less aid in the years that followed. A sense of alienation from both the government and white society prevailed, a feeling that more traditional tribal members preferred.

Even Collier's administration wrought few changes for the Seminoles; the commissioner's attention focused primarily on Trans-Mississippi reservations. His obvious inattentiveness simply confirmed the Indians' perception of independence from federal authority. As in the Hickiwan District of the Papago Reservation, the Indians' worldview was immediately challenged with passage of the Selective Service Act.

In early October 1940, concurrent to developments in Arizona, the superintendent of the Seminole Indian Agency at Dania, Dwight Gardin, informed young men of the reservation that draft registration applied to all United States citizens. This, he said, included the Seminoles, but eligible tribal members instantly balked at the news and adamantly refused to comply with the directive to register. Gardin offered a sympathetic ear but explained that the recently enacted law also included provisions to prosecute those individuals who avoided compliance. Confronted with two distasteful alternatives—registration or imprisonment—some Indians acquiesced and visited the local draft boards. Many Seminoles, however, saw a third alternative; they chose to defy federal authority and among themselves agreed to seek the protection of the Everglades should agents actively pursue their arrest. Believing that Seminole men would not pass either the physical or educational tests given by the armed forces, Gardin hoped to slip the Indians quietly through the tangle of paperwork and in so doing skirt the rising ire of selective service officials for Indian resistance. In late October, Gardin took it upon himself to complete registration forms for the "delinquents" without their knowledge or consent. He hoped covert registration would calm Indian emotions and provide him adequate time during which he could convince Indians of the necessity of compliance with the draft.[10]

Once local Indians were officially registered on paper, selective service officials believed draft resistance among the Seminoles had ended and dropped plans to prosecute them. Gardin's action provided a short-term solution; however, it created a serious long-term problem on the reservation. Unaware that the superintendent had secretly intervened on their behalf, Seminole draft resistors awaited the arrival of federal agents bearing warrants for their arrest. When no representatives of Washington came to Dania, the Indians logically assumed that the federal threats were hollow and believed they indeed did not have to obey any summons for military service. The absence of judicial action also angered those Indians who had earlier succumbed to Gardin's warning of federal prosecution and had registered with the draft. To both groups of men, the superintendent appeared to be a liar. Gardin, without question, had placed himself in a rather precarious situation.

The superintendent interceded on behalf of the Seminoles partly in the spirit of aiding Indian men on the reservation. He certainly did not wish to see any of the resistors imprisoned for draft evasion, particularly being as convinced as he was of their unfitness for military service. However, he also recognized John Collier's determination to have Indian unanimity in draft registration; the steps Gardin took certainly provided, on paper, the appearance of total complicity among the Seminole Indians on the Dania Reservation. This, the superintendent realized, would please Collier and possibly elevate his own opportunity for advancement in federal employment.

In spite of his motives, Gardin boxed himself into a corner. He breached federal law by registering Native Americans without their consent. At the very least, discovery of his unlawful behavior would probably result in his dismissal from the Indian Bureau; the other scenario might include his own imprisonment. He knew, too, that revelation would most assuredly occur once induction orders were mailed to registered Indians.

In early February 1941, Gardin dropped an obviously stuffed envelope into the mail, addressed to John Collier. Inside was a lengthy letter to the commissioner confessing his action from the previous October and the mind-frazzling attempt to conceal his behavior through the remainder of the year. Gardin explained his purpose in registering the Seminole "recalcitrants," but he emphasized most strongly his desire to turn away Washington prosecutors and temper the emotions of resistors until a satisfactory explanation of draft registration could be given the Indians.[11]

In reading the letter, Collier understood the predicament the superintendent faced, but the discovery of Gardin's action now snagged Collier himself between the proverbial rock and a hard place. The commissioner believed it imperative to convey the image of an Indian population in total compliance with draft registration, and in the public record the superintendent's behavior at least provided the paper loyalty of the Seminoles, albeit a loyalty created without their knowledge. Collier then considered the consequences of Gardin's effort and immediately concluded that concealment of the Seminoles' illegal registration from the Justice Department would benefit all persons involved. The commissioner, however, also believed it essential that Seminole Indians realize they were under the direct authority of the United States government and that they consciously submit themselves to the Selective Service system. If the law did not snare the Seminole resistors, then Indians would have no respect for the reservation superintendency or for federal authority. Continued draft resistance would certainly create an image among the Indians of a weak and ineffective government. The whole affair, Collier surmised, would become a serious embarrassment to Washington if not soon resolved. In a letter to Assistant Attorney General James McInerney, Collier encouraged the prosecution of all unregistered Seminole Indians.[12]

Influencing the commissioner's decision was the news media's national coverage of Seminole draft resistance in Florida. Reporters flashed stories that the majority of eligible Indians had fled into the Everglades to elude prosecution after the first call for registration the previous autumn. In fact, many Seminoles did move into the swamp to hide from federal agents. Collier knew that as long as resistance continued, the problem in Florida would fester. And fester it did. In summer 1941 Gardin informed the Office of the State Director of Selective Service that "the medicine man has [again] advised his young braves to disregard the Selective Service Act," and Collier was also notified. The "medicine man" reiterated the tribe's conviction that the Seminole people lived as an independent body, apart from federal authority. Seminoles, he insisted, were not citizens of the United States and, therefore, were not bound to the Selective Service Act.[13]

Collier and Justice Department officials recognized a modicum of public sympathy for the Seminoles and further realized that actual enforcement of draft registration and compulsory service would largely prove a futile effort in Florida, since the Everglades served the Indians as an effective sanctuary. At this point, Secretary Harold Ickes intervened and offered a compromise. He knew further efforts to enforce registration would only prove unsuccessful, particularly when numerous attorneys had failed to dissuade Indians from continued draft resistance. The tribe still assumed that federal authority held no jurisdictional privilege at Dania, and Seminoles firmly believed they were not United States citizens. Given the Indians' defiance and Washington's need to settle the affair, Ickes suggested that all federal agencies accept Superintendent Gardin's assessment from a year earlier—because of the Seminoles' high illiteracy rates and overall poor health, few Indians would actually pass armed-forces induction tests. Therefore, Ickes concluded, rather than doggedly pursue legal action against Indians who would most likely be rejected for military service, Seminoles should be encouraged to assume home defense tasks such as airplane spotting or search-and-rescue service.[14] Without question, Ickes desired a quick resolution of Seminole draft resistance and believed his recommendation offered all involved parties a suitable method for extricating themselves from the increasingly public spectacle. More than Collier, Ickes recognized the long-term imprint of Indian isolation from mainstream society and governmental relations; this was an issue that could not be satisfactorily settled on the eve of war.

Taking the cue from Secretary Ickes, the Justice Department withdrew its plan to prosecute the Seminoles, although the War Department and Selective Service system preferred to maintain the public appearance of enforcement and verbally combated any public hint of retreat for another two years. The Indian Bureau likewise quieted its pursuit and called on Seminoles to cooperate with the domestic war effort, as Ickes suggested. In September 1943, the Florida State director of Selective Service announced that continued actions against the Seminoles would only "produce further distrust of and animosity toward the white man." Additionally, of the one hundred and seventy-five eligible Indians, all but seventy-five had complied with registration requirements to date. Holdouts would simply return to the Everglades and pursuit of them would only waste the government's time and money, with little prospect for success. Moreover, the director said, the majority of all Seminoles spoke little English, which, in itself, precluded their entry into the armed forces.[15] Government plans to coerce Seminole Indians into compliance with draft registration and compulsory military service ended in the autumn of 1943. Neither the Indians nor Collier relinquished any ground in their respective views regarding tribal independence or citizenship.

Seminole and Papago draft resistance both emerged in October 1940, following passage of the Selective Service Act one month earlier, and each centered on essentially the same arguments — tribal sovereignty, exclusion from federal authority, and rejection of United States citizenship. Tribal isolation from the general population and the absence of a direct and sustained relationship with Washington, as evidenced by few federal programs on the reservations, all contributed to the persistence of traditional cultural values and sense of separation from the surrounding world. Maintained was a tribal identity instead of an American, national identity. Collier's insistence on forcing compliance with draft registration and his refusal to examine objectively the Indians' perspective actually drove the Seminoles and Papagos farther from a union with American society at the very time such a union was most desired by Washington.

In contrast to the Seminoles and Papagos, who asserted tribal independence and sovereignty on grounds of prior non-inclusion with American society or government, several tribes battled draft registration in the legal arena using signed treaties with the federal government as their foundation for noncompliance. The Yakima Nation and the Iroquois Confederacy both assumed these documents provided a measure of protection from federal intrusion into tribal affairs, including compulsory military service. But John Collier could not escape his vision of total Indian compliance with America's mobilization for war, a vision that subtly exposed contradictions within his own view of Indians in America. Ideologically, Collier desired the revitalization of native cultures and tribalism as well as the maintenance of tribal autonomy. Nonetheless, the commissioner was emotionally swayed by the patriotic clamor of a nation moving ever closer to war and the popular expectation that all Americans participate fully, including American Indians since they, too, were citizens. Draft resistance carried a potential backlash against Indians from both Washington and the general population, a reaction that might result in lowered federal appropriations for the BIA's reform programs and reduced public support for reservation redevelopment. Cooperation with Selective Service requirements and Native American inclusion in the armed forces, Collier believed, would demonstrate Indian loyalty for the United States and prevent the backlash he feared.

The contradictory message given by Collier magnified itself most clearly on the issue of tribal sovereignty ostensibly granted by treaty. He assured Indians that draft registration would not be construed as a violation of previously accepted treaty provisions nor would Native American participation in the armed forces compromise the sanctity of any written agreement between the tribes and Washington should war crash upon the nation's shores.[16] The Indian Bureau wished to ignore the inherent conflict between compulsory military service in the armed forces of the United States and tribal autonomy guaranteed by treaties, but tribal groups on both the Pacific and Atlantic coasts forced the federal government to resolve the issue.

Shortly after passage of the Selective Service Act in September 1940 the Yakima Nation responded that long-standing treaty provisions precluded its compliance with draft registration and compulsory military service in America's armed forces. Since the ratification of its last treaty with the United States in 1859, the Yakimas had lived in peace on its reservation in south-central Washington State, one hundred and forty miles southeast of Seattle. There the Yakimas dwelled in a fertile valley and concentrated on building an agricultural and lumber-based economy. Like many small tribes across the nation, a self-imposed isolation from white society was maintained well into the twentieth century. With a sustaining economy, little contact with the United States government, and a treaty that promised relative independence, the Yakimas assumed they retained a level of tribal sovereignty that excluded them from national military obligations.[17]

Among the tribal members affected by draft registration was Watson Totus. After a careful examination of the 1859 treaty, Totus remained convinced that the Selective Service Act held no authority over himself or the Yakima Nation. The treaty itself guaranteed tribal sovereignty, and at no point over the previous ninety years had the tribe forfeited any measure of sovereignty or surrendered any degree of self-government to the United States. Conscription, Totus concluded, constituted a clear abridgment of treaty rights. Certain that Yakimas were exempt from draft registration and military service, Totus and seventy others filed suit in Federal District Court in May 1941 to restrain enforcement of the Selective Service Act.[18]

Totus's legal counselors argued three central points. First, the Yakima people lived as alien residents who had not declared their desire for American citizenship and, consequently, were not subject to the military draft. Second, the 1859 treaty explicitly prohibited military cooperation with, or participation in, America's armed forces. Finally, under treaty provisions the Yakimas were extended tribal sovereignty.[19]

The court heard all arguments and read all documents pertinent to the case, but, on May 28, Judge Lewis B. Schwellenbach rendered his decision in favor of the United States. Schwellenbach premised his ruling first on the Citizenship Act of 1924, which stated that all Native Americans born within the territorial boundaries of the United States were natural citizens. The Nationality Act of 1940 simply reinforced that status by extending the 1924 declaration to include all Indians born after that date. The 1940 legislation was intended to eliminate any misunderstanding among Indians or whites regarding Indian citizenship. With the two acts combined, Totus and all Yakimas were recognized United States citizens and, therefore, subject to the provisions of the Selective Service Act.[20]

Schwellenbach further held that the 1859 treaty was "superseded by the Selective Training and Service Act of 1940, which provides that all laws or parts of laws in conflict with the . . . act are suspended for the period in which the act is in force." As a result, the treaty fell under the judge's gavel. Judge Schwellenbach's ruling stripped Yakimas of their perceived tribal sovereignty and abruptly made them liable to the draft.[21] Assuming that an appeal would net the same decision, the Yakima Nation grudgingly accepted citizenship and its corresponding military obligation. The Indian Bureau believed the court's decision not only invalidated the Yakima treaty but all treaties with Indians nationwide.

The singular issue of tribal sovereignty granted by treaty, however, brewed as a kettle of discontent among the Indians of New York State. For more than twenty years, the Iroquois Confederacy, or Six Nations, worked to cool Albany's attempts to extend its authority over tribal lands and to dismantle treaty rights. Passage of the Selective Service Act brought the simmering confrontation to a boil and generated a level of Indian draft resistance that far surpassed Yakima efforts and proved unique among Native Americans to that date.

Residing in a network of reservations that crossed upstate and western New York, the Six Nations existed as a tightly knit confederation of Tuscarora,

Seneca, Mohawk, Onondaga, Oneida, and Cayuga Indians. Historically, these independent tribes melded together during times of peace and responded in unison as a single force during periods of war or when faced with any threatening external force. In 1940, application of the Selective Service Act to the confederacy was viewed by the Six Nations as an external threat, one that imperiled its independent nation status and sovereignty, as granted by a series of treaties with the federal government in the late eighteenth century. With the menace of conscription stalking the Iroquois tribes, the Six Nations banded together once more to provide mutual protection for all confederation members. Resistance among other tribal groups featured small numbers and normally failed to consolidate separate tribes into a single, unified front. The Six Nations broke that pattern by solidifying its 4,200 members in the region and directing their energies into one collective force.

On October 8, 1940, the St. Regis Mohawk Council passed a resolution questioning the fundamental political arrangement between it and the federal government. The council voided application of the Citizenship Act of 1924 to the Iroquois people since the legislation had not been "executed by special treaty with the Six Nations Confederacy." Without Iroquois consent, citizenship could not be extended to confederacy members, and, therefore, compulsory registration and service in the armed forces were illegal demands placed upon them by Washington. The Indians viewed themselves as "foreign nations, not United States citizens." Both the Citizenship Act and the Selective Service Act "had been promulgated unilaterally by Congress and without their consent; thus, the Iroquois rejected the doctrine of plenary power or federal supremacy over Indians and Indian affairs."[22]

The following day, Senecas in Buffalo announced their challenge to the legality of Indian conscription. Wilfred Crouse, president of the Seneca Indian Nation Council, denied Washington's right to place confederacy members under the umbrella of the Selective Service Act. Crouse argued that the Citizenship Act of 1924, which purportedly made Native Americans liable to military service, was invalid, and he sought a volunteer willing to test the argument in court. Four days later, St. Regis Mohawks proclaimed their agreement with Crouse. Three tribal chiefs—Thomas Lazor, Alex Soloman, and Louis Terrence—sent a message to Commissioner John Collier refuting congressional application of United States citizenship to the Iroquois Confederacy and denouncing the compulsory registration and military service of Six Nations members. Individual Indians held the personal freedom to volunteer for service, but they would "not comply to force and coercion," said Crouse. "Under our treaty with the United States of America," he added, "we are a distinct race, nation, and people owning, occupying, and governing the lands of our ances-tors." The confederacy dwelled "under the protection of the Federal Govern-ment in reciprocation for our friendship to the government."[23] The argument as presented by the Senecas and Mohawks rested exclusively on a single point; by treaty, the Iroquois Confederacy existed as a sovereign nation within a na-tion.

The Indian Bureau was under siege from numerous quarters. Concurrent with Crouse's call for Iroquois noncompliance with draft registration was the emerging resistance among Florida's Seminoles and the Papagos of Arizona. Al-ready, cries of racism sounded in tidewater Virginia and rumblings of dissen-sion emanated from Washington State, the Dakotas, and New Mexico. But the combined resistance that rapidly formed in New York most seriously rattled the hallways of the Indian Bureau. Unlike the claims of independence and tribal sovereignty based on a maintained isolation from white society and govern-ment, as promoted by the Seminoles and Papagos, the Iroquois treaties offered legal standing to the Indians' arguments. More so than any other tribal draft resistance, the Six Nations' opposition threatened to unweave the bureau's vi-sion of pan-Indian loyalty to the United States. To present an unruffled image to the news media, Collier publicly dismissed the seriousness of the Indians' arguments and published registration figures from reservations nationwide, which clearly indicated massive compliance with Selective Service mandates. Within the bureau, however, he retorted that the Iroquois contention of non-citizenship and the absolute sovereignty of the Iroquois Nation were no more than a "dream."[24]

In its reply to the Mohawks, the Indian Bureau asserted the constitutional-ity of the Citizenship Act and discounted the confederacy's claim as an inde-pendent, sovereign nation. Collier hoped to mute the issue of citizenship in a personal message to the Indians and appealed to their patriotism, calling on the Iroquois to set aside legal disputes and comply with the Selective Service Act for the duration of the national crisis. Draft registration, he said, applied to all res-idents of the United States, including legal aliens as required by the Alien Reg-istration Act of 1940. In either capacity, as citizen or alien, Native American submission to draft registration proved mandatory. As for the question of sov-ereignty, the century-old Supreme Court case *Worcester v. Georgia* qualified sov-ereignty and ruled that it existed only by consent of Congress. The Citizenship Act in effect withdrew sovereignty from the Six Nations. The commissioner noted, however, that the question of citizenship demanded further clarification, and Iroquois claims of national sovereignty certainly needed to be examined more fully.[25]

Long before the crisis of draft registration locked the commissioner in battle with the Six Nations, the issue of tribal sovereignty plagued relations between New York's Indians and the Indian Bureau. In July 1940 Collier promised the government's continued adherence to the 1794 Treaty of Canandaigua, despite conflicting interpretations of sovereignty. As dictated by treaty agreements, the United States provided annual financial aid for the purchase of "clothing, domestic animals, implements of husbandry and other utensils." Congress, he reminded the Indians, exceeded the $4,500 yearly appropriation required by the original treaty with an additional $6,000 annual grant as prescribed by an 1831 amendment. Such federal disbursements, in addition to congressional and bureau programs to aid Native Americans since Collier's appointment as commissioner, demonstrated Washington's sincerity in the maintenance of treaty obligations, Collier said.[26]

The commissioner's abrupt, matter-of-fact response to the Indians in July and again in October clued the Iroquois' to the lack of seriousness with which Collier viewed the issue of tribal sovereignty. His casual and offhand manner compelled the confederacy to test the limits of Indian sovereignty in federal court. Aware that litigation would be lengthy and a favorable public image was necessary, the Seneca and Mohawk chiefs urged confederation members to submit temporarily to draft registration. "Sign up tomorrow," Indians were told, "and file your claims for exemption later." Following their lead, the Tuscaroras declared their opposition to compulsory registration and service but promised short-term compliance with the law. Chief Clinton Rickard echoed tribal sentiment: "We were not United States citizens, no matter what the government said. We were Six Nations citizens." Like Senecas and Mohawks, he recommended that Indians register for military service, "but only as 'alien nonresident.'" By February 1941, seventy-three Tuscaroras had registered for the draft, and many filed appeals for deferment. As the month entered its final week, two Indians filed appeals and offered themselves as test cases in court. Each young man expressed his understanding that the Treaty of Canandaigua formed the Six Nations as an independent, separate nation within the territorial borders of the United States; therefore, compulsory military training was not required of member Indians. They were instead citizens of their own nation and not the United States.[27]

Six Nations' attorneys preferred a more dramatic case through which Indian claims could be served and bypassed the Tuscarora registrants. Not until spring did they find an appropriate and willing test subject. They selected for the courtroom battle Warren Eldreth Green, an Onondaga. As required by law and advised by tribal leaders, twenty-one-year-old Green registered with his local draft board and soon afterwards received a 1-A classification. Unintentionally, he failed to file an appeal for exemption and was ordered to report to the Syracuse Induction Center on April 26, 1941. Green made his way to Syracuse as directed, swore an oath of allegiance to the United States, and was inducted into the army. Though not opposed to military service, he nonetheless agreed to play the central role in the Six Nations' suit. Being a member of the armed forces, defense attorneys believed a favorable court decision affecting his release from service would most certainly validate Iroquois sovereignty.[28]

Wilfred Hoffman of Syracuse served as legal counsel for Green, and he immediately filed a writ of habeas corpus to dismiss the young Indian from the army. In so doing, he stated that Green, as was true of all members of the Six Nations, was not a "'citizen' within the Selective Training and Service Act of 1940, but . . . a member of [an] independent nation by virtue of treaties between [the] United States and the Six Nations." Moreover, the Citizenship Act of 1924, which purportedly granted citizenship to all Indians within the borders of the United States, did not apply to the Iroquois Confederacy because Six Nations tribes dwelled outside the territorial boundary of the United States.[29]

In May 1941, Green's case entered federal district court at the very same time the Yakimas' court battle raged more than three thousand miles away in Washington State. The principal difference between the trials of Warren Green and Watson Totus rested on Washington's written acceptance of total sovereignty in the Treaty of Canandaigua and the Iroquois' unqualified exercise of a separate national identity for nearly one hundred and fifty years. In contrast, only vague references to tribal sovereignty were bound in the Yakimas' 1859 treaty.

Hoffman stressed that the treaties of Fort Stanwix (1784), Fort Harmon (1789), and Fort Canandaigua (1794) collectively granted nationhood standing and absolute sovereignty over internal and external affairs of the Iroquois Confederation. In each treaty, the United States government conceded that the Six Nations existed as a separate nation, apart from both the United States and Canada. Any attempt by Congress to confer citizenship or enforce any federal statute without the expressed consent of the Six Nations violated treaty provisions. The confederated tribes had never accepted American citizenship or the Selective Service Act. Therefore, "the drafting of Indians into the United States armed forces was a violation of our sovereignty as Indian nations." More than any other document, the Treaty of Canandaigua "exempted the Six Nations 'from all blanket legislation,'" said one prominent Iroquois. With specific reference to military service, the Seneca Indian Alice Lee Jemison argued that "only the Iroquois Confederacy, and/or each nation's tribal council, had the ultimate authority to make decisions for war."[30]

Green's attorney repeated the Indians' commonly held sentiment that "general acts of Congress do not apply to Indians" and that the Six Nations historically had been dealt with in terms of international law. The Treaty of Canandaigua, Hoffman insisted, provided the Iroquois' the "right . . . to exist independently of the will of the Congress of the United States," and it "stands today in all the force it had when ratified."[31]

John Collier admitted that the legal status of Native Americans proved confusing, and their relationship to the federal government had perplexed generations of Indians and whites alike. However, the commissioner stopped short of acknowledging "foreign nation" status for the Six Nations. The Iroquois Confederacy, he said, existed in a politically gray area. They were "separate political communities" with more inherent rights than most municipalities, and "they possess powers of a sovereign nation except those specifically infringed by acts of Congress or by treaties." Reservations, Collier explained, were "semi-sovereign" states, independently able to declare war on America's enemies if the United States made war, as the confederacy did during World War I, yet subject to United States citizenship and military service. Washington affirmed the Indians' power to "control internal affairs," but the United States Constitution remained the supreme law of the land and therefore superseded treaties.[32] In defining reservations as municipalities, Collier shattered Indian claims of nationhood, relegating tribal sovereignty over the years to mere illusion and tribal independence to a position comparable to the relationship cities and states have with Washington.

Collier's explanation fueled Iroquois tempers, especially with his added comment that Indians were conquered nations "whose rights are being protected by the highest courts." The Six Nations, he said, possessed no more sovereignty than any other community in the nation. Moreover, the confederacy's sovereignty historically existed not because of treaty provisions or custom, but because Congress had no reason previously to interfere with it.[33] This assessment by Collier was not a new one for the commissioner. In response to the Iroquois vote against the Indian Reorganization Act, Collier pointedly answered that the federal government "can extend its sovereignty at will over any of these nations, no matter how sovereign they were made by treaties." A tribe that exercises sovereignty "does so because Congress has not legislated to take away that sovereignty."[34] The commissioner's posturing revealed Washington's continued paternalistic attitude toward Native Americans, despite Collier's many public pronouncements supportive of Indian self-government and self-determination.

In court, Hoffman parried the commissioner's remarks. The member nations of the Iroquois Confederacy had ended their armed confrontations with the

United States in 1794 by mutual agreement, not as conquered peoples, he countered. The government's willingness to accept league sovereignty and legitimize nationhood status in the Treaty of Canandaigua indicated that neither party viewed the Iroquois as a defeated nation. In spite of ever-changing federal policies throughout the nineteenth century, the status of the Six Nations remained unchallenged by Congress.[35]

Green's attorney added that confederation sovereignty further manifested itself during, and after, the Great War. He reminded the court and Collier that eight thousand Native Americans, representing numerous tribal groupings, voluntarily enlisted in America's armed forces during World War I, but only the Six Nations declared war on Germany in an act separate from the United States. Following the war, on November 4, 1924, a delegation from the Six Nations traveled to Geneva and presented a petition to the League of Nations. The document proclaimed the confederacy's independence as granted by treaties with the United States and requested admission of the Six Nations into the league as an independent state willing to comply with all principles and requirements of that organization. Although the league rejected confederacy admission, the attempt by the Six Nations exhibited the Indians' prevailing perception of their sovereign status.[36]

Hoffman then tracked relatively recent patterns in New York that buttressed the Iroquois' claim to national integrity and tribal sovereignty. Shortly after the armistice was signed in 1918, a group of assembly members in the state government of New York moved to annex Indian reservation land, claiming its right to acquire lands as needed even without Indian permission. The Albany faction believed the Six Nations fell under state jurisdiction and were, therefore, subject to the will of the legislative assembly. Recognizing the threat posed by Albany, the Iroquois Confederacy asserted its perpetual ownership of all territories provided by treaty with the United States. Determined to maintain the umbrella of federal protection guaranteed by the Treaty of Canandaigua, the Six Nations stood resolute in its defiance of New York's intentions. In an effort to resolve the matter without incurring Washington's intervention, which historically sided with the Iroquois, the assembly in 1919 authorized a state-appointed investigative committee to research jurisdictional responsibility for the Six Nations.[37]

Chaired by Edward A. Everett, the New York Indian Commission began work the following year in search of a definition of the Indians' legal status within the state and nation. After three years of work and coincidentally timed with congressional discussion of citizenship for American Indians, Everett's committee reported its findings to Albany. Hoffman alerted the court at

Green's trial that the Everett Report emphatically confirmed Iroquois claims to the six million acres of land granted them by the 1794 treaty. In so doing, the committee disavowed the state's attempt to withdraw any amount of land from Indian ownership. More relevant to Green's case, the commission upheld Iroquois sovereignty.[38]

The committee decided that the treaties of 1784, 1789, and 1794 did not promote the integration of native New Yorkers into white society; therefore national integrity for the confederacy was granted and remained unmolested by the federal government for the one hundred and fifty years since the last treaty was signed. The Everett Report further ruled that the extension of American citizenship to the Six Nations involved international relations between two distinct political and cultural bodies—the Iroquois Confederacy and the United States. New York held no right to interfere with tribal land holdings, nor did it command any jurisdiction over Indian affairs. Likewise, the report added, Congress could not force citizenship upon the Six Nations. Wrote Everett, "We have no compulsory law applying to any man of foreign birth as to becoming a citizen of the United States." One Mohawk phrased it more succinctly: for Congress to confer citizenship on an independent Iroquois people, it "may as well pass a law making Mexicans citizens."[39]

The Everett Committee endorsed confederacy refusal to entertain any notion of American citizenship. "Every time a bill concerning citizenship has been introduced into Congress, Indians themselves have led in opposing it," Everett said. Clinton Rickard, a Tuscarora, highlighted the report's decision, stating that Iroquois acceptance of citizenship would ultimately lead to its loss of sovereignty. "How can a citizen have a treaty with his own government?" Rickard asked. "To us," he continued, " it seemed that the United States government was trying to get rid of its treaty obligations."[40]

The nearly twenty-year-old committee report fully recommended the maintenance of Washington's treaties with the Six Nations and sanctioned Indian contentions of a separate national identity and national sovereignty. Green's defense believed Hoffman's inclusion of the Everett Report cemented the Indians' argument in court. Both Hoffman and Wilfred Crouse vividly portrayed New York and the federal government as sharks circling their prey—New York wanting access to Indian lands, and Washington expecting territorial and political control.

Green's defense also tracked the Iroquois argument into the New Deal era. The bureau's Indian Reorganization Act, Hoffman reminded the court, promoted a redirection in federal Indian policy from assimilation toward tribal revitalization and a renewal of traditional values. Along with the IRA's promise of self-government and self-determination, the Iroquois Confederacy already held the essential framework of the new relationship between tribal communities and Washington—a framework in place since 1794. Hoffman questioned the benefit of the IRA for the Iroquois people and suggested this to be one reason for the Six Nations' rejection of the act. More important, to the Iroquois Confederacy the IRA was legislation created by a foreign power and by its very origin, then, a plan not applicable to the Six Nations.

The federal government's current determination that Six Nations' sovereignty as an independent nation prevailed only at the will of Congress contradicted treaty guarantees and was inconsistent with the historic relationship between Washington and the Iroquois. Moreover, Hoffman wondered how the Indian Bureau could commit itself to two opposing directions concurrently—the removal of sovereignty guaranteed by treaties and the simultaneous granting of tribal sovereignty through the IRA. Not only did the effort reflect an absence of logic and continuity in Indian policy, it hinted at deeper motivations inside the Indian Bureau—the final dismantling of all remaining treaties with Indian tribes.

Hoffman returned specifically to Green's search for release from the United States Army and concluded his remarks with the reminder that there existed no objection to the Indians' voluntary service in the armed forces. Resistance rested squarely on America's application of the Selective Service Act to the Iroquois Confederacy, a separate and sovereign nation. Washington's denial of Iroquois sovereignty and the "brushing aside" of previously accepted treaties stood in sharp contrast to its historic recognition of the 1794 Treaty of Canandaigua, Hoffman said. Ultimately, the United States commanded no authority to compel Iroquois compliance with draft registration or military service.[41]

Federal District Court Judge Frederick H. Bryant confessed that Green's failure to appeal his classification and to claim exemption from the draft within the law's proscribed sixty-day limit would never have been considered by the court under normal conditions. The national emergency, however, demanded a resolution of the Indians' status under federal law. Realizing that Green's challenge potentially affected many tribal groups, Judge Bryant on May 14, 1941, denied the Onondagas' petition for a writ of habeas corpus and cleared the path for an appeal to the circuit court system.[42]

That day, Green left home for Fort Niagara to begin military training, and there he remained until his next hearing in October. Two weeks later, Hoffman learned of the court's decision in *Totus v. the United States*. Fearful that the Totus ruling set the tone for the Six Nations' forthcoming case, Hoffman and the confederacy pressed the Indian Bureau, Congress, and the White House throughout the summer for an out-of-court settlement. Washington, however, sensed certain victory and refused to compromise the government's position. In a telegram to President Franklin Roosevelt on June 4, Wilford Crouse requested a personal conference between the president and representatives of the Seneca tribe, but the White House informed him that such a meeting was impossible given the president's extremely busy schedule.[43]

Washington actually hardened its posture during the interim, particularly as America's entry into the war seemed more probable. Military intelligence and faltering relations with Japan indicated a diplomatic rupture with the Axis powers in the near future. National mobilization, now more than ever, required the full participation and total compliance of all Americans. The commissioner was determined that Native Americans would cooperate. He had repeatedly and publicly praised Indian support for draft registration and commended the thousands of Native Americans who had voluntarily enlisted in the armed forces to date. But Collier believed that the legal confrontation with the Six Nations threatened to undermine further Indian compliance if the Iroquois' won their appeal, a prospect he did not wish to see develop given the emergence of other incidents of draft resistance across the nation. He was determined that the confederacy would also submit to federal authority.

In October, Hoffman and Green appeared before the panel of judges in the United States Court of Appeals, Second Circuit. The defense repeated its earlier arguments point-by-point and reminded the court that "all Indians in this state [New York] take the position that the draft law is another step in the erosion of their rights in the United States." In similar fashion, federal prosecutors reiterated their earlier position.[44] After listening to both sides, the three judges announced they would evaluate the merits of all arguments presented and issue a ruling within a month.

In the meantime, Collier took the opportunity to publicize the government's position in the general press and in the bureau's monthly publication *Indians at Work.* The article that spilled from his pen proved more than a mere justification of the bureau's stance; Collier created a masterful piece of propaganda. The commissioner stressed emphatically that Warren Eldreth Green was "himself not particularly anxious" to be released from service, nor were a "number of braves from the Confederation tribes [who] have volunteered for service." The Iroquois' willingness to serve in America's armed forces was never the issue. Their courage was never questioned, and their historic support for the United States never wavered. Instead, "the Indians are jealous of their independence, of their status as imperium in imperio," Collier wrote. Green's case centered on "another of those curious anomalies" in the relationship between Indian tribes and the federal government. Most important, it exemplified the Indians' determination to remain free from external domination, truly an American principle. The commissioner applauded the Six Nations' solid pursuit of freedom and acknowledged their "sounder intuition" in not making peace with Germany after World War I as the United States did.[45]

The positive wording and structure of Collier's editorial connoted broad Native American loyalty for the United States and unyielding opposition to the Axis powers. Specifically, the commissioner's remarks sounded the notes of a firm defender of the Iroquois Indians rather than a harsh antagonist of the Six Nations. His choice of words and phrases allowed the commissioner to avoid explicit public rejection of Iroquois treaties and sovereignty while relegating the affair once more to simple misunderstanding of the Indians' status in the United States.

One month later, on November 24, the circuit court of appeals announced its decision. The three judges—Thomas W. Swan, Harrie Brigham Chase, and Jerome N. Frank—regretfully declared their unanimous ruling against the Iroquois Confederacy. Speaking for the court, Judge Frank said, "we have taxed our ingenuity in vain to find any interpretation which would result in a decision in his [Green's] favor." Therefore, he continued, "we find ourselves compelled to decide against Green, although, because of the historic relations of the United States to the Indians, we reach that conclusion most reluctantly."[46]

The Citizenship Act of 1924 and the Nationality Act of 1940, though "at variance" with the status accorded to the confederacy by the three treaties, remained constitutional. Domestic law, Frank stated, took priority over treaties since the *Head Money* cases of 1884. "Whatever doubt there might possibly be concerning the 1924 statute . . . the 1940 statute unequivocally made Green a citizen," even without his consent, Frank added. As the Selective Service Act made "every male citizen" subject to the provisions of draft registration and military service, Green could not escape his obligations. Furthermore, Frank noted, the Selective Service Act itself negated all treaties for the duration of the national emergency.[47]

Judges Swan and Chase concurred with Frank's explanation. Although the wording of the Citizenship Act and Nationality Act made both laws constitutional, Swan noted their inconsistencies with treaties between the Six Nations and the United States. The principal issue the court had to address was the legitimacy of those two congressional acts, and, on this narrow point, the court gave its decision with reference to *Totus v. the United States.* Iroquois nationhood was a separate matter, and Swan suggested the Indians and government officials revisit the issue. With "regret," Swan affirmed Frank's ruling.[48]

The court's decision in *Ex Parte Green* upheld Washington's argument that the Iroquois Confederacy was subject to federal law despite the appearance of national sovereignty bound by treaty. Certainly, the Bureau of Indian Affairs was relieved. The only large-scale resistance to compulsory draft registration and military service seemed to lie in ashes. With the verdict, Collier announced "the courts have now held that . . . the Selective Service Act is applicable to *all* Indians." He felt confident that without the argument of treaty rights, Iroquois resistance would now crumble and across the nation Indians and reservation superintendents would recognize the legal status of Native Americans in the United States.[49]

Still, the issue simmered among the Iroquois. In an effort to reassert its sovereignty as a separate state, delegates from the Six Nations gathered in conference on June 13, 1942, to draft a formal declaration of war against the Axis nations. The following day, a spokesman for the confederacy read the declaration in a thirty-minute national radio broadcast, and in ceremony on the steps of the United States Capitol the next day, Vice President Wallace received the pronouncement from Jesse Lyons of the Six Nations. "We represent the oldest, though smallest, democracy in the world today," the declaration read. Undaunted by the court's ruling seven months earlier, that statement alone announced the confederacy's intention to remain a separate nation within a nation. Having proclaimed the Indians' foremost principle, the declaration turned listeners' attention to the present global war: "It is the unanimous sentiment among Indian people that the atrocities of the Axis nations are violently repulsive to all sense of righteousness of our people, and that this merciless slaughter of mankind can no longer be tolerated." "Now," the declaration continued, "we do resolve that it is the sentiment of this council that the Six Nations of Indians declare that a state of war exists between our Confederacy of Six Nations on the one part and Germany, Italy, Japan and their allies against whom the United States has declared war, on the other part."[50] Acting as an independent, sovereign state, the Iroquois Confederacy entered World War II of its own consent. While the activities on the Capitol steps were carefully orchestrated and partly contrived by federal officials to reduce Indian draft resistance through a show of Iroquois support for the war, the fundamental intent remained pure—the reassertion of Six Nations' sovereignty through a declaration of war with the Axis nations. Without question, Indian Bureau officers, State Department officials, and representatives of the White House who attended the ceremony considered the Iroquois declaration little more than propaganda for public consumption. The Six Nations believed the move to be simply another step in the continued battle to retain a separate Iroquois identity.

In the summer of 1942, Iroquois Indians cast their sight over the preceding one hundred and fifty years to evaluate their current official status in the United States. Land holdings had fallen to white incursions, and a series of treaties with Washington had been established, then erased by congressional policies sanctioned by the federal courts. True, the United States honored its financial obligations to the Indians, but the Six Nations recognized a history of federal curtailment of confederation sovereignty, most significantly under the bureau leadership of John Collier. The commissioner's advocacy of Indian self-determination proved, for the Iroquois, a severe contradiction with reality. As a result, the Six Nations in that summer promised an extended campaign throughout and after the war to recapture its sovereign status.

Draft resistance among American Indians, in general, was confined to a small segment of the native population and generated scant serious attention from the broader, white population. And, with the exception of the Iroquois case, the BIA expressed only limited concern. Most often, Collier ascribed Indian protest to simple misunderstanding of the Selective Service Act. Indian protests, however, centered on the issues of sovereignty, treaty provisions, race, religion, and isolation. Indian draft resistance magnified the critical gulf that still separated Washington and native communities. Washington's inaction or inability to deal effectively with those issues compelled American Indians, such as those in tidewater Virginia and New York, to reassess their status in the United States. Despite the visible loyalty and patriotic fervor displayed by Indians in combat and on the home front, Indian draft resistance illuminated the Indians' determination to secure a renewed identity apart from white society, and it laid the foundation for an ethnocentric movement which crystallized into "Red Power" two decades later.

Six

Indians Go to War

Tired of eating the usual "cafeteria gruel" served at the reservation boarding school at Ganado, Arizona, Keith Little took his .22 rifle from the closet in his dormitory room, gathered several friends, and hiked into the nearby hills to hunt rabbits. Hunting small game that Sunday morning in December proved a pleasant diversion from the daily routine and quickly rewarded the boys with the aroma of fresh meat slowly cooking over an open fire. "Somebody went to the dorm, came back and said, 'Hey, Pearl Harbor was bombed!'" Little recalled years later. More puzzled than shocked, one of the boys asked, "Where's Pearl Harbor?" The next few moments of dialog among the youngsters were probably similar to discussions among hundreds of other small groups of Indians across the United States. "Who did it?" asked one boy. "Japan," answered the bearer of news. "Why'd they do it?" was the next question. "They hate Americans. They want to kill all Americans," the boy replied. "Us, too?" "Yeah, us too," came the response. Said Keith Little, "Then and there, we all made a promise. . . . We promised each other we'd go after the Japanese instead of hunting rabbits."[1]

The startling news of Japan's strike against Hawaii on December 7, 1941, seared itself into American memory. Although Americans viewed their involvement in the overseas war as inevitable, it remained more in the realm of abstraction than reality until that Sunday morning. Like Keith Little and his friends, so many Americans knew more of Hitler and the Nazi conquest of Europe than they did of Japan's Pacific expansion. The nation's news media focused more intently on the Nazi's racial doctrine, Hitler's invasion of Russia, the fall of France, and London's courage under fire. Nazi propagandists filtered Hitler's doctrine into urban communities and Indian reservations alike, and the ranting of American fascist organizations claimed front-page coverage in the press. The fundamental points of confrontation between the United States and Japan, however, were ambiguous as the duality of distance and cultural difference clouded American understanding. Air assaults on the Philippines seemed quite probable, but an attack directly on Hawaii had crossed the minds of few Americans. Japan's aerial strike and the shocking loss of life among American sailors, soldiers, and civilians threw the nation into a frenzy of revenge. Little wonder that Keith Little immediately and emotionally chose to hunt Japanese instead of small game.

From coast to coast, Americans shared a common anxiety for the nation's survival. Oliver LaFarge traveled to Santa Clara Pueblo that Sunday afternoon, and upon his arrival he was informed of Japan's attack. "There was an unexpectedly keen sense of Hawaii and the Philippines, where a New Mexico anti-aircraft regiment has been stationed," he noted. "There was a general acceptance of the war as their own," he added, "deriving from a definite feeling that they were sharers in America and democracy." And, he said later, "There were expressions of regret for the many boys, not just of their own people, but American boys in general, who were going to be killed."[2]

On Monday, December 8, John Collier inserted a flyer into the next edition of *Indians at Work*, scheduled for distribution on Tuesday. Printed on bright, pink paper, Collier offered his perspective on the war that now engulfed the United States. "We are in the World War," he wrote, and "the stake is everything—literally everything—that we as Americans (white and Indian) hold dear. The World War is indivisible; we irrevocably have been sucked into its vortex. It is the most desperate war—not merely the biggest, but the most ruthless and desperate—that our planet has known. On its outcome depends not merely the future of republics and empires, not merely the physical shape of a thousand years to come, but the actual biological survival of whole races," Collier warned. Ultimately, the war would determine "whether the human spirit shall remain alive." Once he painted the war as a life or death struggle, the commissioner cautioned Indian readers not to assume a quick or easy victory. "It is going to be a long war," he said, "requiring of us more than any of us yet can foresee." Evil itself must be destroyed, and once accomplished, "not only our country but the soul within us will have its victory."[3]

In the weeks and months following Pearl Harbor, American Indians increasingly melded into the war effort. The enlistment of Indian men into the nation's armed forces skyrocketed. Reservations marshaled their resources and offered their lands for the military's wartime use. Tribes freely redirected their appropriations to war agencies, and Indians purchased millions of dollars in defense bonds. Communities also set aside for the duration all outstanding claims against the federal government. Such direct, tangible contributions to the war effort aided the United States materially and financially.

Perhaps more attractive to the news media and more intriguing to the general population, numerous tribes themselves declared war on the Axis powers. Within weeks of Pearl Harbor, Jemez Pueblo Indians officially issued a declaration of war on the Japanese. In June 1942, the Iroquois Nation of New York followed suit in a public ceremony, with Vice President Henry Wallace, on the steps of the Capitol Building in Washington. Two months later, the Ponca Tribe announced its own official declaration of war against Germany and Japan. The Chippewa of Michigan also formalized a state of war with the Axis nations and proclaimed their determination to "stand by Uncle Sam to the end."[4]

Tribes that stopped short of an outright declaration of war nonetheless openly condemned the Axis nations. Cheyenne Indians criticized the Axis as an "unholy triangle whose purpose is to conquer and enslave the bodies, minds, and souls of all free people." Other tribal communities took symbolic action to show publicly their distaste for America's enemies. In Arizona, four tribes agreed among themselves to discontinue the stitching of the swastika, an ancient symbol of friendship, on blankets and the painting of the emblem on pots and baskets. They quickly added that the Nazi's use of the image was backwards. Just as quickly, the news media popularized the Indians' display of patriotism to a public eager to read stories of Native American responses to the war.[5]

War declarations, formal condemnation of the Axis, and symbolic gestures that showed the Indians' opposition to America's enemies were intended to demonstrate clearly Native American loyalty to the United States and to encourage pan-Indian unity for the war effort. These actions were more than simple acts of showmanship; they represented the heartfelt sentiment of the Indians involved. Similar to the patriotic performances played on theater stages, programs presented in school assemblies, or in public rallies across the nation, a spirited commitment to victory was generated and sometimes reinvigorated within the local native community through public demonstrations. Moreover, the patriotic clamor emotionally connected those at home with loved ones overseas. Among readers of daily newspapers, Indian displays of loyalty, cooperation, and the commonality of purpose with white society suggested a heightened identity as American rather than that of Indian, but, more often than not, tribes that actually declared war on the Axis nations did so as evidence of their political autonomy and their desire to retain a separate tribal identity apart from the United States.[6]

Both Washington and the press praised Indian combat performance, in part to show white America the wartime sacrifice and contribution of Native Americans and in part to provide Native Americans with evidence of the Indian's full, equal inclusion in the war effort. Among the more visible examples receiving widespread public attention was the death of General Clarence L. Tinker. Within weeks after Japan's attack on Pearl Harbor, Tinker, an Osage, received command of the Army Air Corps based in Hawaii. Throughout the spring of 1942, Tinker regrouped the units and trained them for the long, bloody war he expected in the Pacific. In May, much of the General's force, including himself, relocated to Midway Island in anticipation of a second Japanese assault in the eastern Pacific. When the attack came the following month, Tinker "personally led the squadrons of bombers which supplied the American spearhead of the [counter] attack." He refused "to assign anyone else the task." General Tinker was killed in action at Midway and posthumously awarded the Distinguished Service Medal. In presenting the award, the government formally announced Tinker's Indian identity—an identity unknown to most Americans at the time, including his comrades. Commissioner John Collier added that Tinker "exemplified the modern Indian soldier."[7]

The Bureau of Indian Affairs frequently personalized reports of Indian servicemen in combat to garner greater appreciation for the sacrifices they made on behalf of the nation. Collier's detailed description of Private Ben Quintana typified the commissioner's approach. A Keres Indian from Cochiti Pueblo, Quintana's youth revolved around his love of art. Most of his paintings exhibited traditional Indian culture, lore, and style. By age fifteen, Quintana had developed his skill so thoroughly that friends encouraged him to enter a piece in a contest sponsored by the Coronado Cuarto Centennial. Of the eighty contestants, of whom only seven were Indian, Ben won first place. With that success and the confidence it instilled within him, he soon afterward entered a painting in the *American Magazine* art-talent search with 52,587 other contestants. When the judging concluded, the top award of one thousand dollars was given to Quintana.[8]

The bureau then drew its audience to the current world crisis. The young Keres enlisted in the United States Army in the aftermath of Pearl Harbor, was trained as "an ammunition carrier in a light machine gun" squad, and was shipped overseas. During an enemy attack on his division's perimeter, his gunner and assistant gunner were both mortally wounded while holding the right flank. "Private Quintana refused to retire from this hazardous position and gallantly rushed forward to the silenced gun and delivered a withering fire into the enemy, inflicting heavy casualties." His heroism under fire stalled the enemy's attempt to envelop the American line, but in so doing Quintana was killed. Inspired by his selfless act, the Indian's comrades turned the battle and seized the enemy's strong point.[9] Ben Quintana's parents received their son's Silver Star and the thanks of a grateful nation. Collier's publicity of the young Keres Indian both personalized the war for Americans and demonstrated a commonality between Indians and whites.

Most accounts of Indian combat performance fell into the lengthy shadows of two other individuals—Ernest Childers and Ira Hayes. Second Lieutenant Childers, a Creek from Broken Arrow, Oklahoma, commanded an infantry platoon near Oliveto, Italy, in the Salerno area. While scouting the surrounding countryside on September 9, 1943, Childers's unit stumbled upon a German observation post that immediately opened fire. In his move to gain cover, Childers fractured his instep. Enemy machine guns and snipers pinned his men to their shallow defensive positions, and casualties mounted. Worried that his entire platoon might be destroyed, Childers surveyed the landscape to find some way of disengaging and removing his men to safety. The German guns made the prospect seem futile; his only recourse was to eliminate the Nazi outpost. Armed with only a carbine, Childers singly charged the enemy line, stopping several times to aim and fire at the snipers, all of whom he killed. Finding a concealed location, the lieutenant grabbed a rock and hurled it into the machine gun nest. Assuming the "thud" at their feet was a hand grenade, the Germans sprang from their hole and were immediately shot by the Creek. Lieutenant Childers saved his platoon and single-handedly took the enemy position. Days later, while resting his fractured foot, Childers learned that his battalion was under fire from German machine guns and mortars. Without thought of his own injury, the lieutenant gathered together a squad of soldiers, guided them to a position on the German's flank, and ordered his men to provide base fire against the German defenses. Alone, he moved onwards, slipped behind the German machine guns, eliminated them with his rifle, and captured a mortar observer. When asked later how many Germans he personally killed, Childers said, "I wouldn't want to make a statement about that." Another officer on the scene, however, credited the lieutenant with seventeen kills in that one battle. For "conspicuous gallantry and intrepidity at the risk of life above and beyond the call of duty," Ernest Childers was awarded the Congressional Medal of Honor, only the second such award in Italy to that date.[10]

Despite Lieutenant Childers's bravery and public notoriety following his return to the states, the personification of the warrior image and spirit emerged in a lone, full-blooded Pima Indian from Bapchule, Arizona—Ira Hamilton Hayes. Like other members of his tribe and those from the neighboring Navajo Reservation, Hayes enlisted in the Marine Corps not long after Pearl Harbor. For the most part, only assumptions can be made concerning his decision to volunteer. It seems likely that the redirection in federal Indian policy during Collier's administration of the BIA positively affected his perception of the United States. His own pre-war involvement with the Civilian Conservation Corps-Indian Division probably convinced him of the real potential for assimilation with white society; at the very least, as an enrollee he learned skills otherwise unavailable to him. In addition, the flow of money and the concentrated effort expended by Washington on his homeland made him realize that the federal government sincerely committed itself to a new, constructive relationship with Native Americans. As important, the Pimas historically were "steeped in a rich tradition and heritage and possess[ed] an unwavering loyalty" to the United States, despite Washington's earlier "lies and unfulfilled promises" that resulted in "the loss of their land and water rights."[11]

Ira Hayes was reared in a home steeped in traditional values; nonetheless, he accepted many physical and emotional trappings of white society. Arthur Stanton, a friend of Hayes and a Marine as well, described the Pima as a "loner" who "dreamed with envy of his ancestors, who once roamed the vast plains of the great West, proud and free."[12] Stanton's assessment, however, countered the realities of traditional Pima culture. Instead of the nomadic life imagined by Stanton, Pimas actually lived a sedentary and rather passive existence in Arizona for thousands of years.[13] Stanton was undoubtedly swayed by stereotyped images of American Indians, particularly those of the Great Plains, and assumed the warrior spirit pervaded all Native Americans. His failure to realize the absence of a warrior tradition in Pima culture suggests that Hayes offered little opposition to Stanton's view, despite their close relationship. Hayes either refused to challenge his friend's perception or preferred to think of himself from Stanton's perspective.

Hayes bravely served in the Vella La Vella and Bougainville campaigns and for his service earned the rank of corporal. Offered the role of platoon leader, Hayes refused. "I'd have to tell other men to go and get killed," he said, "and I'd rather do it myself." In February 1945, the Pima landed on Iwo Jima with the Fifth Marine Division. For thirty days, the Marines attacked Japanese positions and warded off counterstrikes. His unit found itself on the slopes of Mount Suribachi, exposed to a murderous fire from Japanese artillery and machine guns. As he and his men scrambled to the hilltop, one Marine pulled from his shirt an American flag, and, together, Hayes and five other men raised the Stars and Stripes on a makeshift flagpole before the watchful camera of combat photographer Joe Rosenthal.[14]

The published photograph sealed in time the courage of America's fighting man. It also spurred a nationwide curiosity to discover the identity of each Marine involved in raising the flag. Following an investigation by the Marine Corps, three surviving flag raisers of the original six were located and returned stateside. Hayes was among them, despite his request to remain with his unit. Rosenthal's photo became the promotional image for the Seventh War Loan Drive and an instant patriotic symbol for the nation. Ira Hayes, on orders, toured the United States as part of the bond drive. On May 1, 1945, he arrived in his hometown to find more than one thousand Pimas celebrating his return with cheers, speeches, barbecued meat, and religious ceremonies. For Indians in all corners of the United States, Hayes exemplified the warrior tradition and became a symbol of the Native American's expected new role in white society, a role in which Indians retained pride in their heritage yet moved toward greater inclusion within the white mainstream. He received accolades from the National Congress of American Indians and was appointed as the first commander of the American Indian Veterans Association before the end of the month.[15]

Over the ten years that followed World War II, Ira Hayes remained proud of his Indian ancestry, particularly his identity as a Pima, and he was honored to have served the United States when the nation was most desperately in need of all her young men. But Hayes never reveled in his combat accomplishments. His closest friends who survived the war remembered Hayes as a shy man, a "humble person" who would "deny ever doing or having done anything bordering on heroism." "Duty" succinctly captured his combat performance. More often than not, he simply tried to forget the horror of war and release the pain caused by the loss of so many friends. He never felt worthy of the praise, the honor, or the unrestrained respect given him. Again, "duty" was the source of his courage, just as it was for the Marines with whom he served.[16]

In the late 1960s, Stanton met Texas resident and artist Joe Ruiz Grandee and recounted his combat experiences, including the firefight that claimed the former Marine's two feet. Impressed by Stanton's personal story and his evident admiration and friendship for Hayes, Grandee honored the spirit of Ira Hayes and the Marines on canvas. Entitled "Ira Hayes—His Dream, His Reality," the Mount Suribachi scene framed the background; and the foreground, which commanded nearly two-thirds of the work, showed a warrior on a painted horse. At the end of his outstretched arm, his hand firmly grasped his weapon, the air whipped the warrior's long hair across his shoulders, and the Indian gazed courageously toward some unseen, ominous presence.[17] The visible strength and spirit of the Indian captured the essence of the warrior tradition, but the portrait of Hayes on horseback fell far short of Pima cultural realities. Skewed, too, was the personal representation of Hayes's character. Ira Hayes, indeed, served courageously in battle, as did all Marines regardless of racial identity, but at no point did he truly see himself in the form presented by Grandee. Regardless of its inaccuracy, the artist's painting represented a bond among World War II Indian veterans from all branches and instilled pride in their service to the United States. For this reason, Grandee's work became the image stamped upon medallions given ceremoniously to surviving Navajo code talkers in 1969.[18]

Unfortunately for Indians in World War II, the emphasized warrior tradition reinforced among whites a stereotyped perception of Native American combat skills. Exploits, such as those related by Ickes, Collier, and the news media, encouraged numerous comparisons between contemporary Indians and the exaggerated warrior traits ascribed to past generations of Indians. Stanley Vestal, the leading authority of Plains Indian culture at the time, believed that "offensive warfare" best characterized the Indians' fighting style. The Native American, he wrote, "was a realistic soldier; he knew that war meant killing, and he never gave quarter or expected it." In a nod crediting the Indians' historic method of fighting, and concurrently slapping the foolish gullibility of recent politicians who contributed to the coming of war, he said that Indians believed "appeasement was fatal." "This lesson produced a profound, and by now instinctive, quality in their thinking and outlook on life," he continued. "The offensive approach to life" marked every aspect of Indian culture, especially warfare.[19]

Vestal's appraisal acquired greater plausibility as additional combat reports filtered stateside and among command officers. During the course of the war, events in the Philippines unfolded to reveal a guerrilla campaign led by Lieutenant Colonel Edward Ernest McClish, a Choctaw from Oklahoma. A graduate of Haskell Institute and Bacone College, McClish had received a commission in the army in 1931 and served on active duty for the next ten years. In early 1941, the army shipped McClish to the Philippines to command scouting operations and to mobilize a local defense force. Following Japan's invasion of the islands, Colonel McClish moved his resistance operations to eastern Mindanao, but in late April 1942 Japanese units discovered the colonel's base and for three full weeks attempted to destroy his ragged and poorly trained troops. McClish proved too elusive for capture or destruction. Throughout the summer, the colonel's forces struck the enemy, fell back, regrouped, and struck again. At the same time, Colonel McClish continued to raise his manpower and by September linked with a similar unit commanded by one Colonel Fertig of the U.S. Army Corps of Engineers. Together, McClish and Fertig constructed regimental strength forces in three of the four Philippine provinces and consistently harassed Japanese troops throughout the islands. By January 1945, the pair had directed more than 350 engagements against Japanese garrisons with an estimated enemy loss of three thousand killed and six hundred wounded.[20] McClish's command was offensive, aggressive, and elusive-traits typically associated with Indian warfare, according to Vestal.

Secretary Ickes detailed what he thought to be the Native American's natural fighting abilities. Indians, he believed, possessed "inherited talents . . . uniquely valuable" in the prosecution of war. These individuals, Ickes asserted, enjoyed an innate "endurance" and "rhythm" for combat. They demonstrated "a feeling for timing, co-ordination . . . an uncanny ability to get over any sort of terrain at night, and, better than all else, an enthusiasm for fighting." The Indian, Ickes continued, "takes a rough job and makes a game of it. Rigors of combat hold no terrors for him; severe discipline and hard duties do not deter him." *Indians at Work* perpetuated many of these stereotypes. Indian soldiers of the Forty-fifth Infantry Division performed a new dance prior to one battle, reported the magazine. There was a "fury of drums and savage rhythm. Instead of a tomahawk, the dancer brandishes a sleek Garand—and they've named it the Victory Dance. . . . and they've sworn to dance it in Berlin. Watch out, Hitler—the Indians are after your scalp!"[21] Similar descriptions were read before the United States House of Representatives and included for publication in the *Congressional Record.* In presenting Richard Neuberger's article "The American Indian Enlists" on the floor of the House, Congressman John Coffee of Washington announced, "American Indians are crack marksmen. They excel as scouts and trailsmen and lookouts, and they are integral parts of numerous American Army units."[22]

Also read into the *Congressional Record* was an article written by Jack Durant for the widely circulated newspaper *Washington Star.* The story rested on the observation of Major Lee Gilstrap at an undisclosed army training post. According to Durant, Major Gilstrap commended without hesitation the natural fighting ability of Native American soldiers. "The Indians love to use that bayonet, and that probably explains why they are the best bayonet fighters," he said. "They like the shining steel blade so well that it is a terrific job to make them remember that rifles carry bullets as well as bayonets." In target practice, "they are the best rifle shots in their division," he continued, "and most of them are particularly adept at long-range rifle shooting." Gilstrap echoed comments made by Ickes and others regarding the Indians' sensory skills. "The sense perception of many Indians is so acute that they can spot a snake by sound or smell before they can see it. They have an uncanny faculty at weaseling over any kind of terrain at night, and there is a saying that 'the only Indian who can't find his way back to his own lines is a dead Indian.'" Physically, "their long, sleek muscles are built for endurance. . . . I never saw an Indian who lacked rhythm, timing, coordination," he said. In all their assignments, Indians excelled. "At scouting and patrol work, the Indian stands out like a sore thumb." Intended as a compliment rather than a derogatory comment, Gilstrap provided examples that surfaced during recent maneuvers. "One Indian, single-handed, captured a tank and its crew; another Indian came back with 87 'scalps,' or identifying arm bands." The major ascribed the Indians' skills to an "enthusiasm for fighting," and a "fighting spirit" that appeared most natural and enriched over generations by emphasis on the warrior tradition.[23]

Similar stereotyped descriptions permeated scholarly journals and mass-consumption periodicals and consistently highlighted the Indian warrior spirit with those serving in the Pacific and European theaters. Representative of most, a *Reader's Digest* article claimed that contemporary Indian soldiers manifested historic cultural traits in the current war. Closer to nature than other races and trained since childhood in hunting and reading the natural environment, Indian soldiers possessed a peculiar ability to track an enemy without detection. As scouts, Indians used their developed senses of sound, sight, and smell. The writer stated that "some [Indian soldiers] can smell a snake yards away and hear the faintest movement." They proved themselves masters of ambush and signal experts. The Indian soldier, the writer continued, "is a natural Ranger. He takes to commando fighting with gusto. Why not? His ancestors invented it."[24]

Even General Douglas MacArthur commented on American Indian capabilities. "As a warrior the Indian's fame is world wide," he said. "Many successful methods of modern warfare are based on what he evolved centuries ago. . . . His tactics apply in basic principle to the vast jungle covered reaches of the present war." One of the general's regimental commanders further noted three features of the Native American that made the Indian "the best damn soldier in the Army" — his physique, sensory perceptions, and "imperturbability."[25] The comments issued by Vestal, Ickes, MacArthur and others were racist, but those who made such observations believed their descriptions expressed a profound respect for Indian combat troops.

Tribute was also extended to Native Alaskans and Aleuts. Because of their supposed natural skills, the War Department contemplated the formation of native scouting units to operate throughout Alaska and the Aleutian Islands. Even the navy considered special operations for Aleuts and Alaskan natives. Said one commanding officer on Adak, Aleuts were "the best sailors in the world." Based on their superb ability "in taking all kinds of craft into isolated harbors regardless of weather," he called on Washington to form an all-Aleut unit to aid both sea and land actions jointly conducted by the navy and army.[26]

In describing Indian fighting abilities during World War II, government officials, white military commanders, and the press continued a pattern present since the Great War. Indian soldiers in World War I were noted as having "instinctive" abilities in combat, skill at camouflage, keen hearing and eyesight, endurance, swiftness and virility, a "blood thirsty" and anxious desire to fight, and an ever-present stoicism.[27] Because of those perceived traits, Indian soldiers were assigned duties as scouts, commandos, and snipers—a pattern repeated in World War II. A continuity existed between the two wars; an image that only assumed greater prominence in the second war.

So many of the stories published in newspapers and magazines focused on the "exotic aspects" of American Indians. As one scholar recently said, "an audience existed for stories about Native Americans, but, judging from the types of articles printed, they [readers] preferred colorful, amusing, personal items rather than substantive pieces on Indian policy. . . . Whites often overlooked the religious aspect of . . . Indian rituals, believing that by World War II Indian religions had long been defunct."[28] Terms such as "warrior," "prowess," "redskin," "warpath," "pow wow," and "scalp" were used with reckless abandon. Indians frequently posed in costumes that had little to do with cultural accuracy. In one *New York Times* article, a story appeared that described one Indian's attempt to enlist in the army. At the induction center in Denver on February 25, 1944, a new recruit was ordered to "skip the fighting talk" and just give his name. "But that is my name," he answered. "It's Charles Jonas Kills the Enemy." According to the writer, Kills the Enemy was a Sioux Indian and "a descendant of a long line of famous chieftains." Another brief *New York Times* page-filler reported that "Chief Two Hatchet leaped from [a] landing barge onto an Italian beach and yelled: 'We've come to return the visit of Columbus in 1492.'" The contributor quickly added that Two Hatchet was known to the army as Private Paul Bitchenen of Cheyenne, Oklahoma. One story that circulated among American troops in Normandy shortly after D-Day and soon filtered back to the states concerned a Red Cross worker, Miss Eisenstadt. Standing over a wounded soldier, she picked up the chart that hung at the foot of his hospital bed and asked the young man, "How on earth did you ever get shot with two arrows?" "That's my name, not my injury!" replied the full-blooded Indian. Whether or not these stories contained any degree of authenticity remains unclear, but what seems apparent with these and similar stories is that much of the press coverage given to Native Americans in World War II turned on the quaint, the romantic, and the exotic images emanating from stereotyped representations fixed in the public imagination.[29]

The army and the Marine Corps fully believed the stereotyped traits to be valid and, as a result, actively recruited Native Americans for special assignments. An example is easily found in the Normandy Invasion. In the early morning hours of June 6, 1944, Allied paratroopers and commando teams leaped into the countryside of Nazi-occupied France. They were instructed to cut German communication and supply lines, hold bridges for the expected British and American inland advance, and neutralize heavy gun emplacements before the beach landings commenced at daybreak. One such unit, composed of thirteen handpicked Southwestern Indians, was ordered to eliminate German batteries along a stretch of Normandy's cliffs. Their selection to the team rested squarely on stereotyped assumptions of the Indians' rock-climbing skills, sense of balance, and the courage that emanated from a traditional warrior spirit. The commando unit accomplished its mission but at great expense. Only two men survived the predawn raid.[30] No doubt, a warrior spirit directed some Indians in uniform, and the desire to further the tradition occasionally affected some of their actions. What many whites, however, mistook for Indian uniqueness in combat was, in reality, a normal adrenaline-filled human response to immediate combat circumstances.

The image also affected Axis troops. One American correspondent reported that German officers reminded their troops of General Karl von Prutch's assessment of Indian soldiers in the Great War. "The most dangerous of the American soldiers is the Indian," von Prutch allegedly said. "He is brave above all else. He knows far more about camouflage . . . than any modern soldier." Von Prutch concluded his remarks with an explicit warning: "He [the Indian] is a dead shot. He needs no orders when he advances. He is an army within himself. He is the one American soldier Germany must fear."[31] Whether or not General von Prutch's remarks were indeed presented to German troops or served simply as creative propaganda for American domestic consumption remains unconfirmed. The ferocity of Russian troops in combat, however, prompted Adolf Hitler to warn his eastern front divisions that the Soviets fight like Indians. Their ruthlessness and savagery demanded the full vigor and resolve of German soldiers.[32]

Most Germans, like Hitler, continued to view Native Americans in nineteenth-century terms, and numerous unconfirmed stories regarding Indian stereotypes and the Indians' presence in the European Theater sifted through both German and Allied ranks. One such tale purportedly originated in southern Italy at a prisoner-of-war camp. According to those who recounted the incident, the American commandant oversaw a rather large collection of Nazi prisoners who consistently refused to follow regulations, and often their agitation bordered on violence. Hearing that the U.S. Forty-fifth Infantry Division was encamped nearby, the commandant devised a plan to utilize the resources of that division.

The Forty-fifth, also known as the Thunderbird Division, included more than two thousand Indians, largely from New Mexico and Arizona. He requested a loan from the Forty-fifth of one dozen Indians for temporary duty as camp guards. On their arrival, the Indians were briefed by the camp commander, and to a man they agreed to follow his plan to quell Nazi disobedience. They slowly walked among the prisoners, glared at many, and rubbed their hands over the shaven heads of Nazi POWs. They soon regrouped with the commandant under the pretense of discussing the prisoners' fate. The Indians mumbled among themselves in their native tongue. As if he understood, the commandant loudly protested, "Well, can't you wait till their hair grows out? I'll have you detailed here as guards." With that, the Indians once again studied the Germans, particularly their haircuts, and then retired to their temporary quarters. Several Germans understood English and the contrived conversation. Word spread quickly throughout the camp. From then on, the commandant experienced nothing but complete obedience from his Nazi prisoners.

While some Indians in the armed forces preferred not to have their identity on display, such as General Tinker, the majority accepted the special attention and occasionally performed ceremonies in full view of fellow soldiers. At other times, Indian troops exaggerated the stereotype for their own amusement at the expense of whites. In his book *Guadalcanal Diary*, Richard Tregaskis recounted a story told him by a senior medical officer aboard one of the vessels that carried marines to their landing site. As the armada approached the island, he told Tregaskis, "I went below [deck] to look around in the hole." He expected "to find kids praying, and instead I found 'em doing a war dance. One of them had a towel for a loincloth and a blackened face, and he was doing a can-can while another beat a tom-tom."[33]

News correspondent Ernie Pyle witnessed a similar event just prior to the American landing on Okinawa. Like so many other observers, Pyle claimed the "Indian boys knew . . . that the invasion landing wasn't going to be very tough. They were the only ones in the convoy who did know it. For one thing they saw signs and for another they used their own influence." Before the invasion force departed their training area, the Indians held a ceremonial dance, Pyle wrote. "The Red Cross furnished some colored cloth and paint to stain their faces. They made up the rest of their Indian costumes from chicken feathers, sea shells, coconuts, empty ration cans and rifle cartridges." They danced and chanted underneath palm trees in front of "several thousand Marines" who formed "a grave audience." The Indians, Pyle said, "asked the great gods in the sky to sap the Japanese of their strength for this blitz. They put the finger of weakness on the Japs." The ceremony concluded with the singing of the Marine Corps Hymn in Navajo. When questioned whether or not he personally believed the ceremony helped determine the ease of landing, one Navajo responded: "I knew nothing was going to happen to us for on the way up here there was a rainbow over the convoy and I knew then everything would be all right."[34]

Undeniably, many Indians carried with them into battle traditional spiritual beliefs and looked for signs within nature suggestive of events yet to unfold. Accounts retold by white onlookers, however, often diminished the seriousness of Indian prayers and ceremonies and frequently brought into question the sincerity of the Indians who held fast to traditional values.

Indians themselves occasionally contributed to the perception of Native American uniqueness. One Navajo recalled that during basic training the camp held a competition among several platoons for the honor of "best drilled." One unit in the contest contained Chinese-Americans. As it performed, the marines counted cadence in Chinese. The Navajo's drill sergeant, in response, decided that his platoon should count in Navajo. "Well, we'd go three or four steps while we were counting 'one'," said the Indian. Since the white sergeant did not understand the language, "we mixed things up, using some bad words. Then we got laughing so hard we couldn't march. . . . [We were] calling him names as we went along." When the platoon sergeant realized what the Indians were doing, he ordered no more counting except in English.[35] The story proved humorous for those who heard it, and those Indians who survived the war enjoyed recalling it whenever the opportunity arose. In this respect, there was a common bond between white and Indian soldiers who longed for the chance to humiliate their drill instructor.

The positive attention and the warm reception given Indians by white soldiers and their officers indicated a ready acceptance of Native Americans in the armed forces. By government order, Indians and whites served in nonsegregated units. The "white" listing of Indians on military records immediately precluded any other prospect. This inclusion, explained the noted anthropologist John Adair, destroyed psychological "barriers" that may have initially existed between Indians and whites. From his interviews with Native American veterans after the war, Adair concluded that a sense of camaraderie and equality surfaced between the two races in the military. For Indians themselves, a feeling of belonging, self-worth, and pride resulted from their acceptance by whites. Most expressed the belief that they were judged as individuals rather than as members of a minority racial group.[36]

Racial prejudice against Native Americans proved much less pervasive among whites than that directed toward African Americans. Indians were recognized as white recruits, trained in aviation, commanded ships, earned commissions, and often rose to senior ranks. Until political pressure forced a change, black Americans were excluded from pilot training, a role readily open to Indian servicemen long before the war. Equality resulted partly because few white Americans had direct contact with reservation Indians. Their limited knowledge of the native population emanated from Hollywood films, and that depiction of nineteenth-century Indians was riddled with stereotype and misinformation. Moreover, the historic military confrontation between whites and Indians was viewed as the Native Americans' defense of their land and families, a perspective that proved worthy, understandable, and relevant to the current world war. Cognizant of that era's passage, but in possession of romantic notions regarding Indians, most white inductees responded to Native Americans with curiosity rather than prejudice.

There was, perhaps, another reason for the positive reception given to Indian recruits. With only few exceptions, Americans relegated Indian-white hostilities to a distant past. The massacre at Wounded Knee had occurred fifty-one years before Pearl Harbor. The Battle of the Little Bighorn, Red Cloud's War, Sitting Bull and Crazy Horse, the perceived Indian impediment to white migration across the continent, and a host of related events and personalities were buried in history. The rapid modernization and technological impulse of the United States since the turn of the century placed those earlier peoples and conflicts in a more primitive and, therefore, a more mentally remote era.

When placed against the backdrop of black-white relations, the imagery of "savage Indians" faded quickly. The horrors of the Civil War still marred the emotional landscape of whites and blacks. That war shattered a nation like no Indian issue ever did. It had directly involved nearly all Americans, split families, ended more than six hundred thousand lives, and laid waste to one entire region of the country. In the years between the Civil War and the present global conflict, the black population grew rapidly, particularly in urban areas and had begun to challenge segregation itself. Racial identification in the United States centered principally on a black-white foundation. In contrast, American Indians suffered a dramatic depopulation until the early years of the twentieth century and thereafter increased slowly. Furthermore, the Indian population largely resided on isolated reservations. Questions of Indian segregation hardly commanded attention. The actual number of Native Americans never seemed to threaten white dominance, and the Indians' presence and actions never challenged the existing social structure of white society as African American numbers and actions seemed to do.

The historic relationship between Indians and whites also contributed directly to the wartime acceptance of Indians in white military units. Throughout American history there had been a concerted effort among whites to incorporate Indians into the general population. Regardless of their ideological underpinnings, "praying towns" of the colonial era, the Lake Mohonk Conferences of the 1880s, which culminated with the Dawes Act of 1887, Indian participation in the Great War, the Citizenship Act of 1924, and even the Indian Reorganization Act all held similar goals. World War II itself was viewed by many white politicians as the Indians' next step toward assimilation. In addition, there was a history of intermarriage between the two races and a rising population of children with mixed parentage. Although white men occasionally fathered children with black women, the marriage of African Americans to whites remained illegal in most states. The legacy of slavery, civil war, Reconstruction, and Jim Crow, all tied to an unbridled racism, still embittered white society in 1941 and cast a biracial mentality upon the nation. Racism certainly prevailed against Indians in many communities nationwide, but seldom did it exist with the intensity and depth as that directed toward African Americans.

White acceptance of Indians as fellow soldiers manifested itself in numerous ways. On furlough or on weekend pass, Indians and whites together frequented the same bars and resorts. They competed for the same women, danced at the same nightclubs, and dined together at the same restaurants. They trained together, fought side-by-side, and relaxed as friends and brothers. The equal treatment and inclusion of Native Americans among white military units was mandated by Washington, but no order required such a close off-duty relationship. The perception held by some whites that Indians were ignorant, unclean, and in a perpetual state of drunkenness faded quickly in the shared living among soldiers.

Cultural differences typically dimmed once in training. Those differences that persisted generally received light-hearted attention. Often, Indian soldiers were called "chief" or "Geronimo" by white comrades, but the conveyance of a racial slur was normally not intended or inferred. In fact, Indian soldiers widely expressed a certain approval for the names given them. Both names connoted power, courage, and respect among Native Americans. What more could they ask from white soldiers?[37]

Of the cultural differences that endured, few captivated whites as much as Indian spirituality. When questioned, Indian recruits recounted religious ceremonies practiced by their families or tribes, such as the Blessing Way ceremony, that sought protection for the Indian soldier in combat and his safe return from war. Others spoke of purification rites, which they anticipated upon their return home. Through these ceremonies, Indian veterans would be purged of the hatred for the enemy they carried into battle, the responsibility of their actions in combat, and the horrific memories of war. For varied reasons, soldiers commonly gathered souvenirs from battlefields; Indians did so for ceremonial purposes. Purification rituals required some object from the enemy to be used in the cleansing process. Normally the item was buried and a prayer given for the separation of the Indian from the symbolic hold the article possessed over the veteran. Through this process, the returned Indian warrior placed the past behind him and regained harmony with the earth.[38] Many Indians carried items over which prayers for protection had been made, and some kept a pouch of peyote as a guard against injury or death in combat. While fighting in France in 1944, Frankie Redbone, a Kiowa, was captured and placed in a German prisoner-of-war camp. As a rule, German guards destroyed all personal possessions of their prisoners. Redbone placed his belongings on a table as ordered by his captors. A guard inquired about the contents of the small bag that Redbone withdrew from his pocket. "Indian medicine," Redbone replied. Everything the Indian put on the table was scooped up and taken away but the pouch. He remained in the camp for the next eight months, and upon his liberation he contended that the protection afforded him by the pouch prevented his own death while a POW.[39]

The Indians' spirituality extended far beyond the search for physical protection in battle. While most soldiers of all races typically offered a prayer before going into combat, Indians frequently did so prior to less perilous situations. One Navajo code talker admitted to asking for divine guidance each time he transmitted a radio message. Moreover, Indian acceptance of the supernatural included unquestioning reliance on prophetic visions. During America's Philippines campaign, one Indian marine had a spiritual experience and later recounted it to his friends. Although the Japanese held the land ahead, "I walked through the jungle and it was filled with light—like in early morning. I walked through the trees, brought the pure night air into my heart, and presented myself to God that I might be a perfect man," he said. In his vision, the marine asked God to make him "strong against the enemy . . . and returned to my people. Then I came back to the foxhole and woke up." Lying there, he mentally retraced his vision and contemplated its meaning. Scanning the area just in front of his hole, he noticed footprints in the soil leading from his position into the jungle ahead and back. Instantly he understood "it had not been a dream—I had really walked, for I saw my tracks in the soft ground. After that I had no fears. I was never afraid again!"[40] To this one Indian, the vision prophesied his safety for the remainder of the war. Furthermore, the complete faith he placed in the dream suggested a total reliance on the supernatural—a carry-over of traditional Indian culture into the contemporary world. Still, the intensity with which Native American soldiers adhered to traditional ceremonies, values, and customs varied according to the individual's level of acculturation.

White soldiers often delighted in observing the Indians' religious ceremonies. They initially showed a profound curiosity, but as the war dragged on, more and more whites exhibited greater respect for Indian spirituality. In part, whites perceived Native American religions to be similar to Christianity. Indians had been exposed to Christian doctrine on their reservations and in boarding schools, and, as a result, many Indians blended traditional spiritual awareness with Christian teachings. Also important, battle experiences seemed to have convinced some white troops of the validity of visions, certain rituals, and fundamental beliefs.

As American forces hit the beach on Leyte Island, the Japanese unleashed a massive counter-bombardment. One Indian, who had earlier spoken of ceremonies given him by his family for protection, scrambled for cover underneath some planks that had been unloaded from the landing craft. On his heels dashing for cover was a white soldier who had listened to the Indian's stories. Together, the two marines sandwiched themselves between the planks and sand until the cannon, mortar, and machine-gun fire ceased. The pair stood, surveyed the damage surrounding them, and was speechless. Scattered all about them were the dead and the dying. "Even though the planks had been literally chewed by shrapnel, neither of us had gotten even a scratch," the Indian later recalled. He credited his salvation to his family's ceremony and the protection it provided him. In fact, he continued, "I came out of the war without being touched by the enemy." And the white soldier who had shared his planks? He and the Indian became close friends for the duration.[41]

The stories that truly revealed the American Indian's role in combat seldom appeared in print. Those that did seldom reached the eyes of the reading public. In November 1944, Sergeant Nathaniel W. Quinton helped repulse a German attack in the Hurtgen Forest and in the process was officially credited with killing or wounding fifty-five enemy soldiers. One month later, he was captured in hand-to-hand combat but soon overpowered a guard, killed another, grabbed several maps showing German positions in the area, and made a successful escape. While fighting in Holland, Private First Class Herbert Bremner, a Tlingit from Yakutat, Alaska, moved with his battalion against four German tanks. Mortar and machine-gun fire damaged two of the vehicles carrying antitank weapons. Without regard for his own safety, Bremner manned a machine gun on top of one disabled vehicle and poured such an intense, accurate fire against the enemy that the German tanks and foot soldiers retired from the field. Private Houston Stevens, a Kickapoo from Oklahoma, was among the soldiers in a landing craft headed toward the beaches of southern France in August 1944 when a German plane bombed and strafed the boat. Though wounded, Stevens scrambled for a .50-caliber machine gun mounted on the craft's rear and delivered a steady fire against the pilot, who had turned for another attack. Despite the heat from nearby flames, the explosion of ammunition aboard the craft, and the burns he suffered from the initial attack, Stevens forced the German plane to retreat. Marine Pfc. Leonard A. Webber, a Shoshone from Fort Hall, Idaho, was attached to the Second Marine Division on Tarawa in November 1943. During the bloody battle, Webber continuously exposed himself to Japanese fire as a runner of battlefield messages between frontline infantry positions, tanks, and the tank battalion command center. The next summer, Webber was engaged against the Japanese on Saipan and Tinian Islands. In advance of the American tanks, Webber (now a corporal) scouted possible routes for the tanks to follow and personally guided a tank platoon over "dangerous and perilous terrain, while under heavy mortar and small arms fire." He led the tanks to a rise, from which they were able to inflict heavy casualties on the enemy below.[42]

Quinton, Bremner, Stevens, and Webber were typical of American soldiers in both theaters of war — not American Indian soldiers, but soldiers. Race commanded no role in displays of courage. Situations arose in battle; individuals responded as best as they could to immediate circumstances. A warrior spirit did not propel these men into action; patriotism and thoughts of family did not influence their behavior. Anyone who experienced the sheer terror of combat understood. Quinton, Bremner, and Stevens fought as they did to preserve their own lives and the lives of the men who stood with them. Webber had a job to do. He knew he could not go home until the enemy was defeated. These men were not "warriors" possessed with inherent skills and natural talents, but soldiers who found themselves in situations they would have preferred not to experience.

On a much larger scale, the same was true for those Indians who gained fame as code talkers. The United States armed forces found Indians in possession of one desired asset — a unique language. The Signal Corps, the army's communication branch, sought a method for transmitting battlefield information in combat without the delay imposed by encoding and decoding messages. Not only did the standard process inhibit rapid communication, but Axis forces proved skilled at breaking Allied codes with relative ease. Since the early 1920s, the encryption and deciphering of information had undergone a technological revolution that, in turn, made the practice a science rather than an art form by

1941.[43] Aware that the Axis powers held much of the same equipment and capability, and sensitive to the problems this imposed on battlefield transmissions among American units, the United States impatiently searched for an impenetrable code for combat operations.

After scanning a variety of possibilities, an incident was recalled from World War I that had confounded German radio operators. A front-line American artillery unit, "having great difficulty in preventing the enemy from intercepting and decoding its messages," hit upon the idea of using two Indians in the outfit as "telephone operators." They spoke to each other in their own language and completely baffled the Germans. The technique proved so successful that the unit continued to employ the Indians' services.[44]

The Air Corps and the navy rejected the application of this idea within their respective branches. Neither air operations nor ship movements demanded the immediate encoding of messages once in combat. Normally, such operations required planning far enough in advance to allow more traditional means of communication. However, both the army and the Marine Corps recognized the potential value of Native American radio operators in the field. Successful ground actions often turned on the quick relay of orders and information. A language alien to all others in the world and spoken by so few people, even in the United States, could prove valuable in a battlefield setting.

The army chose to experiment with Indian code talkers, but only on a limited scale. In autumn 1940, a small group of Chippewas and Oneidas joined the Thirty-second Infantry Division for the express purpose of radio communications. Soon afterward, an Iowa National Guard unit, the Nineteenth Infantry Division, brought several members of the Sac and Fox tribes into its ranks for the same purpose. Their training, and their use in maneuvers in Louisiana, hinted at the successful utilization of Indians as combat radiomen. The tactic seemed so promising that the Thirty-second requested the Indians' permanent assignment to the division, and the army expanded the program in 1941. With posts in the Philippines, where Spanish was commonly spoken, radiomen were needed who could transmit messages directly to the Filipino forces, to American units, and if needed, in code. The War Department found among the Pueblo Indians the necessary linguistic abilities, actively recruited them into the New Mexico National Guard, mobilized the outfit, and shipped the unit to the islands. Optimism prevailed within the Signal Corps, and, in spring 1942, thirty Comanches entered the Signal Corps and were dispatched to the European Theater.[45]

Despite the army's early efforts and the proficiency demonstrated by Indian code talkers, the War Department never fully grasped the program's potential. No more than a few dozen Indians were trained for radio operations. In contrast, the Marine Corps developed the concept on such a broad level that it became an integral part of the branch's combat operations. Unlike the army, Marine solicitation of Indians did not commence until after Pearl Harbor. Moreover, the program resulted not from within the military but from a civilian source.

In February 1942, Philip Johnston approached Major James E. Jones, Force Communications Officer at Camp Elliot in San Diego, with a plan to use the Navajo language for battlefield radio transmissions. The son of a Protestant missionary, Johnston had lived among the Navajos for more than twenty years, and, during that time, gained fluency in the native language. He explained to Major Jones that the Navajos spoke a language unlike any other Indians and added that less than a dozen anthropologists had ever studied that part of Navajo culture. Even German scholars who visited Indian communities in the 1930s, including the Nazi propagandist Dr. Colin Ross, ignored the Navajo language. In essence, this peculiar language seemed safe from enemy understanding if incorporated into the Marine Corps' communication structure.[46]

Johnston convinced Major Jones of the possible worth of his idea, and before the week's end, the Marine Corps extended Johnston the opportunity for a demonstration. On the morning of February 28, the former missionary's son and four Navajos arrived at Camp Elliot. Major Jones gave them six messages normally communicated in military operations and instructed the group to assemble forty-five minutes later at division headquarters. With such a short time to devise a basic code, the Navajos worked feverishly. At 9:00 A.M. Johnston and the four Indians appeared before Jones, General Clayton B. Vogel, and others to conduct their demonstration. Within seconds, the six messages were transmitted in Navajo, received, decoded, and correctly relayed to Major Jones. "It goes in, in Navajo? And it comes out in English?" questioned one rather surprised officer. In later tests, three code experts attached to the United States Navy failed to decipher "intercepted" transmissions; the system "seemed foolproof." Both Jones and Vogel were immensely impressed. Over the following days, the merits of an Indian code-talking program gathered interest with General Vogel's staff. By mid-March, the Marine Corps authorized the recruitment of twenty-nine Navajos for communications work and formed the 382nd Platoon for the Indian specialists. Immediately, the boarding schools at Fort Defiance, Shiprock, and Fort Wingate received visits from marine personnel, and the original complement of code talkers was formed. In addition, Philip Johnston petitioned the Marine Corps for his own enlistment as training specialist at a noncommissioned rank. Though already in his forties, the Marine Corps accepted his offer.[47]

The Indian recruits received basic training and advanced infantry training in San Diego before they were informed of their particular task. To a man, the Indians responded enthusiastically and began the construction of a code. The initial problem centered on the transfer of military terms and phrases to the Navajo language. This proved especially difficult since most of the terms to be encoded had no counterpart among Indians. It was recognized that coded expressions demanded simplicity. Under combat conditions, rapid transmission and translation was critical. Lengthy phrases, or those difficult to remember, might prove too time consuming and, therefore, counterproductive. To avert perplexity, the Navajos selected words that held direct association with nature or with their common reservation life.

Two methods of communication emerged. The first rested squarely on a "words for alphabet" system. Certain terms, particularly names, could not easily be given a specific code word. Simply trying to affix an Indian word to each of the Pacific islands on which Marines would land proved futile. Under the alphabet method, each of the twenty-six letters of the English alphabet would be represented by an Indian term. For example, the island Tarawa would be transmitted as "turkey-ant-rabbit-ant-weasel-ant." In Navajo, the words would be pronounced "Than-zie, wol-la-chee, gah, wol-lo-chee, gloe-ih, wol-la-chee." To avoid repetition, which would make the code penetrable, letters carried multiple terms. The letter "a" also stood for apple (be-la-sana) and axe (tse-nihl). A "t" was represented by tea (dah) and tooth (awoh). In this fashion, the code talkers created forty-four words for letters in the alphabet, the most numerous variations given to those vowels and consonants most frequently repeated. Tarawa, then, might be coded as "dah, be-la-sana, dah-nas-tsa, tse-nihl, glow-ih, wol-la-chee."[48]

A second method rested on a prearranged term to identify an individual geographic location, military weapon, or directive. As with the alphabet system, the Navajos relied on nature, common knowledge, or easily distinguishable features. Stereotyped images dictated the terms for nations and states: "braided hair" (cehyehsbesi) for China; "slant-eye" (behnaalitsoisi) for Japan; "iron hat" (beshbechahe) for Germany; and, "our mother" (nehemah) for the United States. Symbolic words and expressions represented military weapons and orders: "bird" (tsidi) for airplane; "hummingbird" for fighter plane; "bird shooter" (tsisi-be-wol-doni) for anti-aircraft gun; "tortoise-shooter" (chayta-gahibe-wol-doni) for anti-tank gun; "cliff dwelling" (annasozi) for fortification;

and, "horsemen" (linyeanaldaihi) for cavalry. A "chicken hawk," or gini, referred to a dive bomber; "whale" stood for battleship; a destroyer was termed "shark; "Clan" (din-heh-ih) stood for Corps; and "Frog" (chal) represented the word "amphibious."[49]

Once the code was created, the radiomen faced their next challenge—the application of Navajo code talking in actual maneuvers. In the field, transmissions were delivered as if in combat; from ship to shore, from one ground unit to another, from ground to air, and from command center to armored divisions. Messages included information regarding troop strength, direction of attack, places of defense, and routes taken by individual units. Not only did skilled white radio operators fail to comprehend their intercepts, but untrained Navajos likewise were confused by the seemingly nonsensical phrases overheard on the radio. The code talkers' successful demonstration encouraged their rapid deployment to the Pacific. Of the original Indian recruits, two remained at Camp Elliot as instructors for additional Navajo inductees, while the other twenty-seven steamed toward the Solomon Islands.

On August 7, 1942, the First Marine Division hit the beaches on Guadalcanal. By autumn, elements of the Second Marine Division arrived on the island. Attached to both were Navajo code talkers. Throughout the campaign, the Indians plied their skills and quickly earned the respect and admiration of the white soldiers and officers. Whenever the radio code word "Arizona" or "New Mexico" sounded, white operators scrambled for the nearest Navajo. Their talent also placed them in tremendous jeopardy. Weighted down with eighty-pound radios and spools of telephone cable, the Indians were often exposed to enemy fire. "They were always looking for you, always shooting for you," remembered Harding Negale, a Navajo from Gallup.[50]

An added danger presented itself when code talkers were sent on reconnaissance missions behind Japanese lines. Frequently they found themselves as prisoners of the Americans as they re-entered marine defensive positions. On one occasion, marines captured an Indian code talker, assuming he was Japanese. "We have captured a Jap in marine clothing with marine identity tags," radioed one soldier to his commanding officer. After being bound, blindfolded, and gagged for more than an hour, his actual identity was realized and the Navajo was released. One Indian, Eugene Roanhorse Crawford, held the dubious distinction of being captured by Americans on two different occasions. He later recalled his second experience: "They think I'm a Japanese. I took out my dog tags and showed them," he said, "but they didn't believe me. They took me to the command post. Good thing they knew me there. My hands were up and there was a cocked .45 in my back." Crawford was lucky the marines chose not to shoot him on sight. Once his identity was established, he was given "wonderful" treatment from his former captors. "Every time they saw me," he said, "they grabbed me and put me up on their shoulders."[51]

Because of their efficiency, the Marine Corps ordered the recruitment of more Navajos for communications training at Camp Elliot and their eventual assignment to each division within the Corps. "We were being rushed through to get the training done, get over there, fight and win the war," one Navajo said. Only after the war ended did many Indians realize "that the job we did was something special." By the end of World War II, 450 Navajos had entered training, and of those, all but thirty saw action in the Pacific—eight were killed in action.[52]

Across the theater, Navajo code talkers received praise from their commanding officers. A spokesperson for the Third Amphibious Corps noted that the Navajos proved "indispensable for the rapid transmission of classified dispatches. Enciphering and deciphering time would have prevented vital operational information from being dispatched or delivered . . . with any degree of speed." "In my opinion," said Colonel Marlowe C. Williams, after the fighting subsided on Iwo Jima, "these talkers were invaluable throughout the assault on Guam and other campaigns prior and subsequent to this one." Within the first forty-eight hours of the Iwo Jima campaign, the Indians transmitted more than eight hundred messages without error. "Were it not for the Navajos," said Major Howard Conner, "the Marines would never have taken" the island.[53]

The recognition specifically given to code talkers left an imprint on numerous Navajos. It was on Guadalcanal that Carl Gorman looked at himself "clearly for the first time. His sense of pride in his personal achievement as a Marine" swelled within him. Equally important, Gorman later admitted, "The Marine Corps opened my eyes. I realized I had a culture, all the things the white people have." Not only did it dawn upon him that he contributed directly and personally as a marine to the final victory on Guadalcanal, he now understood the value of his native culture to the nation and to himself. "He was here with his fellow Navajos. They were doing a job they could be proud of as Navajos. He, Carl Gorman, who had been beaten and chained in school for speaking Navajo, was now being of service to his country and helping save the lives of his fellow Marines by speaking Navajo," wrote Gorman's biographer.[54] The irony was not lost on Gorman. More importantly, he confessed, he was once more proud of being a Navajo.

Indeed, the marine code talkers proved their value to the Corps, especially to the units directly engaged in combat. Having witnessed the Corps' development and full implementation of the system with remarkable success, the army reconsidered its own use of Indians in the Signal Corps. In June 1943, the army contemplated the creation of an Indian communication unit for deployment in Alaska and in the South Pacific. Not until early September did the War Department authorize the recruitment of twenty-four Indians, principally Creek, for tactical air operations in the Solomons, scheduled to commence the first day of October. Unable to meet the rushed timetable, the Signal Corps continued its recruitment drive and planned to have a trained unit ready for deployment by the end of the year. The army was still without an organized Indian communications platoon by the end of December, and only ten potential code talkers were in training by mid-January. The remaining fourteen Indians were assigned to the unit two weeks later.[55]

Philip Johnston, puzzled by the army's failure to create and utilize a program similar to that of the marines, revealed his concern to a longtime friend and attorney, Paul Wheat. Wheat had contacts in the War Department, and both shared personal ties with a variety of army officers. Johnston informed his friend that he had heard of an American commander at Anzio who was frustrated by the difficulty in transmitting battlefield instructions without German interception. Such a problem could be circumvented, Johnston told Wheat, if only the War Department moved more swiftly toward the formation of an Indian communications program. He asked Wheat to contact their mutual sources and suggest greater deliberation and speed in the formation of a code-talking unit. Johnston also encouraged Wheat to pass the word that he would offer his expertise to the army once his "mission" ended with the marines. In addition, Johnston hinted that a loan of Navajo marines to the army might be arranged, if the army showed interest.[56] Needless to say, army officials fumed once they learned of Johnston's offer. Inter-branch rivalry remained present during the war, and the suggestion that marines might accomplish what the army was unable to do only infuriated those individuals contacted by Wheat.

The army's inability to capitalize on a proven method for field communications derived from its system for Indian recruitment. Unlike the Marine Corps, which first investigated appropriate tribes from which to draw its recruits—a study that examined tribal population figures, levels of acculturation, and the extent of native language usage—the army simply looked for any group of Indians who spoke their native tongue, regardless of dialectical variances and sufficient manpower available for the assignment. Bureaucratic bungling also plagued development of the program, as evidenced by the army's expectation that an Indian platoon could be raised, trained, and ready for operational duty in the Solomon Islands within a span of thirty days. It also appeared that the army believed all Indian recruits could be as easily trained as the Navajos, an assessment that proved misguided once the War Department sanctioned the creation of an Indian code-talking platoon. Marines solely employed Navajos who shared a common language and culture, whereas the army combined Choctaws, Comanches, Chippewas, and Cherokees. Failure provoked the army's chief signal officer in the South Pacific to vow an end to Indian communications efforts, and he termed the recruits a "nuisance." Rather than affix blame on the army's method of recruitment and training, he instead criticized Indians as a group and insisted that the program collapsed from the Indians' inability to learn quickly.[57]

By the end of the war, nearly eight hundred Indians served with the marines, but only half that number performed code-talking duties. Another twenty-four thousand Indians served with the navy and the army. Actual figures, however, remain somewhat clouded. The number represented those soldiers, sailors, and airmen who either maintained an Indian identity or whose Native American ancestry was known and listed with the armed forces and the Bureau of Indian Affairs. Since Indians received classification as "white" inductees, and many members of the armed forces never made their Indian identity a matter of record, it must be concluded that the full military service of Native Americans in World War II will never be complete. To those known Indians, the nation awarded seventy-one Air Medals, thirty-four Distinguished Flying Crosses, fifty-one Silver Stars, forty-seven Bronze Stars, and two Medals of Honor. Five hundred and fifty Indians were killed in action and more than seven hundred others sustained wounds in combat.[58]

Without question, the Indians' service record gave evidence of Native American loyalty and patriotism for the United States. They entered the armed forces for a myriad of reasons, as they did in World War I and as their white counterparts did in this war. Regardless of their motivation, American Indians in World War II admirably defended their nation, their communities, and their families, and they earned rightful acclaim for their service.[59] Their participation in the war, however, placed them at the proverbial crossroads. Having been so closely associated with white society during the war, viewed and treated as equals, often trained in skills transferable to urban employment, exposed to a much larger world than that from which most came, and molded by a war unparalleled in history, each veteran confronted a choice — return to reservations and continue tribal revitalization efforts with an emphasis on one's Indian identity, or make the move into white society. The same choice confronted those Indian men and women who remained on the home front.

Lt. Ernest Childers (Creek) from Broken Arrow, Oklahoma, awarded
the Congressional Medal of Honor for heroism under fire in Italy, 1943.
(Courtesy of the National Archives II at College Park, Maryland.)

Lt. Jack Montgomery (Cherokee), awarded the Congressional Medal of Honor
by President Franklin D. Roosevelt for service above and beyond the call of duty in
Italy, February, 1944. Montgomery served with the 45th Infantry Division, the
"Thunderbird Division." (Courtesy of the National Archives II at College
Park, Maryland.)

Joseph Bruner (Creek) served as President of the American Indian Federation.
(Courtesy of the National Archives II at College Park, Maryland.)

Lt. Woody Cochran (Cherokee) holds a Japanese flag he acquired on New Guinea. Cochran earned the Silver Star, Distinguished Flying Cross, Air Medal, and a Purple Heart as a bomber pilot in the Pacific Theater.(Courtesy of the National Archives II at College Park, Maryland.)

Pfc. Ira Hayes (Pima) at the Marine Corps Paratroop School, 1943.
(Courtesy of the National Archives II at College Park, Maryland.

"Ira Hayes—His Dream, His Reality." Painting by Joe Ruiz Grandee to honor Ira Hayes' heroism on Iwo Jima and the courage of all Native American servicemen. (Permission to print granted by Joe Grandee. Photo filed at the US Marine Corps Museum, Washington, DC.)

(Opposite, top) Indian Marines with the Marine Corps Signal Unit (code talkers) on Bougainville, 1943. Front row, from left to right: Pvt. Earl Johnny, Pvt. Kee Etsicitty, Pvt. John Goodluck, and Pfc. David Jordan. Second row, from left to right: Pvt. Jack Morgan, Pfc. George Kirk, Pvt. Tom Jones, Cpl. Henry Bake, Jr. (Courtesy of the National Archives II at College Park, Maryland.)

(Opposite, bottom) Cpl. Henry Bake Jr. and Pfc. George Kirk operate a radio set in the dense jungle of Bougainville, December, 1943. (Courtesy of the National Archives II at College Park, Maryland.)

Pvt. Simeon Pletinkoff (Aleut) on board a transport ship bound for Japanese held island in the Aleutians. (Courtesy of the National Archives II at College Park, Maryland.)

Among the thousands of Indians who secured employment in the ship-building industry are, from left to right: George Tahamont (Abenaki) and Charles Nelson (Sioux). Both worked at an East Coast shipyard. (Courtesy of the National Archives II at College Park, Maryland.)

Among the Marine code talkers in the first assault wave on Sapien were, from left to right: Cpl. Oscar B Iithma of Gallup, New Mexico, Pfc. Jack Nez from Fort Defiance, and Pfc. Carl C. Gorman of Chinle, Arizona. (Courtesy of the National Archives II at College Park, Maryland.)

Pfc. Cecil G. Trosip of Oraibi, Arizona operating a communications systems with the 4th Marine Division on Saipan, July, 1944. (Courtesy of the National Archives II at College Park, Maryland.)

Lt. Thomas S. Whitecloud (Chippewa) from Lac du Flambeau, Wisconsin,
boards an airplane for parachute practice at Ft. Benning, Georgia on July 4,
1944. Whitecloud served with the Army Medical Corps in the European
Theater and was promoted to Major before the war ended. (Courtesy
of the National Archives II at College Park, Maryland.)

Bill Watkins, a Shoshone and naval aviator cadet, speaks with Sgt. Bill Sixkiller (Cherokee). Sixkiller was killed in action on Saipan in July, 1944. (Courtesy of the National Archives II at College Park, Maryland.)

Sgt. Gilbert Eaglefeather (Sioux) from the Rosebud reservation, South Dakota, served as a waist gunner in a B-17 with the 8th Air Force in the European Theater. Shortly before the photo was taken, Eaglefeather had shot down one ME-109 over Munster. (Courtesy of the National Archives II at College Park, Maryland.)

In training with the Marine Corps at Camp Lejeune, North Carolina are, from left to right: Minnie Spotted Wolf (Blackfoot), Celia Mix (Pottawatomi), and Viola Eastman (Chippewa/Sioux). (Courtesy of the National Archives II at College Park, Maryland.)

John Bates (Kiowa/Wichita) at work at a west coast aircraft plant.
(Courtesy of the National Archives II at College Park, Maryland.)

Ferris Paisano (Pueblo), a graduate of Sherman Institute,
worked as a metal fabricator at Douglas Aircraft in Santa
Monica, California. (Courtesy of the National Archives II
at College Park, Maryland.)

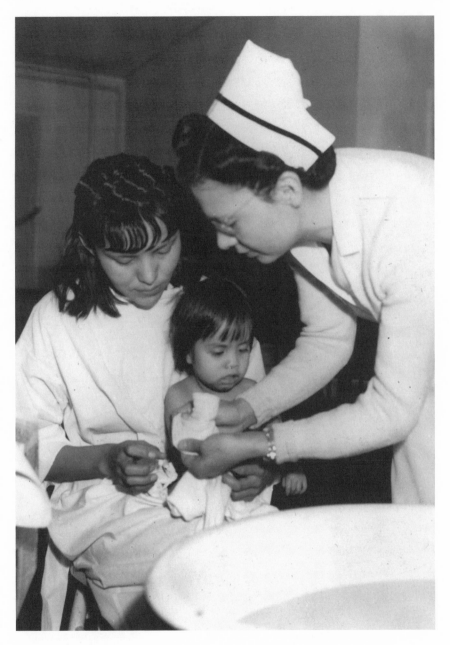

Nurse Leola Freeman (Creek) aids a Navajo High School girl in home nursing skills at Flagstaff, Arizona. (Courtesy of the National Archives II at College Park, Maryland.)

Ensign Thomas Oxendine (Cherokee), served as a naval aviator in the South Pacific. Oxendine recalled that he was frequently referred to as "Chief" in flight school and on board ship, a title he accepted with the respect in which it was typically offered. (Courtesy of the National Archives II at College Park, Maryland.)

Navajos of the 158th Infantry Regiment on New Guinea wearing regalia made from items found on the island. From left to right: Pfc. Dale Winney and Pvt. Joe Tapaha, both from Gallup, New Mexico, and Pfc. Joe Gishi and Pvt. Perry Toney, both from Holbrook, Arizona. The photo was taken January 20, 1944. (Courtesy of the National Archives II at College Park, Maryland.)

Seven

Indians on the Home Front

The war in Europe and in the Pacific seldom strayed very far from the minds and hearts of Native Americans. With twenty-five thousand Indians in service between Pearl Harbor and the occupation of Japan, the war touched most every family in some manner. Concern etched itself across the faces of family members whose loved ones were now in uniform. "Now and then as we went about our tasks in the evening," recalled one Sioux, "the crisp air would carry to us the voices of elderly people singing plaintive war songs about young people who would not return home alive."[1] Reports from the Philippines, Midway, the Solomon Islands, North Africa, Sicily, and the Italian Boot all exposed a war far more ravaging and ruthless than the one endured just twenty years earlier. Although news stories filtering to stateside readers were both censored and cleansed for public consumption, the brevity of life among America's troops in Normandy, in the Hurtgen Forest, and on Tarawa and Iwo Jima was painfully understood on the home front. Each day, it seemed, another boy or young father from the community left for war; occasionally one came home.

To lessen families' fears and soothe the hearts of loved ones, religious ceremonies on reservations solicited divine protection for sons and daughters overseas; some stretched over several days and occasionally extended for an entire week. Indians at Santa Ana, New Mexico, participated in one spiritual ceremony that lasted the entire month following Pearl Harbor. The Sioux at Standing Rock Indian Reservation held a Sun Dance the following summer and prayed for the safe return of all two thousand Sioux men in service as of that date, along with the ultimate destruction of Japanese and German soldiers. At the ceremony, residents from Little Eagle raised a flag comprised of twenty-two stripes, each stripe representing one soldier from the community of three hundred. The Crows of Montana also held a Sun Dance in August 1942 to honor its seventy-five men in the armed forces. More commonplace were the individual prayers privately given by parents for the well-being of their children in war. "Soldier boy, you are the one that is looking over our land," sang one Arapaho father to honor his son in the army. Of his two sons in combat, only one returned. Some of "the old folks at home would compose [songs] about his [the soldier's] hardships, about his campaigns." Prayers were offered "that he would return safely" from war to the family that loved him. These were songs "of inspiration to strengthen our spirit and hope," one Kiowa remembered.[2]

The Bureau of Indian Affairs' periodical *Indians at Work* continued publication throughout most of the war, partly in an effort to inspire cooperation for the war effort among Native Americans and partly to instill the sense of America's inevitable victory. It diligently informed subscribers of the service rendered by Indians in all branches of the armed forces and those employed in defense industries, and it kept Indians nationwide abreast of war-related activities on reservations. On the surface, the publication smacked of patriotic propaganda to rally Indians behind the war effort. Indian courage in battle dripped from combat-related stories; interviewed Native American soldiers were wrapped with red, white, and blue imagery; defense workers consistently lauded Indian New Deal programs for their glowing employment record; and, editorials vaunted the achievements of John Collier's administration and the positive repercussions that Indian war participation would have on postwar tribal development. It incessantly encouraged the Indians' full support for all war-related programs on the home front and a unanimous spirit of sacrifice to the war effort, which would help bring a quick conclusion to hostilities abroad. But underneath the obvious patriotism, and certainly of greater importance for those who remained home during the war, the periodical allowed readers an almost personal connection to sons and fathers overseas and to family members far from home working in defense plants. The psychological imprint left by *Indians at Work* helped to ease the sense of family separation.

Ever mindful of their loved ones scattered across both theaters of war and in response to the bureau's call for cooperation, reservations marshaled their resources and offered their services unconditionally to the federal government. The Blackfoot Agency located at Browning, Montana, volunteered all available floor space and manpower for defense. There, Indian labor was utilized in filing and polishing castings, assembling mechanical parts, simple manufacturing, and the stamping and fabrication of war materials. The 2,500 residents of the Crow Indian Agency in southern Montana similarly offered themselves to the defense program. On January 6, 1942, just one month after Pearl Harbor, the tribal council placed "the entire tribal resources . . . in the hands of President Roosevelt to use as he sees fit in the prosecution of the war." At the same time, the Crows donated ten thousand dollars of tribal funds for the purchase of "bombs and guns." Alaskan natives offered their fishing boats to the navy and Coast Guard, and other tribes in the Northwest extended the Army Air Corps the use of Indian lands for the duration of the war without compensation. Cognizant of "a serious condition [that] threatens the security of the United States," Klamath Indians of Oregon contributed $150,000 for the creation of a national-defense training-center on their land. In the Great Plains, the Cheyenne dropped outstanding claims against the United States until the war ended.[3]

From coast to coast, reservations organized civil defense units, and Indians served as airplane spotters and air-raid wardens on rotating shifts. Commissioner Collier distributed a list of bridges, power plants, and dams on or near reservations considered strategically important for America's security and requested local home guard units to protect the sites. On the Kaschia Indian Reservation near Stewart's Point, California, seventeen tribal members organized a home guard unit, armed themselves, and regularly patrolled the countryside for saboteurs. Thirty-year-old Leo John enlisted in the Bellingham Home Guard in Washington in autumn 1941. Without an automobile or other transportation available, he willingly hiked fourteen miles from his home on the Lummi Reservation to the guard's training center. Indian women on reservations across the country offered their services to local American Red Cross centers, where they knitted garments for soldiers shipped to cold weather environments and prepared thousands of surgical bandages for field hospitals overseas. The Red Cross also solicited cash donations and items desperately needed for the rapidly expanding military manpower. One drive for contributions at Zuni Pueblo, New Mexico, "was announced from the housetops and in a blinding snow, the canvassing started," noted one participant. "Each household contributed and in each case the wheat, corn, or hay was ready when someone called." Families gave whatever they could spare. The family of Edgar Lunasee, who lost contact with him in the Philippines after Pearl Harbor, donated six dollars and two rings to the Red Cross. In one home, a little girl contributed her only nickel. Patriotic posters with both English and native language captions were plastered onto storefront windows and walls. Indian men and women collected scrap metals and rubber. Courses in auto repair, welding, electronics, and communications were held on reservations; day schools remained open to the community six days each week throughout the calendar year to accommodate those who worked odd-hour shifts; and premilitary training programs proliferated at Indian schools nationwide to ease the transition of young men to military service.[4] Haskell Institute in Lawrence, Kansas, like so many schools, adjusted its class schedule to a six-day week plan.

In so doing, three full ninety-day semesters could be accommodated without interruption and schools would be in a position to release students for summer farming and war-related work.[5]

In these activities, reservations were but a microcosm of larger, non-Indian communities found in any section or region of the United States. The young girl who dashed to the local Red Cross office after school to prepare surgical dressings was as common a sight in Richmond, Syracuse, or Fresno, as it was on most any reservation. The children who tugged their wagons heaped with scrap metal to the nearest collection site, the young men who enrolled in higher math classes in preparation for pilot training once in service, the eyes that studied silhouettes of enemy aircraft and searched the skies as spotters, and the wives who preserved animal fats and meat drippings after cooking the family meal for later use in the war represented all races and were found in all communities. The surrounding countryside, homes, and languages spoken may have been different, but there was a common purpose.

On the home front, the war effort also demanded Washington's heightened regulation of federal spending. By 1943, Congress canceled the remaining civilian works programs inaugurated under the New Deal. It was inevitable. The nation could not fund the Civilian Conservation Corps, the Works Progress Administration, the Public Works Administration and similar other programs and still meet the financial requirements of modern war. Closure of these agencies certainly pinched the personal income of former enrollees, but pay scales in the burgeoning private defense industries more than compensated. Even farm labor noticed a significant increase in pay during the war. For Indians, the cancellation of the CCC-ID ended one source of income, but, like the general population, off-reservation wages netted much more money for Indian families. The end of federal works programs was understood and accepted.

The war's impact, however, included one wrinkle not experienced in the general population. Congressional appropriations to individual tribes were sharply reduced, and this action potentially threatened tribal security. Government funds allowed reservations to purchase additional lands, to develop irrigation systems necessary for agricultural productivity and grazing herds, and to provide specific community services typically provided by tax revenues in urban communities. Just three days after Pearl Harbor, John Collier informed Indians to expect a significant curtailment of federal services and funds for the duration of the war and suggested they not voice public complaint. To do otherwise, he warned, would cast Indians in a "bad light" and lead some whites to view Indians as unpatriotic. Sacrifices were necessary for the war effort.[6] To compensate for the inevitable shortages and disruption of tribal life, Collier recommended an almost Spartan conservation effort. "We must avoid waste of our resources now, so as to be sure and have a steady supply to draw upon in case of a prolonged war," he reminded Indians. Not only was it imperative that the nation prepare itself for a lengthy war, "we must try to save all that we can for the use of our children after victory has been gained." Strict conservation of tribal resources and the acceptance of funding reduction among tribes were critical for America's war effort, Collier concluded.[7]

The commissioner's words were unwarranted. Indian compliance with the Selective Service Act had been nearly one hundred percent, and pre-Pearl Harbor enlistment in the armed forces astounded Collier himself, as he was quick to state publicly on numerous occasions. Indian loyalty was not in question. Moreover, the history of Indian-white relations rested heavily on a pattern of wartime sacrifice among Native Americans. Involvement in this war required no less sacrifice. As intertwined as Indians had become in the economic, political, and social fabric of the United States, wartime sacrifice was accepted among Native Americans as it was expected among those of the general population.

Sacrifice was indeed expected, but some observers worried that scaled-down congressional appropriations to reservations, along with the elimination of federal works programs, would subvert gains made by Indians in the pre-war years. "Our world is so changing," said Oliver LaFarge before a community gathering at Santa Ana Pueblo after learning of Japan's attack on Pearl Harbor. The United States was now at war, and, as "sharers in America and democracy," Indians earlier included in New Deal reform programs were now expected to support the nation in war—a war that would certainly halt the process of tribal revitalization and reservation improvement for the duration of hostilities. Perhaps speaking more directly to Washington than to the assembled Indians, he added, "Reform is only half achieved. We still have beggared tribes, slum communities, ignorance, despair, disease, and prejudice." Federal programs must be curtailed and money diverted to the war effort. "But curtailment is one thing," he warned, "back sliding into the evil conditions of the past is another." Indians must press the BIA and Congress to protect gains already achieved.[8]

By the end of 1942, the warnings issued earlier by both Collier and LaFarge became reality when the commissioner notified reservations of a "complete breakdown of existing medical services." The number of physicians in residence on reservations declined sharply. Twenty full-time doctors and six part-timers had been inducted into the armed forces, and another fifteen held reserve commissions and expected to receive their orders shortly. Concurrently, two hundred nurses employed by the Indian Service had either entered the military or moved to urban facilities where pay was much better. As the year ended, Native Americans faced a thirty percent reduction in medical care personnel. To compensate for the shortage, the BIA cut nurse training programs from nine months to six months, in an effort to get more nurses on duty more quickly, and encouraged the continuation of first-aid courses on reservations. Shortages of medical personnel and cuts in federal appropriations to all nonessential war-related departments also resulted in the closure of Indian Health Service hospitals and clinics. Of the ninety reservation hospitals in service in 1940, only seventy-seven hospitals remained open in 1944.[9]

Indians recognized the opportunity that presented itself. The United Pueblo Agency responded to the medical emergency, offering members of its nineteen villages scattered across three thousand square miles in the Southwest a more direct personal involvement in health care. Agency dieticians provided nutrition instruction for Pueblo women and began the training of Indian men and women as hospital ward attendants. Others received training for clerical and laboratory duties. Fortunately for the Pueblos, their extensive population and close proximity to the West Coast made the agency's hospital vital to national interests in the event of evacuation from the Pacific seaboard. Given its potential importance, the federal government conducted inventories of the hospital's equipment and supplies, converted the boy's dormitory at the Albuquerque Boarding School into a convalescent facility for the military, and laid plans for its staffing by certified physicians. Another eleven Indian Service hospitals, mostly in the Southwest, were selected by the American College of Surgeons as emergency-care centers. Wartime necessities compelled the maintenance of medical services in much of the Southwest, but reservations throughout the rest of the nation experienced a general reduction in health care personnel. With the close of 1943, fifty additional physicians and another one hundred fifty nurses had left the reservations for military positions.[10]

One alternative to the diminishing numbers of medical personnel did surface—one that would protect pre-war gains made in reservation health care service. The Crow Indian Agency tribal council considered the employment of African American nurses. Indians themselves offered no objections and fully embraced the idea until the council realized that the employment of black nurses would reap the animosity of white reservation employees. Although desperate for health care providers, the council soon rejected the plan fearing reprisals against African American women and possibly against themselves from area whites. But the decision not to use black nurses also carried a potential gain for the reservation. Like the United Pueblo Agency, the tribal council reasoned that a shortage of white nurses might encourage the training of more Indian women for medical care responsibilities. Young women who completed the program would net a higher personal income and provide a base of medical care on the reservation following the war. For the short-term, the Crows preferred a temporary shortage of competent caregivers.[11]

Not only were medical personnel leaving reservations for military service, so too were Indian men. This forced women to assume responsibilities on the reservations that were traditionally dominated by Indian males. Construction and maintenance work crews increasingly turned to female labor. Women began driving heavy trucks, operating construction equipment, and servicing vehicles when necessary. They volunteered themselves as fireguards and firefighters on Indian lands, and many assumed war-related duties at aircraft observations posts on reservations and in nearby communities. Two Indian women living in Mendocino County, California, regularly drove thirteen miles each way "in an old jalopy" to staff an observation post nightly from 8:00 P.M. to midnight. In anticipation of an Axis airborne strike within the United States, forty Chippewa women created a rifle brigade for local defense. "We have rifles," said one woman, "we have some ammunition and we know how to shoot." Even the tasks typically relegated to males fell to female hands. Among the Navajo and Zuni Indians there was a significant rise in the number of women silversmiths. Tradition dictated jewelry making to be a skill reserved exclusively for men; however, the loss of men to the armed forces and to off-reservation employment required women to fill the vacuum. Besides producing jewelry, women silversmiths also supplied the military branches with silver insignia.[12]

Reservations faced further short-term social restructuring as women, like their male counterparts, secured off-reservation jobs in war-related industries. Of the forty thousand Indians who gained employment in urban areas during the war, approximately twelve thousand were women. That figure represented one-fifth of all able-bodied Indian women. They gained positions as chemists, truck drivers, inspectors, and press operators at ordnance plants in Des Moines, Iowa; Fort Wingate, Arizona; and DeSoto, Kansas. Many worked for Douglas Aircraft Corporation and Martin Aircraft as riveters and sheet-metal cutters. One woman riveter of B–26 parts, whose brother was in the Army Air Corps, kept as her motto: "You keep 'em flying, and I'll keep 'em up."[13]

Indian boarding schools often provided women with specific training requested by defense industries. Chilocco Indian School in Oklahoma encouraged many of its female students to take an aircraft sheet-metal course. In 1942 one class included twenty-one women and only three men. The school newspaper later reported that its women graduates earned an average of forty dollars per week at their jobs in nearby aircraft plants. At Sherman Institute in California, female students were allowed to enroll in classes in arc welding, acetylene welding, and machine shop.[14]

Indian women already in the labor force as World War II broke upon the United States also found expanded employment opportunities as the war progressed. Early in the war, Lydia Westlund, an Ojibwa, worked at an Indian hospital in Minnesota. Manpower shortages quickly opened better paying opportunities in factories, and Westlund soon moved through a series of jobs. Each new employment returned higher wages. "It was easy getting a job," she said. "I went to work at Wood Conversion [Company] for the money. . . . I was only making thirty dollars a month at the Indian hospital. My wage must have tripled at the mill." After the birth of her baby, she gained employment at a paper mill, which offered better working conditions and an even higher wage scale. Westlund placed most of her earnings into a savings account, and she spent much of the rest on groceries for her parents back home.[15]

Lily Laveau worked in the wood processing plant alongside Westlund until recruiters from Boeing Aircraft Corporation attracted her and her sister Lorraine to a plant in Seattle, Washington. Once on the West Coast, Lily and Lorraine received two weeks of instruction and then were assigned to the night shift in the factory. Somewhat apprehensive of "the big city," the sisters "stuck close together [and] never went anyplace alone." "All we did," said Lily, "was sleep and work. We had no entertainment because we were too afraid to go anyplace alone." What truly struck her was that "no one at Boeing" seemed aware of the women's Ojibwa heritage; "no one asked what nationality anybody was," and "bigotry posed no problem." Other Ojibwa women found work just as easy to acquire. Maria Carpenter was a high-school volunteer in the coupon rationing office in Cloquet, when government recruiters passed through the town. Like many Indian women who had seldom ventured far from home, she quickly accepted a similar position at a plutonium plant in Hanford, Washington, and later secured production work in a factory in Illinois.[16]

Moreover, nearly eight hundred Indian women volunteered their services to the armed forces as members of the Womens' Auxiliary Corps and Women Accepted for Volunteer Emergency Service. In the services, women most frequently assumed the expected roles of nurses and clerical staff, but many also were trained as chemists, weather forecasters, cartographers, gunnery specialists, plumbers, electricians, and radio operators.[17] Hilda Rogers, an Ojibwa from White Earth Reservation in Minnesota, joined the WAVES in 1943 shortly after she turned twenty-one. "I went into the WAVES," she recalled in an interview years later, "because my oldest brother was in the service." It seemed patriotic to serve as a medical corpsman to wounded American men, work that some other nurse may perform for her own brother. Others from her home community were in the armed forces as well. "My boyfriend went to Africa, and another bunch went into the South Pacific. I lost a first cousin over there," she added. She was also intrigued by the idea of traveling outside Minnesota, seeing areas of the country she had only encountered in books, and earning wages she would not have otherwise made at home. Rogers was sent to New York for a three-week basic-training course and from there she traveled to California, where "we had to learn what a nurse learned in one year in six weeks." After her introductory training, Rogers was assigned to a hospital in Norman, Oklahoma, which received wounded soldiers and sailors from the South Pacific. The work proved rewarding, and Hilda earned the admiration and respect of her colleagues, but the seemingly never-ending flow of wounded combatants "proved too great a burden." "I was tired of seeing the boys come back the way they were," she remembered, and "saw marriage as the quickest exit from nursing." As nurses, secretaries, truck drivers, mechanics, and electricians, American women in the auxiliary services provided desperately needed services and contributed fully in the nation's war effort.[18]

Although the activities of Indian women mirrored those of white women, as pictorially emblazoned by "Rosie the Riveter" posters, it was Indian women who most consciously and conspicuously crossed traditional, sexual divisions of labor. White culture had maintained clearly defined gender roles, but the constraints placed on women weakened with each national crisis over the preceding one hundred years and with late-nineteenth-century industrialization. Only a few decades before the war, white women made their way into professional positions, enrolled in colleges and universities, or took clerical and manufacturing jobs outside the home. Modern conveniences within the home, such as electric ranges, washing machines, vacuum cleaners, and sewing machines reduced the time spent on domestic chores; the advent of supermarkets, canned and packaged foods, and processed meats sharply reduced from hours to minutes the time necessary to prepare family meals. Radio stretched their worldview from one solely centered on family and neighborhood to national and global affairs. With greater free time and with increased knowledge of the surrounding world long before World War II, women moved themselves into civic volunteer work, ran for political office, and assumed a more visible and vital role in a world historically dominated by men. While it is true that some Native American women gained employment in factories and elsewhere before the war, the majority of these positions were in tribally owned or operated firms on or near the reservation. In the main, the fundamental role of

Indian women remained virtually unchanged to 1940. The demand for full employment in the nation's defense industries, along with manpower shortages throughout the national business community, encouraged Indian women to leave home and secure good paying jobs in urban communities. For the first time, Indian women were in a position to step from traditional gender-based roles within the tribal community and choose an alternative personal course for themselves. The nation needed them. Migration to urban centers now offered a potential for success never before available to Indian women. Prosperity and patriotic participation would result from the move. A sense of inclusion with the broader population prevailed.

Bertha Eckert, secretary for Indian work of the National Young Women's Christian Association, believed the migration signaled the emergence of "independence" for the Indian woman. "Indian girls are taking eagerly to a chance to earn their own livings and will probably choose the responsibilities of a citizen to the security of a ward after the war," she noted, following a three-month tour of the Dakotas, Wisconsin, Minnesota, and Illinois. Relocation to urban centers and volunteer service in the armed forces auxiliary branches was a "trek of Indian women into the new circumstances of financial independence and participation in everyday American affairs."[19]

Without question, some Indian women did seek and acquire personal independence through war work, and employment far from home offered the greatest chance to experience independence. Maria Carpenter admitted that the time she spent in Washington State permanently altered her relationship with her parents. After leaving that job, she returned home but soon learned that she "no longer tolerated her father's strict household rules." This contributed directly to her search for work in Illinois. Lily Laveau credited her relocation from home with teaching her how to manage money. "I learned how to do things for myself . . . how to get along with other people and be out in the public. . . . I have a lot more confidence," she said. Hilda Rogers agreed: "The biggest difference the war made in my life was to know that I was independent and I could do what I wanted to do!"[20]

Eckert's assessment, however, was much too optimistic. While Indian women understood that wartime off-reservation employment promised higher pay and a measure of self-reliance, urban employment and personal independence would potentially shred family bonds and weaken personal ties to the tribal community. For women from more traditional settings, the very underpinning of spirituality itself would be threatened with migration from ancestral homelands. The depth of independence Eckert envisioned for Indian women demanded separation from one's past and closure to a previous cultural identity.

The war, in this respect, served as a potential crossroads for Indian women — one direction led toward the increased likelihood of assimilation with the larger general population; the other maintained long-standing personal connections and an Indian identity.

Indian men recognized the same choice ahead of them. Those who desired assimilation saw employment in defense factories as the catalyst for a transition to urban life and movement into the white mainstream. Others saw wartime employment as a means of securing a higher income while the opportunity existed, with money used for the immediate improvement of family circumstances on the reservation. Still more Indian men allowed themselves to experience the world beyond the reservation, with a conscious choice to be made once the war ended. For the moment, Indians fully intended to exploit the financial opportunity that the war provided.

The extensive training Indian men received through New Deal programs such as the CCC-ID allowed them to become "mechanics, radio and telephone experts, diesel engine specialists, [and] draftsmen." English classes had improved communication abilities, and courses in home budgeting and related matters provided Indians with the tools necessary for off-reservation survival. The Indian Education Service had also conducted specialized courses at Indian schools throughout the nation as America mobilized for war. Carleen J. Sylvas, a graduate from one of Sherman Institute's engineering programs in Riverside, California, said shortly after the United States entered the war, "I'm enjoying my job immensely. . . . At first I thought I couldn't believe it when the engineer [on a merchant ship] told me I was to be in charge. . . . I've been assigned to pack the steam pumps and clean the condensers. I'll be getting $6.25 a day." Sylvas's annual wage of $1,500 far exceeded his pre-war earnings.[21] For Indians nationwide, wages similar to Sylvas's appeared to be an overnight windfall of good fortune.

By 1943 national defense industries employed forty thousand Indians. The Bureau of Indian Affairs estimated that another fourteen thousand could have gained positions had more placement and transportation services been available to carry them to urban settings. In areas where these services were available, many Indians still could not relocate to urban communities, as they lacked money sufficient for travel costs and living expenses until they received their first pay check. Some men were reluctant to leave their families, worried that older parents and young siblings would suffer avoidable hardships. The higher cost of living in cities often meant the migrant could not take his family with him. In spite of these barriers, forty-six thousand Native Americans followed their wage earning spouses or parents to defense work centers. The movement of Indians from reservations to either the armed forces or to urban settings during World War II totaled one-third of the entire Indian population and represented the first mass exodus of Indians from reservations into the surrounding white world.[22]

Navajos commanded a majority portion of Indian employment in war-related industries with ten thousand tribal members engaged in off-reservation work. Thousands found positions with railroads, construction companies, and agricultural operations. So many Indian men left their homelands for outside employment that reservations experienced their own manpower shortages, and superintendents found it extremely difficult to meet local labor needs. "Have now reached point where necessary to comb reservation to meet labor demands," cabled one superintendent to BIA offices in Chicago. In one telegram, a superintendent wrote, "Workmen leaving in every direction in search of war work." Another wired a simple statement: "No labor available present time — acute shortage here." So many young Indian men left reservations that it was commonplace for tribal schools to suspend commencement exercises indefinitely. Many traditional dances and ceremonies also ceased for the duration of war for the lack of male participants. The Lac Court Oreilles Reservation (Ojibwa) of northwestern Wisconsin proved typical of reservations nationally. Here, the "Dream Dance" was not held in 1943 because of the absence of so many young men who held important roles in its performance. The Medicine Dance and the Chief Dance also fell into disuse during the war among the Ojibwa.[23]

The construction of an army ordnance depot at Fort Wingate, New Mexico, used fifteen hundred Navajo men; fully one-third of the total project force was Indian. Both the civilian contractors and army supervisors praised Indians for being "better workers than any other laborers" employed at the site. Once completed in January 1942, more than one thousand Navajos were offered jobs inside the plant and as mechanics, truck drivers, electricians, and stone masons. The army purchased trailers, referred to as "victory huts," placed them on the premises, and allowed Indian workers to live in them so they could be near the work site. So respected were the Indian workers at Fort Wingate that the Indian Service and the local Chamber of Commerce helped Indians gain employment at the Flagstaff Ordnance Depot when it was constructed months later. Aircraft plant managers, impressed with the Indians' skills learned under the CCC-ID and the quality of work they performed, requested the BIA to supply the industry with as many Indians as possible. Two hundred Indians were hired by aircraft manufacturers in southern California alone, and more than seven hundred acquired jobs in plants located in Wichita and Tulsa. Shipyards also solicited Indians for employment. By late spring of 1942, seventy-five Indians were at work building ships in Seattle and San Francisco. From the records and reports maintained by the BIA on Indian employment, John Collier reported that absenteeism among Indian employees "was unknown. . . . They were constantly on the job." The BIA's director of information claimed that "possibly no other race, including the white, has such a record of loyal and efficient service in the vital war industries."[24]

While the bureau could be accused of exaggeration in an effort to present a favorable public image of Indian workers, nearly sixty reservation superintendents personally confirmed the BIA's assessment based on reports filtering back to them from satisfied employers. While their praise might reasonably be construed as an effort to retain job security against a potentially vengeful commissioner, should one contradict his assessment, supervisors outside of Collier's control and influence also lauded the Indian work record. Oscar Carlson, labor foreman at the Naval Supply Depot in Clearfield, Utah, praised the work performed by Navajo, Sioux, Apache, Shoshone, and Ute employees under his supervision. Somewhat aware of historic intertribal rivalries and expectant of trouble at the plant with representatives of so many different tribes present, he was pleased to note in 1945 that throughout the war years, "I have never had an Indian in my office for disciplinary action." Even Indian school administrators received congratulatory letters from supervisors in defense plants. George Trombold, director of personnel at Boeing's Stearman Aircraft Company, mailed a note of appreciation to C. W. Spalding, superintendent of Haskell Institute. "We have been exceedingly well satisfied with the boys you have sent to us," he wrote.[25]

Native American migration followed defense contracts to cities such as New Orleans, Jacksonville, Norfolk, New York, Detroit, Chicago, and Los Angeles. Members of North Carolina's Lumbee tribe first dispersed throughout the Tarheel State, creating small colonies of Indians in Raleigh, Wilmington, Charlotte, and Greensboro.[26] As job vacancies filled, Lumbees moved northward, along the Atlantic seaboard and into the Great Lakes region with a pronounced concentration of tribal members settling in Philadelphia and Detroit. Outside North Carolina, the largest resettlement of Lumbees emerged in Baltimore, where construction jobs frequently opened. There, many Indians established permanent residency in the city, anticipating this to be a springboard for assimilation with the white population. Still others worked in Baltimore until jobs promising higher wages opened elsewhere. By early 1944, a stable Indian community of three thousand, mostly Lumbee, occupied a twenty-three-block stretch of East Baltimore Street, although the community at times numbered nearly seven thousand, depending on employment prospects.[27]

Lumbee migration resembled trends set by other Indians across the United States throughout the war years. New York's Iroquois Indians concentrated their initial job search in Buffalo, Rochester, Syracuse, and New York City, where most found employment with Bausch and Lomb, General Motors, Kodak, Alcoa, National Gypsum, and Curtis-Wright. Within months, the lure of higher wages, better working conditions, and improved living conditions encouraged thousands to relocate once more to Chicago, Detroit, and Akron, and some ventured as far south as Tulsa, Oklahoma.[28] The Sioux targeted the Great Lakes area and cities of the Plains states. Southwest tribal members first filtered into nearby cities such as Albuquerque, Dallas, Tucson, and Phoenix and soon afterwards migrated to Pacific Coast cities and to urban areas along the Gulf of Mexico.

On the surface, the changes brought to Native Americans who migrated into urban areas appeared quite positive. They generally netted a higher income than that which was possible on reservations or within segregated Indian communities. One estimate placed income for off-reservation work at a level three times greater than that earned within the traditional Indian environment, a wartime average of $2,000 to $2,500 annually for urbanized Indians. Although still substantially below the national average, it represented the highest Indian income level ever and, to Native Americans, evidence of the potential prosperity associated with assimilation. John Collier observed that Indians employed in non-reservation defense industries in 1943 earned over forty million dollars in contrast to ten million dollars earned in urban employment in 1940. And, as important, very little racial discrimination against Indians was displayed by white coworkers, employers, or community residents. Although some Navajo workers at Fort Wingate initially complained of a pay scale below that of white employees, the policy within defense industries nationwide required Indians and whites to receive equal pay for equal work. As in the armed forces, Indians were typically identified as white employees at government installations and in private manufacturing. Faith Traversie who worked at the Mare Island Navy Yard, "never felt any prejudice because there were all nationalities working there—Asians, Chicanos, Whites from every part of the United States" and numerous other Indians, a sentiment repeatedly sounded by Indian workers.[29]

The commissioner failed to mention that hourly wage rates rose substantially in the intervening three years, a hike caused partly by the general demand for workers amidst a manpower shortage and partly by competition among industries for labor. He also failed to cite one other obvious fact: the number of urbanized Indians stood at an all-time high during the war years. Although individual income had witnessed growth, the actual extent of increased wages was not as great as Collier suggested. Nonetheless, the commissioner was correct in his overall assessment that urban Indians fared much better than just a few years earlier.

In contrast, black Americans continually faced severe racial discrimination, despite some federal efforts at reversing the pattern.[30] Job training programs, such as the Vocational Education National Defense Fund, had received millions of dollars from the federal government to prepare workers for war production, but, in 1941, less than two percent of the trainees were black. A few months before Pearl Harbor, the United States Office of Education granted Tennessee $230,000 for equipment and the training of state residents for defense employment. Of that sum, only two thousand dollars was used to fund courses for African Americans. Following pressure from Washington, the aircraft industry commenced the hiring of blacks in 1941; however, African American workers in those plants comprised less than six percent of all employees by the end of the war and most of those performed unskilled, menial labor. The movement of African Americans into the auto industry and the upgrading of blacks to skilled positions generally met with staunch opposition from white workers. Employees at one plant in Detroit went on strike to protest the introduction of black labor. The threat of strike also sounded in the rubber industry when suggestions were made to hire skilled African Americans.[31]

Although some blacks moved into previously denied industries and skilled positions, the Department of Labor warned them not to expect the continuation of those jobs following the war. "The Negro has made his greatest employment gains in those occupations (especially semiskilled factory jobs) which will suffer the severest cutbacks" in postwar years, the department's spokesman announced.[32] The absence of adequate training and the prevalence of racial discrimination precluded any rational expectation of African American acceptance by white society and exhibited the antithesis of Indian opportunities.

Socially, African Americans fared no better. Jim Crow weathered the war in spite of antagonistic liberal voices raised in both the North and the South. Thousands of blacks poured into urban centers during the war in search of employment, and the influx of new arrivals strained the limited housing available for blacks in rigidly segregated communities. Race rioting, generally initiated by white workers in defense plants and government housing projects, erupted in Detroit, Mobile, and other major cities nationwide. Theaters and restaurants often barred the admission of African Americans, and public transportation services maintained separate seating for the two races. Even the American Red Cross required the segregation of donated blood.

The barriers constructed against African Americans before 1941 and enforced throughout the war years gave evidence to Native Americans of their own acceptance among whites. The sweeping positive reception accorded to Indians in the nation's labor force and in community social settings all pointed to that assessment. The animosity that did confront some Indians more often came from other Indians rather than from white society.

A schism emerged between those Indians who migrated to urban centers before the war and those who arrived in the wake of Pearl Harbor—a pattern reminiscent of European immigrant experiences in early twentieth-century New York City. The great influx of native migrants during the war represented a threat to established Indians well on the road toward assimilation. Having settled in the urban environment between 1932 and 1940, the early-comers had acquired fluency in English and become skilled workers, often with supervisory responsibilities. Many saw themselves as part of the expanding middle class, financially and socially. Conversely, wartime arrivals often proved less acculturated and more attuned to traditional tribal values regarding work and personal conduct. Often entering the labor force without training for specific, high-demand, job skills or sufficient personal finances, wartime migrants tended to collect themselves in less expensive sections of the community and congregate together, replicating a reservation atmosphere. In short, pockets of Indian communities arose and occasionally gave rise to slum conditions. Unable to perform work at the level of earlier migrants, and facing a festering racist response from white employers because of their lack of abilities, frustration led many new migrants to react with outbursts of public disorder, drunkenness, and occasional violence.

Employers of recent Indian migrants typically categorized their work record as either excellent or poor, with little room for a middle ground. Two white supervisors, "exhausted by Indians bringing complaints to the management and appearing at work drunk, fired all of them preemptively"—a total of sixty-four Indians were dismissed. Standard charges made by white employers included the Indians' inability to arrive at work on time, lack of productivity once on site, an inattention to detail and quality, and short-fused tempers.[33] To protect their own position and status within the white community from a racist backlash, established Indians purposely distanced themselves from wartime arrivals.

Part of the problem among new migrants rested on their previous relationship with white employers on the reservations. Agency officials generally had adjusted themselves to Indian ways of working and "demanded less effort than is true in private enterprise." Moreover, work relief on reservations offered greater personal interaction between labor and management. In such settings, employers proved more tolerant of absences and failure to execute instructions properly.[34]

Because so many of the complaints leveled by employers were aimed at Indians who had relocated from the Pine Ridge and Rosebud Sioux Reservations, the University of South Dakota linked with divisions inside the Bureau of Indian Affairs in late 1942 to conduct a joint investigation into the problem. In its report, issued in the spring of 1943, the two institutions recommended that Indian education among the Sioux include instruction in the specific realities of off-reservation employment. Armed with job skills and an attitude conducive to urban residency, the Sioux would capture a secure hold on their newfound jobs. The report also suggested that a wage-work agricultural program be developed on reservations with time allocated to prepare Indians to cope with culture shock. In spite of the findings and recommendations, Collier contended that the Indian urban experience was, by and large, a positive one to date and should not be impeded or altered.[35]

Indians, nationally, found increased job opportunities, higher income levels, and social acceptance in white communities. The racism that dogged African Americans rarely trailed Native Americans. Indian participation in the war and on the home front garnered white respect, federal recognition and praise, and the likelihood of eventual assimilation for those who pursued that goal. The national portrait represented Native Americans as fully and equally part of the war effort. By the time the University of South Dakota compiled its recommendations, Collier realized Congress was not amenable to creating additional training programs specifically for the native population. There was already a gathering of voices in Washington for the final termination of federal guardianship over American Indians, voices that would only grow louder and bolder as victory overseas seemed imminent.

Throughout the war, Indian loyalty for the United States manifested itself through the purchase of war bonds by individual Indians and entire tribal units. Some tribes allocated portions of their congressional appropriations for war bond purchases. The Shoshones, for example, authorized Secretary Harold Ickes to redirect five hundred thousand dollars of their allotted monies, and the Oklahoma Seminoles released fifty thousand dollars in tribal appropriations for war bonds shortly after Pearl Harbor. Eastern Cherokees made similar requests, and the Office of Indian Affairs in Juneau, Alaska, sold $110,646 worth of bonds to area natives. An intertribal council of Euchee and Creek Indians in Oklahoma agreed to spend four hundred thousand dollars currently on deposit in Washington for defense bonds. Sioux Indians of North and South Dakota chose to suspend immediate payment of five million dollars awarded them by the United States Court of Claims. The legal battle with Washington had begun eighteen years earlier, but, said one council member, "We feel that during this time of national emergency, when our country is at war, we should not demand immediate payment of these claims. A few more years of waiting, if it will help our country, will be patiently accepted."[36]

A few tribal groups held fundraising activities. In September 1943, Indians from twelve Arizona tribes gathered at the Phoenix Indian School and performed dances for a bond rally. Members of the United Pueblo Agency performed dances on neighboring reservations and in nearby communities for donations—contributions which in turn were spent on war bonds. Eight of the dancers extended their tour to include stops in New York, Philadelphia, Washington, Detroit, Chicago, and Pittsburgh. Their performances grossed three hundred thousand dollars, and all proceeds went to the purchase of bonds. Other Pueblo Indians contributed profits from pottery sales or from fees charged to photographers who visited their villages. In Albuquerque, Navajos involved themselves in scrap-metal collection drives. To weigh the gathered items, one woman of known weight sat on a "teeter-totter" as a counter-balance. Nearly five tons of metal was weighed during the months that followed, and the earnings were invested in defense bonds.[37]

An elevated income among Indians from off-reservation employment and expanded agricultural production enabled the purchase of war bonds by individual Indians. Between April, 1941 and March 1942, Indians invested $1,270,000. Over the following four months, an additional $2,500,000 in bonds were bought by tribes and individuals. Amounts varied by tribe. The Klamaths bought $228,000 in individual war bond purchases and petitioned Congress for permission to invest another $150,000 of tribal funds; the Sioux Tribal Council at Cheyenne River authorized fifteen thousand dollars in tribally purchased bonds; and Pine Ridge Sioux contributions totaled $106,350. Kiowas purchased bonds in the amount of $93,500, and more than sixteen thousand dollars in bonds were acquired by residents of the Wind River Reservation. The Quapaw far surpassed all other tribes by June 1942, with a total outlay of $1,018,000. It was rather commonplace for individual Indians to invest their money with the federal government to the limit of their personal finances. On December 8, 1941, three Navajo men from Manuelito, New Mexico, traveled to Window Rock, Arizona, and contributed three hundred fifty dollars to the war effort; Theo Bourgeau, a seventy-five-year-old Colville Indian cattle rancher, purchased seven hundred fifty dollars worth of defense bonds in January 1942. The largest individual purchase of war bonds was made by Chee Dodge, a Navajo, who, in the spring of 1942, invested twenty thousand dollars. The combined amount of Indian purchases, in excess of $3,700,000 by the summer of 1942, more than tripled by April 1943 to a staggering twelve and a half million dollars—a figure equal to the "per capita contribution" of any other race in the United States. Donations continued to flow from the reservations throughout the war years, and in early 1945 Commissioner Collier estimated that nearly fifty million dollars in war-bond sales had been made to Native Americans. An exact figure remained impossible to determine, however, because many Indians were identified as whites in the general population.[38] Collier took pride in reporting the Indians' financial sacrifice. When added to their conversion of reservation facilities and land for defense needs and to their support for military induction, an intense Native American loyalty for the United States and its war effort was clearly visible.

A portion of Indian war-bond purchases resulted from higher profits earned from reservation-based agriculture, which witnessed substantial growth and productivity during World War II. As the United States prepared for war between 1939 and 1941, reservations such as the Rosebud Agency in South Dakota formed National Defense Committees for the purpose of mobilizing area resources for military and civilian use. In most cases, the committees projected agricultural demands, studied the likelihood of price increases for food, and estimated the economic return that Native American farmers would probably net. The committees served as advisory boards, suggesting the type and quantity of crops to plant and determining approximate market prices.[39]

The defense committee formed at the Hoopa Valley Indian Agency in California initially offered similar services, but with war imminent, it moved quickly to involve itself more as an administrative unit rather than as an advisory board. It established a Young Farmer's Club for unemployed tribal youths and petitioned the Indian Education Service for a cash allotment to purchase farm equipment for tribal ownership. With approximately $1,300, the club bought a tractor, plow, disc harrow, and a mowing machine. For a usage fee of two dollars per acre cultivated, members were entitled to use the machinery— the collected funds to be spent on maintenance and gasoline costs.[40]

On reservations without agricultural defense committees, tribal councils guided farm productivity and secured funding from the BIA and other federal offices. The Eastern Cherokees, for example, appealed directly to the United States Army. More than one hundred tribal members had left the reservation for military service by the summer of 1942, and many others had migrated to defense jobs in urban areas. In response to the Indians' request, a cavalry division based at Fort Bragg, North Carolina, supplied horses and troops for the plowing of Cherokee lands. The tribal council contributed six hundred dollars to purchase seeds for families unable to buy their own.[41]

Across the United States, reservation defense committees, youth clubs, and tribal council supervision of local agriculture allowed Native Americans to direct Indian farm productivity for the national war effort. Their efforts resulted in the cultivation of 150,000 additional acres by December 1941.[42] Agricultural output rose throughout the first full year of war. Twelve months after Pearl Harbor, John Collier reported a fifteen percent increase in the number of family gardens among Native Americans and a thirty-five percent jump in cultivated tribal acreage. Reservation-based farm products, excluding livestock, was valued at twenty-one million dollars. Two-thirds of Indian produced crops sold on the domestic market, and the remainder was funneled into the armed forces. Collier translated Indian farm productivity into a recognizable and relevant perspective: reservation farm production fed cereal goods to 367,103 American soldiers; 52,057 men were provided potatoes and other vegetables; and, 38,346 men in uniform received fruits. The pattern continued into each of the three succeeding years. Production of cereals in 1944 alone totaled 4,839,500 bushels at a market value of five million dollars; other field crops netted $3,682,400, and the harvest of fruits, nuts, and berries earned $775,000. Indian farm output continually increased and at the war's end market value rested at $22,600,000 for all agricultural goods, exclusive of ranching.[43] Perhaps most startling is that agricultural productivity increased sharply in spite of severe cuts in congressional appropriations and the movement of one-third the total Indian population into the armed forces or urban employment.

Livestock endeavors fared even better. Anticipating higher demand for meat and livestock by-products with the onset of World War II, reservations increased cattle holdings thirty-five percent and sheep fifty percent by December 1941. The number of beef cattle under Indian ownership had doubled to 321,000 during the previous decade, and dairy cows had realized a four-fold increase during the same time span, from 11,300 to 49,500 head. In the first full year of war alone, another $12,800,000 was earned in the production of beef and dairy goods. John Collier calculated that 220,250 soldiers were fed with Indian raised beef that year. One year later, in 1943, total cash income generated by beef and dairy herds rose to fourteen million dollars. By the end of 1944, holdings of all cattle on reservations leaped to 1,531,000 head at a combined market value of sixteen million dollars, with beef and dairy products accounting for fifteen million dollars of the total.[44]

Much of the agricultural prosperity reaped by Native Americans resulted, in part, from the incorporation of new lands into tribal ownership. Immediately prior to the war, the Resettlement Administration secured nine hundred thousand acres for Indian ownership, and the BIA bought another three hundred thousand, largely for use in ranching. During the first two years of the war, Indians purchased from the government seventeen thousand acres with pre-war appropriated funds, and twelve tribes collectively acquired thirty-eight thousand acres from wartime profits. When added to the two and a half million acres returned to Indian ownership under New Deal programs, reservation land holdings during the war years allowed for profit increases in ranching.[45]

Nationally, Native American ranching and farm acreage increased just before and during the war, but some individual tribes actually lost land to the federal government for wartime usage. The military's urgent need for training bases, bombing ranges, airfields, and supply centers demanded the sacrifice of land from communities and individual citizens nationwide. The South, for example, was particularly hard-hit. Dozens of new air bases were constructed in every state of the region, as were army training centers and defense factories. Washington most often forced the sale of desired property to the federal government, and families residing on those lands were required to relocate at their own expense.[46] In this way, much land escaped private ownership. And, particularly in the Piedmont region of the Carolinas and in north-central Louisiana, war games and maneuvers were typically held on private property with tacit consent granted by landowners. The flow of federal dollars to local construction companies contracted to build military facilities, along with the arrival of millions of servicemen holding paychecks ready to be spent, certainly brought prosperity to the region earlier designated by Roosevelt as the nation's "number one economic problem." The Southwest and Pacific Coast states experienced a similar pattern. Cities were inundated with military personnel and migrants seeking work in urban-based defense plants. Urban congestion proved nearly overwhelming, and city services nearly collapsed. As in the South, Washington's representatives visited Southwestern farmers and ranchers and left orders for the owners to make preparation for the sale of their lands for military usage. The federal government also reclaimed Indian reservation land, often with John Collier's approval. But, unlike the sale of white-owned property, the BIA pledged its return to Indian control once the national emergency passed. As a liaison between the Indians and the military, Collier frequently demanded that the government lease needed tracts from reservations, and in cases where Washington sought actual purchase of Indian property, Collier arranged the acquisition of adjacent land to compensate for the loss.[47]

The Sioux at Pine Ridge lost three hundred thousand acres to the government in what amounted to a "forced sale" at minimal market value. Compounding this, resident families were denied the opportunity to harvest their crops prior to eviction, and the BIA failed to inform the tribe of its right to file suit for damages incurred. Without question, the Pine Ridge residents suffered financially, experienced social dislocation, and once more witnessed dishonest treatment by federal authorities. And, from coast to coast, Native Americans relinquished 840,000 acres to Washington's wartime use.[48] As damaging as this was for tribes and for individual Indians, in the broader context of the nation's war effort, additional land was essential for military use. Whereas the overwhelming majority of acreage purchased by Washington from white families in the South and Southwest was never returned to pre-war owners once hostilities concluded, Washington did reassign title of most Indian lands to the reservations from which acreage was taken during the war. Moreover, land purchases by Indians or for Native Americans by the federal government just before and during the war far exceeded the total acreage used by the armed forces during World War II and, consequently, provided an overall expanded territory for Indian agriculture and ranching on the home front.[49]

Wartime prosperity came to Alaskan natives from another enterprise. American defense preparations in the territory and in the Aleutian Islands assumed greater importance as Japan's war in China intensified and imperial forces moved throughout the Pacific. Although few Americans in early 1940 seriously imagined a Japanese invasion of the United States, Alaska was still considered a probable target in an eastward move by Japan's forces. From the islands trailing off the mainland, the Japanese Navy could effectively control American shipping in the North Pacific; from the Alaskan mainland itself, Japanese forces would command a northern approach into Canada and the United States. Throughout 1940, the War Department increased its military presence in the region, constructed airfields, and connected roads from major cities stateside to Alaskan communities and outposts. Bone-chilling cold air, however, impeded construction of these vital projects during winter months and threatened to delay completion of emergency defenses. In February, army officials contracted with the Nome Skin and Sewers Cooperative Association for cold-weather clothing. Requested by the government were eighty reindeer parkas and forty-eight pairs of mukluks (seal skin boots). The co-op was an operation owned and controlled by Alaskan natives, formed under the Indian Reorganization Act and the Alaska Act of 1936. The initial, trial contract was filled by mid-1940, and in August another contract was let for 6,396 mukluks, 365 reindeer parkas, and 150 pairs of seal-skin trousers with promises for later orders of mittens, snowshoes, caps, and fur socks. Most of the manufacturing was performed by three hundred women and children, and by early 1941, one hundred and fifteen trousers were en route to military supply depots along with 150 parkas and 2,100 mukluks, and boxes filled with socks, mittens, caps. Army officials were extremely pleased with both the quality of work and the quick delivery of clothing from the Indian co-op; more delighted were the soldiers and construction crews who were issued the items. America's entrance into the war fueled greater demand. The attack on Pearl Harbor, and the realization that Japanese submarines patrolled waters along America's Pacific Coast, proved the nation's vulnerability to enemy attack. In response, Alaskan defense preparation assumed heightened urgency, and the War Department made an additional request for five thousand more mukluks and a significant production increase in other winter garments.[50]

GIs in Alaska and the Aleutian Islands received regular shipments of foodstuffs from stateside warehouses, but federal authorities supplemented the soldiers' diet with fish caught and canned within the territory itself. Two Indian-owned canneries operated in Alaska, companies that had floundered on the verge of extinction before federal redevelopment programs of the 1930s financed business survival until each became solvent, prosperous firms. By 1940, Alaskan canneries produced fifty percent of the world's salmon catch, and natives of the territory reaped much of the profit. Pressed with the demands of war after Pearl Harbor, the two Indian canneries earmarked their entire production for 1942 to the United States armed forces. Each fisherman and cannery worker pledged a personal record level of production to aid the war effort.[51] Profits were to be gained through the sale of salmon and other fish products to a ready buyer in desperate need—the United States government. Nonetheless, the sincere personal pledge of loyalty to the United States added by cannery workers and fishermen in their promise to produce a record harvest echoed the patriotic sounds ringing across the nation. More than financial reward was at stake; each understood that his efforts directly contributed to winning the war, and each realized the danger every family in Alaska faced in 1942. It proved a very real danger.

As the Battle of Midway raged in early June 1942, Japan bombed Dutch Harbor and landed forces on the islands of Attu and Kiska in the Aleutian Chain. On Attu, Mr. and Mrs. Foster Jones, who worked for the Indian Bureau in Alaska, confronted the invasion along with the local native population. Foster Jones died, allegedly committing suicide, as Japanese troops entered the Aleut community where he and his wife worked and lived. Several eyewitnesses, however, claimed Mr. Jones was murdered by an advance squad of Japanese soldiers. Mrs. Jones attempted suicide after learning of her husband's death, but she recovered and later claimed that she was treated well by her captors. The forty-five Aleuts who resided on Attu were taken prisoner and shipped to Japan as laborers. Only twenty-four survived the war.[52]

To protect Aleuts on other islands, Washington, with Collier's ready nod, ordered the evacuation of all residents to hastily constructed camps in southeastern Alaska and Washington State. Some of the evacuation centers were more than fifteen hundred miles away. Few willingly concurred with the relocation, preferring instead to remain in their homes and face the enemy should Japanese forces move farther along the chain. Nonetheless, more than eight hundred fifty Aleuts were forced to evacuate and were permitted to carry only essential clothing and personal hygiene items. They left behind all other personal belongings in their homes. The army and navy attempted to secure adequate housing, extra clothing, and medical attention for the relocated Aleuts, but failed miserably in their efforts; their concern was more focused on defense preparations and building an offensive military force to challenge Japanese expansion in the Pacific. Families found themselves living in shacks and vacated canneries. Food was insufficient in quantity and often provided little nourishment. Diseases filtered throughout the Aleut communities, and "scores of Aleuts" perished in the camps. Collier and the BIA tried to supply evacuees with whatever relief was available, but the movement of goods into a tightening defense zone and the priority of military transport over civilian shipments both combined to weaken Collier's efforts. Alaskan natives and Aleuts were returned home following the war, but they discovered that their houses had been used to billet American troops and their personal household goods had either been destroyed or vandalized by military personnel in their absence.[53]

Native Americans faced the war on the home front with commitment, hard work, and an obvious display of patriotism. Many, like the Aleuts, personally confronted the destruction of war and suffered as a result. Overall, however, their participation in the war effort and their responses to the demands generated by war closely resembled that of other Americans, white and black. In this respect, Native Americans united with the larger population against a common external threat, as they had done in the Great War. But World War II was different. Never before did full inclusion with white society seem so possible. Wages for Indians touched an all-time high, specialized training courses were widely available, and the movement to urban centers proved remarkably easy. The war generated an atmosphere of optimism among American Indians, a feeling of equality and a perception of opportunity. Although serious problems resurfaced on many reservations, it appeared to most Native Americans that these were temporary concerns caused by the demands of war. They held the faith that once peace returned, Indians would be in a position to determine for themselves the postwar direction of their own lives.

Eight

The Movement toward Termination

World War II carried Native Americans to the precipice of assimilation with white society, and it seemed quite clear that once the war ended Indians would be in a better position to pursue full inclusion with the dominant culture or remain within their tribal communities. Nonetheless, two issues still clouded the crossroads. First, Indian draft resistance renewed a latent racism in some quarters of the white population, while Washington's continued abrogation of treaty provisions and its never-ending paternalistic posture shadowed Indian moves and refreshed Native American suspicions of the federal government. Although assimilation seemed within reach for those who desired it, the crises of compulsory service that swirled from 1941 to 1943 often compelled many Indians to reconsider their alternatives. The cloak of secrecy Collier draped over the central issues upon which Indian dissent was grounded, and his public assurance that draft resistance was both minimal and incidental, kept Congress and the general population somewhat oblivious to the fundamental concerns of Native Americans. When combined with a burgeoning racism among some whites, retrenchment into a separate Indian identity apart from white society surfaced as a preferred option for many Indians.

Second, the Indian Bureau and the press had masterfully crafted an image of Indian unanimity behind the war effort and inclusion with white society. It appeared to most observers that, from coast to coast, the overwhelming majority of Indians complied with draft registration, enlisted in the armed forces, served courageously overseas in combat zones, worked in defense industries, purchased war bonds, and contributed reservation resources willingly to national defense. The overall imagery was, indeed, a rather accurate reflection of the broader Indian population's support for the war effort, but it purposely ignored the concerns of many Indians and the numerous points of conflict between Washington and tribal communities. Such a carefully cultivated image was considered necessary for the war effort, but it lulled congressional leaders into the belief that Indians en masse preferred assimilation and would be prepared for final inclusion with white society once the war ended. It seemed to confirm the pre-war direction of Congress toward termination of all federal Indian services.

As early as 1937, key congressional leaders challenged John Collier's pluralistic vision and openly moved to revoke the Indian Reorganization Act. Senator Burton K. Wheeler, himself the original co-sponsor of the bill only three years earlier, led the attack against his own handiwork. Wheeler claimed that the purpose of the legislation was misconstrued. The IRA, he believed, intended to stimulate a climate on reservations conducive to the development of job skills, medical services, and educational programs necessary for eventual assimilation. Collier's emphasis on tribal revitalization actually retarded the Indians' progress, he felt. What most concerned him was the redistribution of individual allotments into tribal ownership. This provision alone countered the prevailing concept of private property in the general population and more than any other element in the IRA carried seeds corruptive of assimilationist values.

The senator's confrontational stance in 1937 might have suggested that he either misunderstood his own bill or was effectively manipulated by Collier, but neither explanation seemed viable. Wheeler held the respect and admiration of his colleagues for his political prowess and his apparent intelligence. Moreover, the bill received full scrutiny from Indian leaders, anthropologists, ethnologists, progressive reformers, and economists long before its passage, and their interpretations were widely circulated and accepted. Even Collier repeatedly clarified his goal and the bill's specific provisions, and the legislation received the endorsement of both Secretary Ickes and President Roosevelt.

More likely, two other forces prevailed upon Wheeler and the growing ranks of IRA opponents. First, the renewed downturn in the national economy in 1937 prompted Wheeler's opposition. Unemployment nosed upward throughout the year, tax revenues dropped, and Congress once more faced the need to reduce the government's budget. Military mobilization remained a distant prospect, but FDR himself had already sounded warnings as events in Asia worsened and Hitler's plan for Europe became clearer. In short, Congress anticipated a tightening of the federal purse. If assimilation once again became the stated goal of Indian affairs and the process of integration resumed in force, then congressional appropriations to the Bureau of Indian Affairs and the supplemental programs it sponsored could be reduced. Second, and equally important, the IRA was in part the creature of the 1928 Meriam Report, which pointedly addressed the horrific forces threatening Indian survival. In the decade since its publication, emergency reform programs and the IRA combined to revitalize reservations and actually raise the standard of living for American Indians nationally. By 1937, the spirit of reform waned as congressional leaders increasingly assumed success in meeting Meriam's recommendations. Having accomplished the inferred goals of the IRA, the next logical step was Indian assimilation into mainstream society.

Wheeler's refutation of the IRA and his promotion of assimilation certainly piqued the attention of his colleagues and Washington officials, but Collier's influence still permeated Congress and the Roosevelt administration for the remainder of the 1930s. Pearl Harbor, however, provided Wheeler and other anti-IRA congressmen with greater leverage. Strapped by the costs of war, along with an already tight budget caused by pre-war mobilization, Congress fully funded only those agencies deemed indispensable to the war effort. The BIA suffered a fifteen percent cut in its appropriations, from thirty-three million dollars in 1941 to twenty-eight million dollars the following year. Not since 1935 had the bureau's budget been so low. Additionally, the Civilian Conservation Corps completely vanished along with a host of other programs beneficial to Indians as the war progressed.[1]

As evidence of the BIA's diminished importance for the duration of the war, Congress notified Collier of the bureau's relocation to Chicago so that war-related offices would have room to expand within Washington. The commissioner fumed. The current emergency, he argued, did not warrant the agency's removal; sufficient facilities in the Department of the Interior existed which could be transformed to meet military needs. Since the costs incurred by transferring operations to the Midwest would have to be covered by existing bureau funds, financial aid to reservations would be crippled, Collier contended. The move impaired the BIA's "efficiency at a time when every penny of appropriation must be spent as wisely and as frugally as possible." Despite the commissioner's pleas, Chicago became the wartime home for the Bureau of Indian Affairs, and Collier was compelled to commute frequently to Washington, occasionally at his own expense.[2] With the commissioner and the BIA housed so far from the nation's capital, Collier's influence among congressmen weakened and exposed the IRA to more serious threats.

Renewed debate within Congress arose within months of Pearl Harbor. In discussing the proposed 1943 appropriations bill for the Department of the Interior, specific concern was expressed for Indian Bureau expenditures. Congressman Everett Dirkson pointed out that BIA appropriations stood at significantly increased levels over the preceding twelve years, from approximately seventeen million dollars in 1930 to almost thirty million dollars in 1942, and the latter figure was itself a reduction from thirty-five million dollars in 1940. Despite such a tremendous rise in appropriations for services to Indians, the Native American population only increased by fifteen percent during the same period of time. "This does not make sense," he thundered. He added that in the previous ten years, the number of bureau employees also rose substantially, with twelve thousand men and women currently on the BIA payroll. The ratio of employees to Indians, he said, allowed "one shepherd for every 31 Indians in the country," including Alaskan natives and excluding supervisory personnel with the Civilian Conservation Corps. Again, he said, "This does not make sense." On the heels of Dirkson's comments, the full House considered the merits of continued high appropriations and congressional oversight for Indian affairs. The alternative would be to inaugurate a plan in 1942 for the curtailment of funding so that Indians would one day soon be free of the BIA and become "self-sustaining" individuals in American society.[3]

Increasingly, congressmen challenged the necessity of maintaining not only high appropriations but the very existence of the Bureau of Indian Affairs itself. Surely, said one congressman from Ohio, sufficient funds were available to Indians through local and state children's services offices, education systems, and family aid programs without Native Americans remaining dependent on federal dollars. Moreover, federal departments such as the Department of Agriculture could be petitioned by reservations for financial aid and the extension of its programs directly to Indians. In short, the BIA did not require the extensive funds provided to it over the previous decade, and programs existing outside the bureau were capable of satisfying Indian needs.[4]

Congressman Francis Case of South Dakota supported appropriations cuts but questioned the soundness of relying on state agencies and federal departments not prepared to meet the special needs of Indians. Are there any pamphlets provided by the Department of Agriculture "written in Sioux or written in any other [Indian] language?" he asked. Have those congressmen who now call for reduced appropriations ever visited an Indian's home "with its dirt floor and leaking sod roof?" Have they ever witnessed "a father and mother who were trying to master a white man's economy, children who were trying to work a white man's way, and had yet to learn that the white man would deny them jobs?" He then asked, rhetorically, Have the congressmen "ever visited an Indian reservation and seen Department of Agriculture officials attempting to help them? No; they have had to depend on the Indian Bureau."[5] Case's argument was well received. For 1943, Native Americans would only face further appropriations cuts rather than the complete elimination of BIA financial support.

Collier understood quite well the direction of Congress. Unless the overall value of both the bureau and the IRA manifested itself soon, the House and the Senate would press the termination of all federal services to Native Americans.

The commissioner, therefore, actively searched for a means to prove the act's continued worth.

In early 1942, he found in the War Relocation Authority an opportunity to press the merits of the IRA, extend its very life, and concurrently provide aid to reservations in spite of appropriations cuts. Collier hoped the application of the IRA to Japanese-American internment camps would benefit the Asian minority in a manner reminiscent of the Native American experience prior to the war. If implemented fully, Japanese-Americans would experience a renewed awareness and appreciation for their own traditional culture and cultivate a heightened pride in their own racial identity. Moreover, tried and proven IRA programs, he thought, would enhance the social, economic, and political base of the interned Japanese-Americans within the United States following the war. Improvement in job skills, education, health care, and political activity on the local level of government would be easily transferred to their original communities once released from confinement. And, if housed on Indian lands, the physical labor of detainees might serve those areas on reservations in desperate need of further development.[6]

True to form, Collier's sweeping vision sprang from an unrealistic perception of minority cultures within the United States and an almost panicked desire to salvage the one program that most represented his lifelong work in social and political reform. Japanese-Americans certainly did not require the educational training Collier offered, and they were not in need of essential job skills or practical experience in American politics. Most detainees were born and reared in the United States, and many managed their own businesses in white communities. As for cultural awareness and pride, such were already integral elements of Japanese-American life. Collier's perception was obviously founded upon false assumptions. His wish to validate the IRA and, in the process, boost reservation economies blurred any objectivity and understanding he may have earlier held.

The commissioner provided further explanation. First, he said, the bureau possessed the experience of administering the revitalization of a race distinct from that of whites or blacks. Indians, he argued, held fundamentally different values than those of mainstream society, and they posed a set of problems unlike any faced by other minority groups in America. Based upon the IRA's success to date with Native Americans, the bureau's governance over Japanese-American relocation centers seemed only logical. Second, the IRA promoted democratic principles among Native Americans and encouraged tribal self-government. By 1942, Collier said, the light of democracy shined brightly within IRA communities. Unless the IRA or a comparable program directed by the Indian Bureau encouraged a democratic political agenda among interned Japanese-Americans, faith in democracy would vanish, once relocation commenced. The extension of the IRA's political structure to the confined minority would restore trust in democratic government while at the same time "demonstrate for the whole country the efficiency . . . of the cooperative way of living." Collier touched the very foundation of the IRA—the maintenance of a unique cultural identity with training sufficient for a close relationship with the broader society. Successful application of the program to Japanese-Americans, along with the elevation of "the Indian from his slough . . . and opening to him the door of the future," together carried vindication for the Indian Reorganization Act and an end to congressional antagonism for the bureau's policy.[7]

Collier's persuasive argument encouraged Vice President Henry Wallace to suggest at a cabinet meeting that the commissioner himself head the War Relocation Authority. Secretary Ickes concurred. Because of the rising anti-IRA sentiment in Congress, President Roosevelt rejected Collier's nomination and appointed Milton S. Eisenhower to the post. FDR, however, extended to Collier direct control over the relocation camp to be established at the Colorado River Indian Reservation at Parker, Arizona.[8]

In April 1942, Eisenhower laid initial plans for the camp at Parker and created a system to be utilized at all evacuation centers, most of which were to be located on Indian lands. The construction of additional camps on more than the one reservation surprised Collier. Certainly, he was pleased with the news. Eisenhower assured Japanese-Americans that a "humane" and "constructive" environment for working and living would be provided for the war's duration, and he further promised Native Americans that their lands would be occupied only temporarily. To the nation at large, the director announced that relocation would "provide the maximum useful work contributing to the war effort."[9]

The commissioner was concerned that a single program common to every camp might compromise the objectives of the WRA, and he advised Eisenhower not to create "uniform" rules, regulations, expectations, and work assignments. Such an arrangement, he said, doomed the entire project to failure, for each facility would contain varying numbers of detainees and be geographically different from the others. Success required flexibility, attention to the camp's peculiar location, and the availability of resources in its immediate proximity. The very survival of Indian cultures exhibited this reality, as had the IRA's success to date, and the WRA needed to understand that point fully.[10]

Collier imagined the Parker facility as a national showcase to highlight IRA objectives and accomplishments. Of the ninety thousand acres available at the Colorado River site, he expected to allocate twenty thousand acres for the construction of housing and community resource services, divided equally among five colonies of four thousand residents each. The diversion of an "adequate water supply" from the Headgate Rock Dam, recently constructed by the Indian Irrigation Service, offered the region an agricultural base. Japanese-Americans "will be employed in construction of irrigation canals, leveling of lands, and preparation of the land for cultivation," Collier said. Detainees, he added, would produce their own food and receive payment "on a wage basis" for any surplus crops taken by the federal government for the war effort. The commissioner planned for the Parker colonies to exist as "complete local units with doctors, nurses, teachers, and other specialists provided by the Japanese themselves," as he had planned to develop under the IRA. Furthermore, each colony "shall adopt appropriate organization for managing its internal affairs with as much stress upon democratic values as can be supplied or evoked," he concluded. It was hoped that the Colorado River project would exhibit "a valuable piece of social experimentation . . . with a minimum of concentration-camp psychosis for the interned Japanese."[11]

Throughout the spring of 1942, federal authorities transported Japanese-Americans to the Parker relocation center, and by late June the interned population totaled seventy-five hundred. In an address to the residents, Collier explained that public attitudes and the circumstances of war demanded their confinement for, he expected, four to six years. He added, "You are in the middle of a tragedy. You have come through shock, tragedy, and great loss into a situation where the measure of your happiness is determined by your ability to endure and spiritually conquer what is asked of you." The Indian Bureau's administration of Parker, he continued, "is to facilitate your action in any way that we can and then to protect your liberties in so far as we have the power . . . and all those liberties as citizens of the United States." Through teamwork and common effort, Collier envisioned a colony that would become a "demonstration of the efficiency and the splendor of cooperative living—a truly happy place where individuals and families will be giving themselves utterly to the community and winning a reward of inward power and inward joy greater than anything external in the whole world."[12] The picture Collier presented ignored the humiliation, the anger, and the uncertainty felt by relocated Japanese-Americans. Their personal independence and the ties they earlier worked hard to establish within urban communities along the West Coast no longer existed. The federal government had stripped them of the very rights and privileges Collier now promised to protect. Moreover, it was evident that the commissioner's remarks served as a restatement of the IRA's original objectives rather than a program relevant to the interned residents at Parker.

Dissension in Washington over administrative issues that June forced the resignation of Eisenhower and the appointment of Dillon Myer as the new director of the War Relocation Authority. Myer detested the social experimentation that Collier planned for the program at Parker, an intense displeasure that was rooted in his dislike for the IRA, which he openly and often condemned. The new director underscored the detention element of the WRA and discounted the inclusion of IRA goals. Rather than the development of "little Tokyos," remunerative crop production, and Collier's vision of a "happy place," Myer preferred a straightforward program of confinement and, once the war ended, immediate release of all detainees. Among his first acts, Myer reduced the amount of land for cultivation from twenty-five thousand acres to five thousand acres.[13]

Summer ended with the assigned twenty thousand Japanese-Americans in residence at Parker and another five thousand en route to the Gila Reservation in southern Arizona. Inadequate community facilities at the camps, reduction of land for farming, and insufficient housing plagued the new arrivals. In an effort to provide adequate housing, Collier pressed the Defense Housing Authority coordinator, C. F. Palmer, and Secretary Ickes for a massive infusion of prefabricated units which the bureau might "inherit" after the war. The commissioner specifically requested ten thousand single-family houses at a cost of five million dollars, a move that would potentially save the bureau fifteen million dollars in postwar building costs for Native Americans. In spite of Myer's objections, Collier's plan was approved, and construction began that autumn.[14]

"Termination fever" gathered momentum in Washington, but Collier hoped anti-IRA sentiment would subside once Congress recognized the bureau's effective administration over relocation camps and the cost-saving efforts taken by the commissioner for postwar Indian reservations. But, knowing that the Wheeler faction gained new supporters each week, Collier wanted reservations to be prepared for termination. His demand for prefabricated housing and for the Japanese-American cultivation of reservation lands would give a few southwestern tribes some measure of postwar relief.

Collier's problems were only compounded by the bureau's management of relocation centers. Criticism of the IRA had been plentiful in its own right, but the commissioner now was targeted by private citizens for programs implemented among Japanese-Americans. Upon learning that Collier placed Japanese-American teachers in Indian Service schools, Mrs. Charles Dietrich, a member of the New Mexico Association on Indian Affairs, fired off an angry letter to the commissioner. She warned him that the detainees might indoctrinate Indian children with Japanese values and attitudes regarding the current world war. More seriously, she feared that the interned might learn Navajo, transmit their knowledge to Japan, and break the code talking system in use by the Marine Corps in the Pacific.[15] Mrs. Dietrich's complaint seemed trivial, but it nonetheless revealed two interesting points. First, her concern mirrored the national sentiment that Japanese-Americans were potential agents for Japan and, therefore, rightly belonged in holding camps for the duration of the war. Second, and perhaps more startling, the Marine Corps purposely attempted to maintain the secrecy of Indian battlefield communications, and the Navajos' contribution was not publicly and officially recognized until the late 1960s.[16] Mrs. Dietrich was not only aware of Navajo code talking, but felt comfortable enough to mention it casually in writing.

In his reply, Collier accused Mrs. Dietrich of racism and the failure to comprehend who the detainees actually were. He informed her and the New Mexico Association on Indian Affairs that Japanese-Americans "think American, and are unswervingly loyal to America, despite the ill treatment which they have received." Most were native born, he added, and all demonstrated total acculturation with white values. Many held college degrees, one even possessed a master's degree. Furthermore, few detainees commanded any ability to read or write the Japanese language, and no method existed to enable any evacuee to transmit information to the enemy.[17]

More surprising to the commissioner, sentiment appeared within the bureau and among Indians themselves against housing evacuees on reservation lands. A camp population of twenty thousand, said one BIA official, necessitated a large expanse of land, a territory that Native Americans urgently needed. The loss of acreage severely curtailed Indian crop production and herding operations, which otherwise would promise both an increase of reservation income and foodstuffs for American troops overseas. Another argued that the presence of a relocation facility on Indian lands, taken and developed without Indian consent or input, hearkened back to pre-IRA years when such a process was the norm. What faith in the BIA would Native Americans hold if it insisted on the use of reservation property without direct Indian approval? Affected tribes loudly echoed the charge. Collier carefully explained the anticipated benefits of the relocation program to Indian reservations, and he specifically cited land reclamation and cultivation as positive repercussions of the WRA presence. He also pointed to increased housing marked for Indian ownership following the war.

Added to the criticism provided from private citizens, bureau officials, and Indians was the continued confrontation with Dillon Myer, which exploded into open, verbal combat in late 1944. Collier was informed that WRA-constructed housing would be demolished with the release of interned Japanese-Americans, rather than be transferred to Indian ownership as originally promised. He also discovered that Congress was contemplating the permanent transfer of relocation camp lands to the federal government instead of to reservation control following the war. Myer's own actions as WRA director further complicated the emerging postwar picture for Native Americans. Repeatedly, he denounced the IRA in general and blocked any specific effort by Collier to prove its merit among Japanese-Americans in the internment camps. Challenged by Myer and Congress, Collier openly worried that the IRA would be dismantled during the course of World War II, and that Indians would face severe problems in the postwar era. His concern only deepened as he studied the direct impact of war on reservations.

By 1943, reservations felt the sharp pangs of reduced funding. Job-training programs that had prepared Indians for urban employment in defense work now were but a memory. Road building and school construction halted; irrigation projects sat unfinished; and health care facilities closed. The migration of nearly sixty-five thousand Indians from reservations further complicated a distressing situation. There were now fewer hands available for reservation maintenance work and fewer men to farm the land. Women and children filled the void when possible. For the first time in their history, women of the Mescalero Apache Agency tended fields and livestock. With supplemental labor provided by neighboring whites, free of charge, the Apache women eked out a meager living. Similar aid in other localities compensated for the absence of manpower and federal dollars.[18] Gains made before the war now faltered, as Oliver La-Farge warned they might. Across the nation, reservations that earlier bristled with new construction, land redevelopment, and rising economic value, stumbled and showed clear signs of fragmentation.

Without expressing much concern over faltering reservation conditions, Senator Wheeler and his fellow champions of assimilation renewed their charges against the IRA and Collier's administration. In June 1943, Wheeler introduced Senate Report 310. The proposal, however, went well beyond the mere removal of Collier's reform program; Wheeler seemed to point toward a complete termination of federal services for Native Americans and rapid Indian assimilation.

Senate Report 310 offered six specific recommendations. First, its originators advised the immediate end to research and surveys commissioned by the BIA, along with the dismissal of personnel assigned those tasks. Second, the measure demanded the elimination of all tribal rehabilitation programs. Wheeler and SR 310 further advocated the withdrawal of money for Indian land purchases, a division of tribal trust funds into equal, individual shares, and state control over the management of forests, irrigation, hospitals, and schools normally directed by the BIA. Finally, the proposal attacked the very existence of the Indian Bureau itself by calling for a staff reduction to levels necessary to effect its ultimate closure.[19] If implemented, the plan would relinquish Indian affairs to individual state control and encourage the assimilation of Indians into white society. Interestingly, SR 310 promoted one point most vocally sounded by the American Indian Federation—the complete elimination of the BIA.

Wheeler anticipated positive repercussions should the measure be enacted. As an economic document, SR 310 promised less expensive government. Congressional appropriations would conceivably fall from twenty-eight million dollars to five million dollars by 1945 if the plan were to be implemented immediately. That money could be channeled into military defense, invested, or shuttled into programs that benefited the larger society.[20] As a political statement, SR 310 voiced the sentiment that Indians were now prepared to take their place alongside whites in the general population. The Indians' full participation in the war proved their ability to assimilate.

Aware of the prevailing sentiment in Congress, Collier noted that "the year ahead is going to be a time of danger for Indians, for civil liberties, for conservation, and for many other values" cherished by Native Americans. His only relief rested in the fact that no specific termination bill was introduced to Congress at that time, but the Senate did consider legislation to condemn portions of Indian lands and set prices for their sale at levels below current market value.[21] If enacted into law, tribally owned property would be opened to white speculators once more, a pattern historically allowed by Washington. Additional land losses would further impoverish Native Americans and force immediate assimilation regardless of individual preparedness.

The bill sputtered through the Senate but stalled in the House, where it eventually died. Having narrowly dodged the first direct volley of fire from Congress against the IRA, Collier warned Indians of the shifting currents within the federal government. The United States, he reminded Native Americans, must devote its full energy to the war effort. That conflict commanded priority. But, he added, Indians faced both an external and an internal enemy. Following America's victory abroad, he said, "the final battleground is at home."[22]

Collier understood that his IRA contained provisions that encouraged conflicting directions for Indians to follow. Elements of the law actively promoted tribal revitalization and traditional native culture; other features offered programs and services that provided essential skills for a smooth transition into mainstream society. Neither direction, however, envisioned the forced assimilation of American Indians nor the elimination of the Bureau of Indian Affairs. The war placed Native Americans at the proverbial crossroads and permitted tribes and individuals the right to choose their own path and their own relationship with white America. Confronted with termination-minded congressmen and a general population more accepting of ending a special relationship with Native Americans as a result of the Indians' wartime participation, Collier surmised that the IRA's only chance of survival hinged on the promotion of its assimilationist benefits. In response to the new challenge, the commissioner presented a counter-argument to congressional leaders. Complete termination of federal services to reservations and to individual Indians, he warned, would cripple the successful transition of Indians into the larger social and economic structure of the United States. Many Indians still did not possess the education necessary for a postwar technological world, regardless of pre-war training. Others depended on continued farm subsidies and federally funded irrigation projects for agriculture and herding. Unless Washington maintained a support mechanism, or a safety net, for Indians until they could survive independently, Native American assimilation would fail.

In late 1943, the Association of American Indian Affairs rallied behind the commissioner. A constant advocate for Collier's Indian New Deal, the association commenced the publication of a periodical to highlight the Indians' current predicament. The first edition of *The American Indian* criticized congressional sentiments in an article submitted by Oliver LaFarge. In "The Brothers Big Elk," LaFarge reported his interview of two combat-experienced Indian airmen in Europe who were dismayed by the apparent movement in Congress to effect complete and immediate termination of federal services to Indians. Each brother personally looked forward to eventual assimilation and believed that his participation in the war rewarded him with white acceptance, but neither believed assimilation connoted a denial of their Native American heritage or should be required of all Indians. The Big Elks strongly voiced their concern that Indians were "suffering" at home while the war continued overseas, a suffering caused by the curtailment of opportunities and services necessary for the prosecution of the war and a suffering from the obvious direction taken by termination-minded congressmen. The brothers, LaFarge wrote, "hope the American people will repay loyalty with loyalty, but experience keeps them from being quite sure."[23]

Statements of Indian defiance toward congressional proceedings littered subsequent issues of *The American Indian*. A common theme was clearly evident by spring 1944. Although assimilation was the goal for many Indians, most were not ready for the dissolution of services rendered by the IRA or the bureau itself. Termination meant the return of Native Americans to state control. Arizona and New Mexico still practiced racial discrimination as evidenced by the absence of suffrage rights for Indians in those states, an issue that enraged Collier. "These states should do the American thing and grant Indians the franchise," he thundered, particularly when "we are preaching democracy" worldwide. These states "should grant a little more of it at home," he said. New York still hungered for jurisdiction over Iroquois lands, and in most every state there existed land-hungry whites who actively sought ownership of tribal holdings. What acts of injustice awaited Indians, wondered Collier and the editors of *The American Indian*, if federal protection vanished? Repeal of the IRA, eradication of financial aid and governmental programs aimed at improving Indian skills, and an undoubted revival of racism within individual states promised catastrophe to assimilation-bound Indians and to those who remained on reservations. Without continued protection for Indians, termination amounted to another act of government betrayal, and such action would result in the elimination of Indian faith in the integrity of the United States.[24]

Collier amplified the Indians' protest. "Right now," he said, "when the Indians are fighting and dying in far places all around the globe for the freedom of us all—right now, serious attempts are publicly being made to destroy all the protections and all the rights they have so recently won." Congressional moves toward the "destruction of the personal and property rights of the Indians" warranted staunch opposition from Native Americans and whites alike. The intention "to lift government trusteeship" concealed a devious scheme "to betray and wreck their [Indians'] lives while they are at war and unable to raise their voices in defense."[25]

One earlier criticism of the Indian Reorganization Act inadvertently buttressed Collier's argument. Skudder Mekeel, a university professor and former colleague of the commissioner's, was a longtime critic of traditional federal Indian policy and enthusiastically welcomed the IRA's emphasis on tribal revitalization and traditional culture. By 1944, however, the successful wartime movement of Indians into the white mainstream convinced the professor that the IRA, in reality, concealed a shrewd and cleverly orchestrated plan for assimilation rather than tribal revitalization. To Mekeel, the assimilationist goal embodied by pre-Collier federal policy was simply repackaged under the guise of self-determination and renewed tribalism. Appalled by the IRA's deceptive promotion of cultural pluralism, Mekeel dropped his support for the act and joined the chorus that called for the IRA's repeal.[26]

Mekeel's rationale for opposing the IRA countered congressional arguments, but his presence in the opposition force added to the appearance that the act had fewer adherents. Ironically, however, by calling for the IRA's repeal, Mekeel actually strengthened Collier's stance against termination. While the IRA intended cultural renewal, the policy and bureau programs actively encouraged assimilation—the very goal espoused by anti-IRA congressmen. Indian migration into the urban work force and inclusion with white military units confirmed the assimilationist tendency of the IRA. Having produced such a mass movement of Native Americans into mainstream society during the war, armed with the skills necessary for survival and success, why should the IRA be scrapped, Collier asked? What better method existed to prepare a traditionally ignored and depressed people for assimilation? The commissioner believed immediate termination of services guaranteed the failure of assimilation and the retrenchment of Indians into poverty, and Collier looked to every possible source in a bid to salvage his program.

With termination looming in the shadows, Indians themselves took a more direct role in their own defense. Meeting in Denver in November 1944, eighty Indians representing nearly fifty tribes across twenty-seven states discussed the congressional threat to end financial programs and to dissolve tribes themselves. From the gathered delegates emerged the National Congress of American Indians, a pan-Indian organization composed of both assimilationists and traditionalists, all determined to protect civil and tribal rights of Indian people. As formed, the NCAI was to be a "national instrument to make their voices heard in legislation and implementation of federal Indian policy."[27] The NCAI supported voluntary movement into the white world, not the forced mainstreaming advocated by Congress. As an echo to Collier's position, the founders stated the need for continued federal services to make assimilation a viable option and defended the inherent right of all citizens to select their own lifestyle. The individual, not Congress, was to choose assimilation or a tribal existence, said NCAI members. Indian communities held the right "to control their own destinies," and founded on this objective, the organization would serve as a lobby and guardian of Indian rights, cultures, and values.[28]

Collier applauded the NCAI's advocacy of self-determination. It challenged termination efforts and furthered his own view of Indian affairs. The NCAI's position, however, did not surprise the commissioner. Many of the founders themselves had served in the bureau since 1934 or directly benefited from the IRA. To Collier, organizational objectives simply mirrored his own conception of justice for American Indians.

By its own admission, the NCAI's task resembled that of a political action committee. It planned to lobby congressmen and senators on behalf of Indians nationally and to pressure state legislatures for equitable treatment of Native

American residents. A direct product of the termination mentality gripping Congress, the NCAI envisioned itself as a national mouthpiece for Indians, regardless of tribal affiliation: a single, vocal force in the pursuit of equality, freedom of choice, and nondiscrimination. A consolidated effort, founders believed, could achieve more than individuals, individual tribes, or the BIA itself working independently of one another. "Indians as a distinct cultural group cannot survive . . . unless they speak as one people with a common voice," noted one member. As an organization representative of Indians only, the NCAI purposely dissociated itself from the Bureau of Indian Affairs and later barred membership to any federal employee.[29]

Self-determination was the organization's stated goal; Indians may pursue assimilation or renewed tribalism, but the NCAI's very existence represented a concerted effort to maintain a racial identity apart from white society, another minority group in the United States whose rights were in jeopardy and in need of protection. This was a logical response to wartime developments. White society wrongly assumed that Indian military service and work in defense plants was indicative of a desire and a readiness to assimilate with the general population. New Deal programs that aided tribal revitalization and reservation redevelopment suffered the financial constraints imposed by war. The IRA, which theoretically sanctioned tribal government, would soon be repealed, as Congress debated the final termination of all federal services for American Indians. And by 1944, there was already evident within Washington a movement to rescind federal recognition of tribal identity among Indians.

Congress misread NCAI goals. Once founded, the organization quickly pressed Arizona and New Mexico for Indian suffrage and called for the creation of an Indian Claims Commission to settle outstanding tribal disputes with the federal government. Collier himself had frequently encouraged voting rights for Indians. More than one full year before the founding of the NCAI, the commissioner declared that "Indians of New Mexico and Arizona . . . assert their rights to State franchise." "These states," he said, "should do the American thing and grant the Indians the franchise, for all over the world we are preaching democracy and should grant a little more of it at home."[30] Rather than as measures required to protect the civil rights of a minority race, Congress interpreted the NCAI's two-pronged move as the Indians' "last minute" bid to assure full assimilation. The attainment of voting rights in the Southwest suggested the collapse of the final barrier to full citizenship and the Indians' acceptance in white society. An Indian Claims Commission would resolve all outstanding financial disputes with Washington and clearly signify the Indians' intention to accept termination. With this skewed understanding, Congress cheered the

NCAI.[31] Certainly, the House Subcommittee on Indian Affairs misinterpreted the NCAI's purpose. When a more comprehensive understanding arose in Washington, Congress ordered a thorough investigation and evaluation of the NCAI and continued its pursuit of complete, final termination.

An organization comprised of Indians for the advancement of Native American rights had been formed in opposition to the termination policy that was meandering its way through Congress. Here was "the word 'terminate' again — terminate the Indians," said Hazil Lohah Harper, an Osage Indian. "I don't know what is going to happen to the Indians [over] the next fifty years," she said at the time.[32]

While the NCAI settled into the trenches for its battle with Congress, Collier grasped what he believed to be one final opportunity to salvage the IRA. A postwar world order, founded on the principles of the Indian Reorganization Act, captured his imagination. Successful application of the IRA structure overseas to peoples of the Pacific islands recently retrieved from Japanese occupation would validate his program and perhaps breathe longer life into it at home among Indian populations. To Collier, the extension of Indian Service programs to islanders seemed quite logical as a method for bringing them into an American orbit, just as it had inadvertently worked to prepare Indians for assimilation.

The commissioner reminded the Roosevelt administration of the achievements made by Native Americans under the bureau's guidance. Expanded educational services reached more Indians and provided relevancy to the larger world, job skills allowed Indians access to higher paying positions and rewarded them with financial security, and reservations themselves had reaped fundamental improvements in living conditions and productivity. Moreover, Collier contended, bureau programs engendered among Indians a respect for American democratic values, institutions, and constitutionalism. The success of the IRA, Collier believed, hinged on one key element — an understanding of cultural diversity. Although the IRA contained an overarching goal for all Native Americans, it nonetheless accommodated differences in climatic and environmental conditions, economic bases, political structures, religious values, and tribal customs. Pacific cultural variations, the commissioner assumed, could not be much more diverse than that existing historically among American Indians. With a proven ability to adapt to such variances and exceed expectations as proved under the IRA, the Indian Bureau offered the replication of Indian programs among the Asian islanders.[33]

Secretary Ickes concurred with Collier. "Because of the Department's unique experience with primitive people," Ickes said, the BIA "should participate actively in the administration of any islands in the Pacific which may be occupied and governed by the United States." Convinced of the compatibility of Indian Service programs to Asian postwar development, Ickes suggested the bureau play a central role in the formulation of American policy and train civilian personnel selected for territorial administration. Together, Collier and Ickes anticipated the natural transition of the IRA to overseas environments, although little thought was given to its application to Japan. Indian reservations proved themselves to be "a laboratory and a demonstration ground in behalf of the world's reorganization ahead," said Collier.[34]

The commissioner and secretary hoped bureau programs would be granted a reprieve from termination if the Roosevelt administration endorsed IRA-styled redevelopment projects for occupied territories. Unfortunately, the two reformers viewed the Indian Service role overseas in a less than critical manner. Assimilationist policy had framed the federal government's focus since the Dawes Act, and, as a result, Indians had experienced a prolonged interaction with American educational, economic, religious, and political institutions. Native American acceptance of white culture had progressed so thoroughly by World War II that assimilation appeared as a logical next step.

To the contrary, Pacific island cultures possessed no such solid foundation. The assumption of a smooth transfer of services into the Pacific territories and the anticipation of a response similar to that given by American Indians denied historical realities. Moreover, the Native American population had been decimated by white expansion over a period exceeding two hundred years. Rather than a willing association with white culture, the majority of Indians had been coerced into accommodation as their numbers dwindled. Again, most Pacific cultures dwelled outside of the Indian experience. Although Native Americans were still culturally different and tribal variations continued to exist, a common experience shared by Indians nationwide with white America muted the most striking dissimilarities with mainstream society. The extent of acculturation, the forced relationship with white culture, and a heightened commonality among twentieth-century Indian cultures all permitted a greater opportunity for the successful implementation of the IRA. Asian cultures did not have these features in common with Native Americans and, consequently, made the IRA's effective transfer to the Pacific less plausible.

Despite the flaw in Collier's vision, the plan was founded on a humanitarian goal—the supply of food, clothing, medicine, shelter, and municipal services that would aid the "destitute and undernourished peoples in foreign lands." Bureau officials further intended to promote agricultural development, care for orphaned children, and initiate the establishment of modern educational programs. The reuniting of families separated by war, as well as physical and psychological therapy to those persons in need, also comprised part of the BIA's overarching objective.[35]

President Roosevelt sanctioned the concept. Hoping to avoid a repetition of the unplanned, haphazard administration of Pacific territories, which had confounded the United States in the late nineteenth century, FDR, in January 1943, ordered the Departments of State, War, Navy, and Interior to initiate policy formulation and the creation of a committee to address "the recruitment and training of civilian personnel for work in occupied areas or for postwar service" overseas. The president specifically pointed to a direct involvement by the Bureau of Indian Affairs and added that a full utilization of America's resources similar to the Indian New Deal effort was warranted. FDR further suggested the committee solicit the participation of universities, scientific institutions, and other educational organizations to develop training curricula and criteria for the selection of qualified personnel in a manner patterned after Collier's administration of Indian affairs. The committee, then, would serve as the "primary organization charged with the duty of recruiting and training expert civilian personnel for non-military over-seas services," the president said.[36]

Roosevelt directed Ickes to create a private organization, in collaboration with the Indian Service, to study and to recommend a permanent policy for the nation's "colonial relationships" in the Pacific. Later known as the Institute of Ethnic Democracy, members included anthropologists, ethnologists, scientists, and specialists in the field of Indian studies.[37] Throughout the spring of 1943, Collier and Ickes sought advice from Vice President Henry Wallace, Benjamin Gehrig of the State Department, Dr. Fred Eggan of the Philippine Commonwealth, and Under Secretary Abe Fortas; however, no definite committee was impaneled or policy formed as summer approached.[38]

The slow pace owed less to Collier and Ickes than to wartime constraints. Faced with congressional attacks against the IRA and the very existence of the bureau itself, Collier hoped for a full deployment of bureau resources for Pacific islands administration as quickly as possible. A commanding and visible presence in territorial governance and redevelopment might bolster his contention that the IRA still held merit, and it would potentially validate BIA programs stateside among Indian communities and encourage their continuing support of Indian assimilation following the war. Committee inaction hampered Collier's rebuttal to complete termination, and he spent the remainder of his tenure as commissioner promoting bureau participation in overseas programs to the media and to civic organizations.

Collier's promotion of the plan, however, smacked of paternalism and white

American cultural superiority. His statement that the program's recipients would receive "mastery over their own resources, self-government, and the right of cultural diversity" implied that such could be gained only with American guidance. Coming from the commissioner of Indian Affairs, it also hinted that the redirection in Native American conditions emerged from the benevolent hands of the white-dominated bureau leadership, having elevated Indians from the grip of poverty and cultural suffocation to new economic heights and the democratic promise. Although couched in terms that credited America's native population, Collier asserted that "what the Indians have shown, the peoples of China, India, and Indonesia, and the peoples of Africa and . . . Latin American countries just as certainly will show if granted liberty, responsibility, and intellectual nurture."[39] This carried the undertone that a caring protector provided those elements to Indians, and the same overseer would extend similar rewards to Asians as well. Under American guidance, and the work of the Indian Bureau particularly, the nonwhite, economically stagnant, politically undemocratic Asian peoples would survive and eventually prosper as Native Americans did.

A new era of American imperialism hovered on the horizon. Responding to the implication, Roosevelt contended that "we have no imperialistic intention," but without hesitation he added, "the interests of this country will dictate either the permanent acquisition of some of these territories in defense of our western coast or some continuing friendly relationship. It therefore behooves us," he continued, "to plan carefully in advance a colonial policy which shall recognize the inherent rights of these native peoples and safeguard them in their growth toward democratic self-government either under the American flag or in close association with American interests."[40]

The president envisioned an imperialistic posture in the Pacific, with Indian Service administration at its core. The IRA had encouraged a relationship between reservations and the federal government similar to that desired by Roosevelt in overseas territories. Because of the redirected Indian policy, a degree of local democracy and autonomy permeated reservation governments; yet, federal authorities commanded and exercised veto privileges in the national interest. Indian Service methods and programs, therefore, suited the government's objective to assert influence over liberated areas.

Collier longed for widespread approval of the IRA and the revitalization of Indian cultures, and the application of Indian Service philosophy and tactics to overseas endeavors carried that potential. But the commissioner associated federal Indian policy in 1944 with another goal—the establishment of a world order conducive to global peace. To eliminate the fundamental causes for war, man's basic needs in life had to be provided. This meant that food, clothing, medical care, education, economic prosperity, and a democratic political system were essential for all peoples worldwide. A global union demanded the subordination of cultural differences to a world order premised on cooperation. In America, the Indian Reorganization Act linked diverse cultures under a common program for revitalization. While protecting individual tribal identity, the IRA joined Native Americans with a common goal and provided them with the necessary tools with which to acquire their objectives. If applied to liberated areas, perhaps the foundation for a peaceful world order might be successfully established.[41]

The commissioner's view was obviously much broader than that of Roosevelt. The president only hoped to employ the Indian Bureau's skills in developing island cultures for the postwar world, particularly for America's own economic and political benefit in the Pacific. With that narrow objective, FDR dismissed much of Collier's plan for global peace and order in favor of an international political-military coalition to suppress armed aggression. Rather than initially concentrate on redevelopment as a means of remedying the underlying causes for war, Roosevelt preferred the creation of an international judicial body (the World Court), a general assembly for the discussion of disputes, and an inner-council to respond to immediate threats. Not until mid-1944 did the president concede a need for social and economic support programs in the emerging United Nations. By then, a program patterned along Collier's idea seemed too limited in its capacity for a massive postwar global effort. A movement away from the international implementation of Indian policy became visible. "This interest [in Indian policy]," noted one observer, "is a product of World War II and it can subside as abruptly as it arose; indeed, the reaction is already starting."[42]

As autumn 1944 passed into winter 1945, Collier scanned the conditions in Europe and the Pacific. Victory in both theaters now seemed likely. That thought comforted him. However, when he surveyed domestic Indian affairs, the commissioner sensed doom. Throughout the war, the BIA had struggled from one crisis to another. Bureau appropriations suffered crippling reductions, supplemental funding from other agencies disappeared, and many reservation programs vanished completely. The mass exodus of Indians into the labor force and the armed forces further hindered reservation productivity and security. Moreover, Congress launched a direct assault on the IRA and on the bureau's very existence.

Collier's involvement with the War Relocation Authority and overseas redevelopment, along with his revamped argument to salvage the IRA, signaled the defensive posture of a bureau on the verge of collapse. Even the creation of the

NCAI and the Indian Claims Commission in 1946 contained the implicit message that Indians themselves no longer viewed the bureau or Collier as viable, as capable advocates of Indian affairs. An apparent loss of faith revealed itself among Native Americans with each failure of the commissioner during the war to counter effectively congressional attacks.

Battered and weary from his dozen years as commissioner of Indian Affairs, John Collier tendered his resignation on January 19, 1945. In his brief statement to the president, Collier summarized the bureau's battles since late 1941. In every way possible, he informed Roosevelt, Congress "hampered and retarded" Indian progress. Unable to cope with the continued pressures facing him, he hoped to devote his remaining energies to inter-American Indian activities, the improvement of ethnic relations, and the promotion of true democracy for all people. Three days later, President Roosevelt "reluctantly" accepted Collier's resignation and praised the commissioner for his long service to Native Americans.[43]

John Collier had attempted a fundamental redirection in Indian affairs and the redevelopment of reservations during his tenure as commissioner. In so doing, he inadvertently provided Native Americans the resources, training, and services necessary for assimilation. This simply completed the long continuum of assimilationist efforts that had framed federal policy since the 1880s, and the Indians' relatively smooth transition to war and to wartime employment was the product of Collier's work. Moreover, the extent of Indian participation in World War II, and the overwhelming acceptance of Native Americans by whites, convinced Congress that it was time to terminate all Indian services.

Segments of the Indian population confronted a crossroads early in the war. The Iroquois Confederacy was forced to choose between the abrogation of historic treaties with the federal government and its inclusion with the larger body polity; Virginia's tidewater natives were compelled to confront their racial identity in a biracial state and determine a course of action appropriate to their own needs. With Collier's retirement and the war's end in sight, termination appeared certain. In 1945, American Indians nationwide had decisions to make that would affect their postwar lives. Would they seek residency and employment in urban areas, and in so doing follow the direction of assimilation? Or, would they return to reservations, which in all certainty would face a severe curtailment of federal services but retain a more traditional community existence?

Nine

Postwar Directions

The guns fell silent in Europe four months after Collier's January resignation as commissioner of Indian Affairs. By the end of summer, the war in the Pacific passed into history as well. American soldiers and sailors began the homeward trek—most filled with jubilant anticipation, some plagued by weariness, and a few haunted by the dark memories of battlefield carnage. Like their fathers before them who fought in the Great War, Indian veterans straggled home through wilderness America and across the windswept prairies to the homes and families they left years earlier. Unlike their fathers, these men did not plan to resume automatically the lives they surrendered for military service. This generation of Native American veterans expected to exercise free choice in determining their future—the right of self-determination. The inclusion that Indians found in the armed forces and the racial equality that seemed so sincere and all-pervasive suggested an American society open for Indian assimilation. Most realized that a transition period and additional training for postwar employment was necessary for a successful movement into the white mainstream, but the path toward assimilation nonetheless appeared unobstructed. At the same time, pre-war reservation development—the extension of health care, educational services, and tribal self-government, along with a redirection in reservation economics—all hinted that Indians could opt for a more traditional existence.

What returning Indians found instead were limited choices. Reservation services and economies deteriorated during the war and frequently resembled pre-Collier standards. Wartime necessities stripped tribal communities of most federal services. Schools and medical facilities had either closed entirely or suffered from shortages in personnel and supplies, lands remained uncultivated, and irrigation projects had fallen victim to appropriations cuts. Even reservations that witnessed a burst of activity and prosperity early in the war noticed a downward slope in the quality of life by 1945. A sense of abandonment coursed through Indian communities, and uncertainty loomed over Native Americans who preferred to spend their days on the reservation, surrounded by the land and people so central to their lives.

Among the Pine Ridge Sioux, emotions intensified to a point just short of hostility. Wartime demands had collapsed reservation progress and in so doing made self-determination nearly impossible to exercise. If the nation's power and wealth eluded Native Americans during the war and during an era of national prosperity, many wondered, then perhaps the United States' relations with foreign powers was in reality as destructive and inhumane as the government's historic relationship with American minorities. If that were true, then "the United States was the cause of the war," tribal members contended. As one Sioux recalled, "It seemed logical to us that if we were unhappy with the United States Government for what they had done to us, other countries would be angry at the United States for the same reason."[1]

Those who remained on reservations during the war had already chosen their postwar path. By the end of 1945, the superintendent at Window Rock, Arizona, noted that "the peyote culture, messianic revivals, [and] ceremonials are a withdrawal from the white man's world in the only direction they know— toward a faded Indian tradition."[2] In many respects, the war stimulated an ethnic renewal. The nation's call to arms raised the spirit of the warrior tradition in many younger Indians, and elders breathed new life into the old war chants and ceremonies. Children, steeped in the stories of their parents and grandparents, wrapped the current war in the images of nineteenth-century conflict. While visiting the home of his bride, Pfc. Wilson Guerrero wrote to his parents, "The little children of Cochiti day school . . . always ask for the scalp of Mussolini to make little Indian dolls out of it." In tribal communities across the Plains, the Sun Dance was performed, and in southwestern villages Indians "left their homes and went secretly to their ancient shrine[s]," where they prayed and fasted as in earlier days. Said one student of Indian cultures in 1943, "war has aroused long dormant instincts in the First Americans."[3] Many American Indian communities experienced cultural revivalism and a pride in their identity on a level that paralleled the nationalism that emerged among people worldwide during the war. Ironically, what John Collier failed to accomplish during his tenure as commissioner, now appeared as the Indians' response to war.

Those who worked in defense industries confronted a less certain postwar era. Having become skilled workers and socially accepted by whites during the war, many hoped for a continuation of employment and complete assimilation following the closure of hostilities abroad. Two serious developments were overlooked. First, demobilization sharply reduced the need for labor. Munitions factories, aircraft plants, shipyards, and manufacturers of war materiel released thousands of workers early in 1945, and the trend only escalated that summer and autumn. An overabundant supply of workers glutted urban centers, and returning veterans added to the surplus. Second, veterans received preferential treatment from employers, particularly white veterans. The specter of racism once again reared itself as both Native Americans and African Americans lost their jobs to white returnees. With Indians displaced from employment and often unable to secure positions elsewhere, many had no choice but to return to their reservations—a direction they had not intended to take. Most of the forty thousand Indians who relocated to urban centers during the war and the majority of Native American veterans now migrated back to their pre-war homes, and reservations strained to provide for them. Estimates made just before the end of World War II hinted that between seventy-five and ninety percent of all Indians who left the reservations during the war would, in fact, return after the war.[4] The flow of men and women back to reservation lands in 1945 and 1946 suggested that the estimates were rather accurate.

Native American veterans themselves compounded the social pressures that pervaded Indian communities in late 1945 and in 1946. The war left its mark on thousands of men. Physical dismemberment, alcoholism, and memories of the war's brutality affected many of them, and the ever-present sight of orphans, widows, and parents who had lost sons proved a constant and grim reminder of the war. Said one Sioux elder, a "younger generation with a taste for new and non-Indian things and ways" prevented a smooth transition to reservation existence. "The wounds of war were too deep, and the exposure of the young people to city life was too disturbing" for a peaceful reunion with pre-war tribal life, lamented another. A restlessness sifted through the returnees and disrupted reservations across America.[5]

Indian income also underwent a postwar readjustment. Military wages and dependency allotments mailed to the families of soldiers vanished with the end of war. Money sent home by those who were employed in defense industries also disappeared as a result of the widespread layoffs and the closure of many wartime factories, military hospitals, and transportation centers. There was less demand for Indian-produced agricultural products, silver goods, and cold-weather clothing. The economic crisis that confronted numerous reservations just before the war's end only intensified as returned veterans placed greater demands on an already strained financial setting. By 1946, tribal income nationwide plummeted to pre-war levels. Navajo earnings fell to $471 annually, while South Dakota Sioux income hovered just under $600. Oklahoma's reservation Indians averaged $625, a level similar to New Mexico Indians, and Arizona's natives saw their annual earning capacity dwindle to $525. Following three years of postwar adjustments in the national economy, the median income for reservation Indians peaked at $950 in 1949. Although the adjusted earnings represented a substantial improvement when contrasted to depression-era figures, the 1949 median amounted to a fifty percent drop from the level attained by Indians in 1944. Urban Native Americans fared only slightly better in that last year of the decade, with an average annual income of $1,200. But that figure represented a sixty-six percent reduction from the 1944 level of $3,200. When contrasted with African American earnings of $2,200 and white income at $3,800 annually in 1949, American Indians again found themselves at the lower end of the national income scale.[6]

Especially hard-hit was the Navajo Reservation. In summer 1947, a severe drought crippled agricultural and livestock operations. The failure of federal agencies and projects to complete irrigation programs before the war and the government's refusal to pursue the efforts during the war only compounded the natural disaster. Not until December 12, 1947, did President Harry Truman appropriate two million dollars for emergency relief. One year later, in the winter of 1948–49, an unexpected blizzard fell on the reservation. Federal aid came more quickly as the Army National Guard and Civilian Air Patrol conducted a rescue mission to supply food, animal feed, and clothing to the Navajos. Still, ten percent of all livestock perished.[7]

Across the nation, reservations faced extreme hardships in the immediate aftermath of World War II; however, Indian veterans perhaps suffered the most. In 1946, the anthropologist John Adair interviewed one hundred Indian veterans from the Navajo and Pueblo communities. Adair found a "long continuum of change" among the Indians that began in the early 1930s. The Indians had observed and benefited from improved reservation conditions under the Collier administration, complied with Selective Service regulations, served in the nation's armed forces, often traveled overseas and experienced combat, and, now that they had returned home, confronted pre-war conditions once more. Although the interviewed men agreed they had been treated fairly and equally by whites during the war, they felt that they had been "dumped" back into the old ways of life with demobilization. For the two thousand Indian veterans at Window Rock, Arizona, the Veterans Administration had sent only two representatives. Neither the VA nor local banks offered loans on Indian lands. Veterans, therefore, could not open small businesses or invest in white companies. Those questioned by Adair now complained of white discrimination. Added to this, the majority of respondents pointed to their inability, by law, to vote or to drink alcohol as evidence of continued discrimination. Veterans warned Adair of a reactionary movement among Indians unless the problems they faced were soon eradicated.[8]

Speaking at the annual meeting of the Association on American Indian Affairs on November 15, 1947, Oliver LaFarge broadly sounded Adair's findings. "Indians," he said, "cherished the delusion that in return [for military service and sacrifice at home] their country would pay attention to the Indians' needs . . . and give them a full opportunity to share in the good things of our way of life." Contrary to expectations, he added, Indians had been duped again. The postwar circumstances in which Native Americans found themselves demonstrated the government's uncompassionate attitude toward Indians. LaFarge listed as evidence the continued funding cuts, rising unemployment, reduced educational opportunities, the end of service programs, and the closure of reservation hospitals.[9]

LaFarge then addressed specifically the issue of termination currently under discussion in Congress, and he expressed no opposition to the ultimate goal directed by Washington. Instead of confrontation, he recommended that Native Americans recognize that its fulfillment "is freedom in the only real meaning of the word, the freedom of being fully equipped to take care of one's self and to have an equal status in the pursuit of happiness." No supervisory body would exist to dictate Indian affairs; Congress would exert no control over Indian finances. The freedom to regulate one's own life, as in the days before the white invasion of North America, he contended, would once again be the reality of Indian life. But, he asked, how could this freedom be attained with reduced appropriations in the present, money that would permit the training of Indians for self-reliance in the future? At the moment, he said, Navajo veterans "sit idle and helpless" since they own no land and possess an education not conducive for off-reservation employment. Indians were about to lose the gains they had earned over the previous twenty years, just as he feared when he first heard the news of Pearl Harbor.[10]

Rather than immediate termination, LaFarge preferred a gradual elimination of federal oversight. Gradualism, he wrote in an article for *Harper's Magazine*, afforded Indians the time to enhance their skills and to gain additional training for the complete realization of self-reliance in the white world. Such a process, he thought, was the only realistic approach to termination. But LaFarge understood that even a gradualist policy might not address the immediate needs of the Indian veteran. The returned soldier faced a peculiar set of problems. "When he came back [from war], he had great hopes. He spoke better English now. He had his mustering-out pay, he had the GI Bill of Rights, he had seen the world, he had lived and fought and played as an equal among white men." Indian veterans, however, now discovered themselves "boxed-in." Most jobs were filled, and discrimination prevailed. Those who had planned to become ranchers faced overstocked ranges once more. Indians who sought loans failed to qualify. Others who wished to improve their education were denied the opportunity. Indian veterans, LaFarge complained, were "victims of their own vigor." War garnered white acceptance for Indians; in peace, "they encountered the realities of hopelessness and destitution."[11]

To prove his argument, LaFarge drew upon specific examples. "The [food] intake of the average Navajo is several hundred calories below that which we provide the Germans in the territory we occupy." He cited one veteran who complained of chronic fatigue. When a Red Cross volunteer asked the former soldier why he so often felt tired, the Indian replied, "Well, you see—sometimes I don't eat for two or three days." In addition to inadequate nourishment, only six thousand of the twenty-five thousand Navajo children were enrolled in reservation schools in the autumn of 1947. No additional room or personnel existed to accommodate the remaining children or the returning veterans. For the sixty thousand residents on Navajo lands, only one field nurse from the BIA was available to provide essential medical attention. Hospital personnel manned only 450 beds, 135 of which were designated for tuberculosis patients. Numerous diseases besides TB ravaged the Indian population between 1946 and 1947; small pox, scarlet fever, typhoid fever, diphtheria, and measles all ran rampant. With the economic problems prevalent on the reservation, few people should wonder, he said, why Indian veterans seemed so despondent. "We went to Hell and back for what?" asked one Navajo. "For the people back here in America to tell us we can't vote? Can't do this! Can't do that! because you don't pay taxes and are not citizens! We did not say we were not citizens when we volunteered for service against the ruthless and treacherous enemies, the Japs and the Germans!"[12]

To make LaFarge's argument more personal and more effective, anthropologist Evon Z. Vogt presented a case study of John Nez, a Navajo veteran. In an extended interview with Vogt, Nez retraced his life. Born in 1917, he had been reared fearful of whites because of his parent's experiences in boarding schools; however, his own education experience under the guidance of a compassionate white teacher altered that view. With her tutelage, Nez excelled in academics and earned high honors, which rewarded him with an all-expenses-paid graduation trip to Los Angeles where "new vistas of the white world opened" his eyes.[13]

The army drafted Nez in January 1941, and during the war he saw combat in North Africa, Italy, France, and Germany. While in service, he told Vogt, whites included him fully as "a respected equal in the white world." The army classified him as white, and he even dated white women during his training at three southern posts. Vogt noted that Nez's "white ways were more than a 'veneer.'" They were, he said, "integral parts of his motivational system."[14]

Discharged from the armed forces in late 1945, Nez returned to his Navajo home and intended to open a small trading post with the aid of a GI loan. Because he possessed no prior experience related to store management, the government rejected his application. Undaunted, he turned to farming, but his loan request for a tractor was not approved. He owned no collateral. Unable to understand the paperwork and the application process for admission to business school, and unable to secure financial aid, Nez wandered the reservation in frustration. Feeling the bite of discrimination and battered by multiple rejections, he began to drink excessively. Jailed repeatedly for public drunkenness and disorderly conduct, Nez followed a path similar to that taken by another Indian veteran, Ira Hayes, whose own hopes for assimilation turned to despair and ended with an untimely death. At the time of Vogt's interview, thirty-two-year-old John Nez lived in poverty and had no idea what he might attempt next. Only with continued financial aid, Vogt concluded, would Native American veterans avoid the condition in which Nez found himself.[15]

Across the nation, Indian veterans concurred with the assessments made by Adair, LaFarge, and Vogt. Having experienced social acceptance during the war and having "tasted" the opportunities afforded by off-reservation life, many veterans expected to pursue the course of assimilation. Race, noted one South Dakota resident, "is no bar . . . to securing jobs in a great many fields of commerce and industry; neither is it any bar to succeed in a great many professions." "When we Indian servicemen get back [from war], we're going to see that our people are set free to live and act like American citizens," said a Winnebago soldier. "We're tired of being treated like museum pieces. I'm a mechanic. I want a real job. They're not going to send me back to live in a shack and loaf around in a blanket," he added. His comments were echoed by a fellow veteran from the same tribe: "Give our boys and girls training as Americans, and not as Indians, and they'll set themselves free."[16]

Determined to break the bands of poverty, illiteracy, isolation, and dependency on the federal government, which once more strapped so many reservations, thousands of Indian servicemen took residency in Los Angeles, San Francisco, Phoenix, Detroit, New York, and other urban communities once the war ended. They continued their education under the GI Bill, worked for good wages, and found the social acceptance they expected. More often than not, the racism that affected Indians was generally most noticeable nearest the reservations, and those who successfully made the transition to urban living were among the most acculturated Indian veterans and the least dependent on federal aid.

The number of less acculturated Indians and the problems that challenged them, as detailed by Adair, LaFarge, and Vogt, proved greater than Washington was willing to admit. Instead, Congress assumed that the gains made on reservations under the IRA, along with the Indians' inclusion with whites during the war, accelerated the extent of acculturation. This flawed understanding was partly sustained by the examples of Indians who successfully made the postwar transition to urban life and by the Indians' wartime expectation of inclusion in white society. From such a perspective, it seemed logical to members of Congress that the termination of federal aid to and guardianship over Native Americans was in the best interest of Indians. That such a plan also promised significant savings in federal spending and reflected the nation's retrenchment from New Deal liberalism were added bonuses. However, in considering termination as new federal Indian policy, Congress failed to realize that the severe curtailment of services to Native Americans actually hampered the ability of less acculturated Indians to make a smooth transition to urban life and created a more dismal existence for those who remained on reservations.

African Americans also suffered rising unemployment and impoverishment following World War II, and the depth of racism against them proved much deeper and more extreme. But the harshness and pervasiveness of racism against blacks over so many years had forged among them a common, shared experience, which, in response, provided some measure of unity and cooperation. The overwhelming majority of black Americans held a common culture and heritage in the United States that made acceptance within their own broader community easier to accomplish. In addition, support groups existed for African Americans in urban centers. Since their inception in the early twentieth century, both the National Urban League and the National Association for the Advancement of Colored People aided blacks as a single race. Moreover, black churches provided direct assistance and comfort to its members in response to local white racism. Native Americans possessed none of these personal support mechanisms. While the NCAI attempted a pan-Indian unity, cultural and historical differences remained a divisive force and impeded a singularly national effort, such as that fashioned by African American organizations. While the Indian Claims Commission sought financial redress for Native Americans once it was established in 1946, it only addressed settlement issues for individual tribes. The task of challenging immediate termination and securing aid necessary for Indian assimilation or tribal revitalization rested more squarely on the work of individual Indians or on individual tribes rather than on national organizations that represented a more culturally unified membership.

Despite the lack of preparedness for actual postwar assimilation, for those who preferred that particular direction, the Eightieth Congress entered Washington in 1946 with the goals of reducing big government and initiating complete termination of federal services to Native Americans. The Senate promptly informed Acting Commissioner of Indian Affairs William Zimmerman to submit specific recommendations for cost reductions that could be implemented immediately. Fighting to hold on to Collier's policies and to aid Indians as long as possible, Zimmerman refused, until the Senate issued him a subpoena. Congress ordered him to determine which tribes could be "removed at once from government supervision" and the amount of money that "would be saved for each tribe so removed." Which tribes could survive without federal aid, he wondered? Zimmerman considered levels of acculturation, tribal economic conditions, and the individual state's ability and willingness to provided supplemental financing to Indians. Although he purposely delayed compliance with the directive, Zimmerman eventually provided a list that ranked tribes according to their ability to survive without federal support. At the top of his list was the Iroquois Confederacy.

Late that year, William Brophy was confirmed as Collier's replacement and penned the annual report for the Office of Indian Affairs. The new commissioner's remarks were quite brief. He highlighted the Indians' war record in a few short paragraphs and summarized positive developments in health care, economics, and the preservation of physical resources on the reservations. His report clearly revealed the overall progress made on reservations since 1933, despite wartime regression. Moreover, Brophy cited and praised Indian service during World War II, but he did not recommend the complete termination of federal services.[17] Like Zimmerman, Brophy dragged out the process of naming tribes for termination. Unlike his predecessors, however, Brophy successfully applied pressure from Washington on Arizona and New Mexico to guarantee suffrage rights for Native American residents. If termination was to be carried forth, he argued, the basic rights of citizenship had to be provided.[18] Although both Zimmerman and Brophy issued lists of tribes "competent" for termination, two years elapsed without any elimination of Indians from federal guardianship, largely because of Brophy's insistence on civil rights protection for Native Americans.

Termination, nonetheless, moved forward toward policy status. In 1946, Congress established the Indian Claims Commission, recommended by the National Congress of American Indians two years earlier. The ICC was to settle all outstanding tribal monetary claims against the federal government and, once completed, end Native American financial dependency on the United States. Approved by both houses of Congress, President Truman signed the bill and, in so doing, said, "I am glad to sign my name to a measure that removes a lingering discrimination against our First Americans and gives them the same opportunities that our laws extend to all other American citizens."[19] Tribes were given a five-year time limit in which to file their cases with the commission, and the commission itself would then investigate, review, and evaluate the merits of each petition before awarding any cash settlement. The program was intended to last no longer than ten years. Conflicting claims, legal disputes, arguments over the method of payment, and even heated debates regarding the official status of persons now claiming an Indian identity all combined to push ICC proceedings into 1978. By the time of its dissolution that year, the ICC had settled more than 280 cases and awarded more than eight hundred million dollars in judgments. But, at its inception, few politicians anticipated such a lengthy process and most assumed the ICC would in fact hurry the movement of termination to its desired end.[20]

In 1948, the Hoover Commission renewed the call for immediate termination. Moreover, it suggested that all Indian affairs be handled by the individual states, and that Washington's involvement should finally cease. The statement implied the dissolution of all treaties historically made with Native Americans, even though such a position had been validated years earlier in the court cases of Watson Totus and Warren Eldreth Green. The prospect of state control pleased individuals in Arizona and New Mexico, who opposed recent legislation to grant Indians voting privileges. In early 1949, both states attempted to disenfranchise the native population. Although the moves were declared unconstitutional, the actions taken by those two states served as warnings to Congress that safeguards must be created to protect the Indians' civil rights before full termination could be accomplished. Indian veterans' fears that postwar assimilation was unlikely now garnered credibility.

Both the House and the Senate assured tribes of temporary economic assistance for the development of skills necessary for movement into mainstream society. The Indian Loan Act passed both houses and allowed all Indians with at least one-fourth blood the right to obtain federal loans to aid their relocation to urban centers. Congress further authorized short-term funds to attack reservation poverty, illiteracy, and inadequate health care. With these provisions, Congress believed Native Americans would be encouraged to migrate to urban areas or to establish self-sufficient operations on their native lands and, therefore, eventually be removed from federal support.[21]

The movement toward termination gained steam when former War Relocation Authority director Dillon Myer became commissioner of Indian Affairs in
1950. Convinced that the mission of the Indian Service was to "free the Indian
from government control . . . and free the government from undue expenditures," Myer eagerly pushed for the immediate cessation of federal aid for and
control over Native Americans. Having the wartime experience of transplant-
ing large populations to various locations within the United States, Myer felt
that a similar tactic could be employed with American Indians. His Indian Relocation Program began operation the following year.[22]

On paper, the program provided enough assistance for an Indian's one-way
transportation to the nearest large city and subsistence until he received his first
pay check from a job the bureau helped him secure. Other than the Indian
Loan Act, no further aid would be granted; the Indian would be on his own.
First year appropriations totaled three hundred thousand dollars. Few reservation Indians accepted the offer. Myer's plan failed to include transportation expenses for the Indian's family and ignored completely the individual's skill level.
In 1952, the BIA extended its benefits to include the relocation of entire families,
fifty dollars for household shipment, an identical amount for tools, and subsistence for four weeks. Additional funds would be provided if the Indian lost his
job through no fault of his own. Continued reservation decay compelled more
Indians to accept the program. Among the Navajos, over four hundred families participated in relocation. To compensate for unforeseen expenses, the BIA
encouraged commercial loan institutions to cooperate with urbanizing Indians.
Myer and other bureau officials eased lenders' doubts by citing evidence of Indian loan repayment under Collier's administration. According to bureau statistics, more than sixteen million dollars had been loaned to Native Americans
since 1934; only six thousand dollars had not been repaid. In short, "Indians are
good credit risks," said Secretary of the Interior Oscar Chapman.[23]

Of special concern to Myer and other proponents of relocation was the anticipated overcrowding of Indians into segregated sections of urban communities. In order to break tribal affiliations and prevent the development of "little
reservations," the Relocation Program refused to permit more than two Indian
families from settling in the same city block. One benefit, officials assumed,
would be quicker assimilation of Indians into the community through forced
submersion. Yet, Myer's goals failed to take shape as planned. In many cities, relocated Indians opened their homes to distant relatives and to family friends
who moved to urban centers without bureau aid. Many accepted the cramped
living conditions in order to pool financial resources for common survival.
Overcrowding became widespread, and entire city blocks turned into predom-

inantly Indian communities. One report cited sixteen Indians of all ages living in one unventilated attic without furnishings, except for blankets and a hot plate. In other instances, children were discovered sleeping in hallways and in bathrooms.[24]

Relocation never achieved Myer's objective. Largely, this was attributed to the commissioner's own poor administration and inability to comprehend the state of Indian affairs. Financial aid from the BIA proved insufficient for the movement of entire families to urban settings, housing was generally inadequate, and the bureau seldom monitored the progress of relocatees. The commissioner encouraged Indians to volunteer for relocation, but he did so without considering their ability to adapt to urban life. Also, Myer measured the performance of reservation superintendents in part by the number of Indians they relocated. Consequently, "a lot of the people were pushed into this program" by relocation officers whose only motivation was job security, complained a Pine Ridge Sioux. Most Native Americans were not ready to assimilate because of wartime and postwar developments. More than fifty percent returned to Pine Ridge within one year after relocation.[25]

As policy, termination never achieved the goals envisioned by Congress. Few Indians in the decade immediately following World War II held the level of acculturation necessary for independent movement into the white mainstream, and reductions in federal aid to reservations and to individual Native Americans actually impeded the development of those very skills required for assimilation. Even relocation and the Indians' total immersion into white urban society never held any chance of successfully effecting assimilation. On reservations, the standard of living deteriorated rapidly with only scant attention given by Washington, and the interest shown by Congress and contenders for the White House seemed closely connected to election year politics. The Kennedy Report of 1970, the product of a federally funded investigation into Indian affairs and chaired by Senator Edward Kennedy, revealed reservation conditions that could have been easily copied from Louis Meriam's findings in 1928. The deplorable standard of living commonplace on reservations nationwide reflected Washington's long-term neglect during the era of termination.

At best, federal aid was limited during the 1950s. The NCAI loudly called on Washington to maintain a safety net of services to aid American Indians in their transition from reservation communities to urban residency, and through its work many programs marked for elimination were allowed to continue their services to Native Americans. As a result, thousands of veterans returned to the classroom, earned their high-school diplomas and college degrees, and, once armed with academic training, found the avenue toward assimilation free of most obstacles. The NCAI's determined protection of the Indians' civil rights also opened opportunities for a movement, by choice, into areas of white society previously closed to Native Americans.[26] That was, after all, the stated mission of the NCAI—free choice, self-determination. Still, those who chose to remain within the tribal environment continued to suffer poverty, poor educational services, and declining health care.

On the eve of World War II, Native Americans scanned the previous decade and concluded that significant advances had been made by and on behalf of Indians. The Indian New Deal had cultivated tribal economics, expanded educational opportunities and job skills training, contributed to the development of a sound health-care program, and permitted tribal communities a greater measure of self-determination than that which existed under any previous era of BIA supervision. Although not a planned goal of John Collier's Indian Reorganization Act, bureau programs in the 1930s made assimilation a real possibility. As envisioned by the commissioner, the IRA encouraged a tribal environment conducive to the retention of traditional Indian cultures, albeit a modified traditional existence. In 1941, the image of a crossroads appeared before American Indians, an image that seemed much clearer early in the war years, with one direction leading toward inclusion with mainstream society and the other toward a reinvigorated tribal life. The choice remained the Indians'.

World War II heightened the Indians' expectations for self-direction as forty thousand Native Americans found off-reservation employment in defense plants, good wages, and social acceptance. Twenty-five thousand men entered the armed forces, often received training transferable to civilian work, and also found social acceptance. The overarching image of the war years was one of opportunity and the anticipation of postwar assimilation. It also provided Indians with the option of taking the skills and experiences earned in service to the nation during the war back to their tribal communities. The war, then, established a crossroads for Native Americans.

Underneath the image, another reality existed. Racism questioned Indian identity and restricted the civil rights of many Native Americans. Washington actively challenged the legality of long-standing treaties, which in itself was an attack on identity. Reservations fell into disrepair, and federal funds for essential tribal programs evaporated. The policy of termination, championed by Congress during the war and implemented as policy after 1945, further confounded Native Americans. Postwar directions for American Indians were, in fact, severely limited.

A casual glance at Indian affairs from 1928 to the late 1940s would garner the impression that Native Americans were victims of white paternalism and corrupted federal policy. In reality, American Indians exercised a degree of self-determination not seen since the government's official closure of Indian-white hostilities in 1890. Throughout World War II, Native Americans actively courted opportunities provided to them, created opportunities when there seemed to be none available, and challenged Washington at numerous turns. Indians extended their academic and vocational training, entered the armed forces, and contributed fully to national defense. When confronted with threats to tribal sovereignty and established treaties, with issues that questioned their very identity, and with postwar directions that potentially submerged them as second-class citizens, American Indians chose to resist the system. The clearest evidence of the Indians' exercise of self-determination that emerged from their World War II experiences was a conscious and spirited reassertion of their ethnic identity in white America. The path so many Indians chose to follow after 1945 was that leading directly toward a renewed pride in Indian culture and history—the forerunner of the Red Power movement that arose in the 1960s.

Notes

Introduction

1. Virgil Wyaco, *A Zuni Life: A Pueblo Indian in Two Worlds*, ed. J. A. Jones (Albuquerque: University of New Mexico Press, 1998), 36–38.

2. Ibid., 22–25.

Chapter One

1. *New York Times*, 18 February 1919, p. 2. See also Brian W. Dippie, *The Vanishing American: White Attitudes and United States Indian Policy* (Middletown, Conn.: Wesleyan University Press, 1982), 194 and David Levering Lewis, *When Harlem Was in Vogue* (New York: Random House, 1981), 4. Although 8,000 Indians served in World War I, nearly 17,000 registered with the Selective Service though not required to do so by law since Native Americans were not citizens of the United States. For an excellent study of Native Americans in the Great War, see Thomas A. Britten, *American Indians in World War I: At Home and at War* (Albuquerque: University of New Mexico Press, 1997).

2. Thomas Britten, *American Indians in World War I: At Home and at War* (Albuquerque: University of New Mexico Press, 1997), 183–185.

3. Ibid., 186.

4. Department of Commerce. *Statistical Abstract of the United States* (Washington DC: Government Printing Office, 1924), 7, 11, 13, 15, 110. See also, Alan L. Sorkin, *The Urban American Indian* (Lexington, Mass.: D. C. Heath, 1978), 10.

5. Department of Commerce. *Statistical Abstract of the United States: 1929* (Washington DC: Government Printing Office, 1929), 136, 623. See also Frederick E. Hoxie, *A Final Promise: The Campaign to Assimilate the Indians, 1880–1920* (Lincoln: University of Nebraska Press, 1984), 147–187; James S. Olson and Raymond Wilson, *Native Americans in the Twentieth Century* (Chicago: University of Illinois Press, 1986), 128.

6. U.S. Department of Commerce. *Fifteenth Census of the United States: 1930,* "Characteristics of the Non-White Population by Race," (Washington DC: Government Printing Office, 1933). See also, Sorkin, *The Urban American Indian*, 10; Geoffrey Perrett, *America in the Twenties* (New York: Simon and Schuster, 1982), 323.

7. John Collier, "The Vanquished Indian," *The Nation* 26 (January 1928): 40.

8. Stuart Levine and Nancy Levine, eds., *The American Indian Today* (Baltimore: Penguin Books, 1974), 100; Olson and Wilson, *Native Americans in the Twentieth Century*, 97.

9. Lewis Meriam et al., *The Problem of Indian Administration: Report of a Survey Made at the Request of Honorable Hubert Work, Secretary of the Interior and Submitted to Him, February 21, 1928* (Baltimore: The Johns Hopkins Press, 1928), 208–15; Collier, "The Vanquished Indian," 39; M. C. Guthrie, "The Health of the American Indian," *Public Health Reports* 44 (19 April 1929): 952.

10. Meriam, *The Problem of Indian Administration*, 314–22, 333; Collier, "The Vanquished Indian," 39; Margaret Szasz, *Education and the American Indian: The Road to Self Determination, 1928–1973* (Albuquerque: University of New Mexico Press, 1974), 19.

11. Meriam, *The Problem of Indian Administration*,332.

12. Ibid., 341, 489, 524; also, Samuel Stanley, *American Indian Economic Development* (Paris: Mouton, 1978), 259.

13. Stanley, *American Indian Economic Development*, 259; Donald Parman, "The Indian and the Civilian Conservation Corps," *Pacific Historical Review* 40 (February 1971): 40.

14. Barbara Graymont, ed., *Fighting Tuscarora: The Autobiography of Clinton Rickard* (Syracuse: Syracuse University Press, 1973), 122–23.

15. Ibid.

16. Ibid., 124.

17. Guthrie, "The Health of the American Indian," 952.

18. James G. Townsend, "Disease and the Indian," *Scientific Monthly* 47 (December 1938): 489.

19. Meriam, *The Problem of Indian Administration*, 11.

20. "Civilizing the Indian," *The Nation* 138 (10 January 1934): 33–34.

21. For a full treatment of one specific Indian boarding school, see K. Tisianina Lomawaima, *They Called It Prairie Light: The Story of Chilocco Indian School* (Lincoln: University of Nebraska Press, 1994). This work is a published version of her doctoral dissertation and is built largely around the recollections of those who attended Chilocco in the 1920s and 1930s. The interviews revealed a myriad of student responses and appraisals of the academic, vocational, and social experiences of former students. Two important points, however, were frequently offered. First, there was a noticeable change in the school's system of discipline in the late 1930s. This appeared after the replacement of Ryan as director of Indian Education with Willard Walcott Beatty and was the product of altered goals within the Indian Education Service, encouraged by Commissioner of Indian Affairs John Collier. Second, the school included Indian children from numerous tribes and geographical regions. Former students often remarked that a commonality as Indian emerged among them instead of the strict retention of individual tribal identity.

22. Collier's vision for a redirection in federal Indian policy was largely formulated before Hubert Work appointed Lewis Meriam to conduct an investigation of reservation conditions. See John Collier, "The Indian Affairs Outlook," *American Indian Defense Bulletin*, 8 May 1926; unaddressed letter by Collier dated 27 January 1926, File: "John Collier," American Philosophical Society, Philadelphia.

23. For a full treatment of the Curtis Act (1898), the Jerome Agreement (1892), *Lone Wolf v. Hitchcock (1903)*, the Burke Act (1906) and the Omnibus Act (1910), see Hoxie, *A Final Promise*, 147–87.

24. Collier, "The Indian Affairs Outlook," 8 May 1926.

25. Elizabeth Shepley Sergeant, "A New Deal for the Indian," *New Republic* 95 (15 June 1938): 154; Oliver LaFarge, "The American Indian's Revenge," *Current History* 40 (May 1934): 168.

26. Loretta Fowler, *Arapahoe Politics: 1851–1978* (Lincoln: University of Nebraska Press, 1982), 174.

27. Ibid.; also, Graymont, *Fighting Tuscarora,* 125–26.

28. Graymont, *Fighting Tuscarora,* 126; J. C. Morgan, "A Navajo Dissenter," *Christian Century* 51 (3 October 1934): 1380.

29. Rupert Costo, "Federal Indian Policy," *Indian Self-Rule: First-Hand Accounts of Indian-White Relations from Roosevelt to Reagan* (Salt Lake City, Utah: Howe Brothers, 1986), 48.

30. Ibid., 49, 52.

31. Morgan, "A Navajo Dissenter," 1380.

32. Ibid.; Oliver LaFarge, "Revolution with Reservations," *The New Republic* 84 (9 October 1935): 234; Sergeant, "A New Deal for the Indian," 154.

33. Loretta Fowler, *Arapahoe Politics,* 175; Harold Fey and D'Arcy McNickle, *Indians and Other Americans* (New York: Harper and Row, 1970), 111.

34. J. R. McGibony, "Indians and the Selective Service," *Public Health Reports* 57 (2 January 1942): 6; Townsend, "Disease and the Indian," 489.

35. Townsend, "Disease and the Indian," 493.

36. J. R. McGibony, "Indians and the Selective Service," 5.

37. Ibid., 6.

38. Szasz, *Education and the American Indian,* 60, 64.

39. Ibid. See also post-1935 interviews of boarding-school students in K. Tisianina Lomawaima's *They Called It Prairie Light,* as described in n. 21.

40. "Civilizing the Indian," *The Nation,* 33–34.

41. Thomas Mails, ed., *Fools Crow* (Garden City, N.Y.: Doubleday, 1980), 151.

42. Donald L. Parman, "The Indian and the Civilian Conservation Corps," *Pacific Historical Review* 40 (February 1971): 40.

43. Calvin Gower, "The CCC Indian Division," *Minnesota History* 43 (Spring 1972): 6; Parman, "The Indian and the Civilian Conservation Corps," 46.

44. Parman, "The Indian and the Civilian Conservation Corps," 42, 50–53, 55; Gower, "The CCC Indian Division," 12; "Indians in the CCC Camps," *Missionary Review of the World* 56 (December 1933): 611.

45. *Statistical Abstract of the United States: 1942,* 155–56, 162.

46. Oliver LaFarge, "The American Indian's Revenge," 165.

47. LaFarge, "Revolution with Reservations," 233.

48. For reference, see Ray Allen Billington, *Westward Expansion* (New York: MacMillan, 1982) 644–61. Great Plains Committee, *The Future of the Great Plains* (Washington DC: Government Printing Office, 1936), 3.

49. Graham D. Taylor, *The New Deal and American Indian Tribalism: The Administration of the Indian Reorganization Act, 1934–1945* (Lincoln: University of Nebraska Press, 1980), 132; Fowler, *Arapahoe Politics,* 197.

World War II and the American Indian

50. "The Indian Reorganization Act, June 18, 1934," *This Country Was Ours: A Documentary History of the American Indian*, ed. Virgil L. Vogel (New York: Harper and Row, 1972), 197–203.

51. Interview of Antoine Roubideaux in Joseph Cash and Herbert T. Hoover, eds., *To Be an Indian: An Oral History* (New York: Holt, Rinehart, and Winston, 1971).

52. "President Roosevelt Addresses Navajo People," *Indians at Work* 8 (August 1941): 10–11; Letter, Franklin D. Roosevelt to the Navajo People, 19 June 1941, Official File 296 (Indians, 1941–45), Franklin Delano Roosevelt Library, Hyde Park, New York.

53. John Collier, *The Indians of the Americas* (New York: W. W. Norton, 1947), 261–63; Shuchi Naguta, *Modern Transformations of Moenkopi Pueblo* (Urbana: University of Illinois Press, 1970), 306; Fey and McNickle, *Indians and Other Americans*, 221–22; *Annual Report of the Secretary of Agriculture, 1940*, p. 375.

54. Benjamin Reifel, "Federal Indian Policy, 1933–1945," and Philleo Nash, "The IRA Record and John Collier," *Indian Self-Rule: First-Hand Accounts of Indian-White Relations from Roosevelt to Reagan*, ed. Kenneth Philp (Salt Lake City, Utah: Howe Brothers, 1986), 54, 103; Charles Weeks, "The Eastern Cherokee and the New Deal," *North Carolina Historical Review* 53 (1976): 306.

55. Floyd O'Neil, "The Indian New Deal: An Overview," and Benjamin Reifel, "Federal Indian Policy, 1933–1945," *Indian Self-Rule: First-Hand Accounts of Indian-White Relations from Roosevelt to Reagan*, 43, 55.

56. Kenneth Philp, "Federal Indian Policy, 1933–1945," *Indian Self-Rule*, 59. It should be noted that Philp has emerged as an outspoken critic of the IRA and the Collier administration. "My assessment of the Indian New Deal," he writes in this work, "has become more negative over the years." He believes the IRA contradicted assimilation except as noted in this particular quoted passage.

57. LaFarge, "Revolution with Reservations," 234.

Chapter Two

1. James V. Compton, *The Swastika and the Eagle* (Boston: Houghton Mifflin, 1967), 4.

2. Compton, *The Swastika and the Eagle*, 176; Adolf Hitler, *Mein Kampf* (Boston: Houghton Mifflin, 1971), 290–92.

3. "Edmonson Jew-Exposure Patriotic Bulletin," 10 September 1938, 2; The James True Associates, "Industrial Control Reports," 5 March 1938, 2, and 25 May 1940, 4; "That Fifth Column," 4 May 1940, 1. These documents are held by the Federal Bureau of Investigation inside the file titled "James True" and released through the Freedom of Information and Privacy Act (FOIPA).

4. Investigations conducted by the FBI and the Office of Indian Affairs verified that groups such as the Silver Shirt Legion, the German-American Bund, and the James True Associates distributed Nazi literature directly to Indians. The government also discovered that much of the material originated from Berlin broadcasts. See FBI files regarding James True, William Dudley Pelley, and Fritz Kuhn. For a detailed discussion of German radio transmissions into the Americas, see Z. A. B. Zeman, *Nazi Propaganda* (London: Oxford University Press, 1964), 113.

5. "Regarding the Sioux as Aryan," undated memo from Dr. Donald Collier, Department of Anthropology, University of Chicago, to an uncited recipient, Office of Indian Affairs, RG 75, Box 15, National Archives. Also, Leland Bell, *In Hitler's Shadow: The Anatomy of American Nazism* (Port Washington, N.Y.: Kennikat Press, 1973), 90.

6. Richard Cancroft, "The American West of Karl May," *American Quarterly* 19 (Winter 1967): 249–58.

7. Ibid., 255.

8. Ibid.

9. Ray Allen Billington, *Land of Savagery, Land of Promise: The European Image of the American Frontier* (New York: W. W. Norton, 1981), 56.

10. Thomas A. Britten, *American Indians in World War I: At Home and at War* (Albuquerque: University of New Mexico Press, 1997), 107.

11. Britten, *American Indians*, 108.

12. Ibid.

13. "Indians Are Non-Aryan, Hrdlicka Says of Activities of Bund," *Washington Daily News*, 24 November 1938, Office of Indian Affairs, RG 75, Box 6, National Archives.

14. Jere Franco, "Patriotism on Trial: Native Americans in World War II" (Ph.D. diss., University of Arizona, 1990), 89.

15. William E. Coffer, *Phoenix: The Decline and Rebirth of the Indian People* (New York: Van Nostrand Reinhold, 1979), 149.

16. Richard Neuberger, "The American Indian Enlists," *Asia and the Americas* 42 (November 1942): 629.

17. "Yankees and Yankeeland," *El Alcazar*, 1 December 1941 and "Falangist Propaganda and the Indians," clippings located in the files of the Office of Indian Affairs, RG 75, Box 7, National Archives; U.S. Department of Commerce, *Sixteenth Census of the United States: 1940*, "Population: Characteristics of the Non-White Population by Race," (Washington DC: U.S. Government Printing Office, 1940), 5–7; Peter Farb, *Man's Rise to Civilization* (New York: Avon Books, 1968), 295.

18. "Falangist Propaganda and the Indians"; "Yankees and Yankeeland."

19. For an excellent study of European perceptions of the American West in general, and Native Americans in particular, see Ray Allen Billington's *Land of Savagery, Land of Promise: The European Image of the American Frontier.*

20. Although Hitler spoke frequently of ridding Germany of all Jews and on occasion suggested physical extermination, Nazi Germany's policy to exterminate European Jewry did not become official until Hitler's invasion of Russia in 1941. Following Nazi combat divisions were *Einsatzgruppen* teams that commenced the mass murder of Jews at places such as Babi Yar, now synonymous with German atrocities. The "Final Solution" that formalized the construction and operation of death camps resulted from the Wansee Conference in January 1942. See Nora Levin, *The Holocaust: The Destruction of European Jewry, 1933–1945* (New York: Schocken, 1978) and Lucy Dawidowicz, *The War against the Jews, 1933–1945* (New York: Bantam, 1975).

21. Franco, "Patriotism on Trial," 90.

22. Colin Ross, "Der Balkan Amerikas." Translated, with an introduction, by Saul K. Padover and located in the files of the Office of Indian Affairs, RG 75, Box 15, National Archives.

23. Ross, "Der Balkan Amerikas." It is interesting to note that Ross's suggestion of a "red state" paralleled in time a similar consideration by Hitler of a Jewish state on the island of Madagascar.

24. Letter to Mr. Charles Elkus from John Collier, 1 December 1941, Papers of John Collier, Yale University; Sander A. Diamond, *The Nazi Movement in the United States, 1924–1941* (Ithaca, N.Y.: Cornell University Press, 1974), 224.

25. Saul K. Padover, "'Unser Amerika': The Nazi Program for the United States," *Forum* (January 1939), article located in the files of the Office of Indian Affairs, RG 75, Box 15.

26. Letter to John Collier from Dr. Colin Ross, 2 December 1938, Files of the Office of Indian Affairs, RG 75, Box 15.

27. Ibid.; Letter to Mr. LaRouche from William Pomeroy, 5 December 1938, Files of the Office of Indian Affairs, RG 75, Box 15; "Hollywood Ad Hits Leni Riefenstahl," *New York Times*, 30 November 1938, 15. With the exception of Walt Disney, Hollywood studio executives rebuffed Ms. Riefenstahl. To be "personally attacked," she said, "surprised" her. She claimed no propaganda mission in the United States. For a sound presentation of Riefenstahl's visit to Hollywood, see Thomas Doherty, *Projections of War: Hollywood, American Culture, and World War II* (New York: Columbia University Press, 1993), 16–35.

28. Letter to Dr. Colin Ross from Kristie Sather, secretary to the commissioner of Indian Affairs, 5 December 1938; Memo to John Collier from Harold Ickes, 12 December 1938, Office of Indian Affairs, RG 75, Box 15.

29. Memos to Superintendents Aberle, Newman, McCray, Hall, Wilson, and Fryer from John Collier, 21 December 1938, Office of Indian Affairs, RG 75, Box 15.

30. Compton, *The Swastika and the Eagle*, 11, 13; Diamond, *The Nazi Movement*, 224 and n. 2. In March 1940, Hitler held a private interview with Ross to discuss the latter's findings. Ross stated that Americans increasingly viewed war with Germany to be inevitable and that Nazi propaganda should be intensified among America's minority groups. Hitler later referred to Ross as "a very smart man who surely had many good ideas."

31. Interview with Willis Mizer, Chelsea, Oklahoma, Doris Duke Indian Oral History Collection, vol. 17, Norman, Okla.

32. Richard Neuberger, "The American Indian Enlists," 628–29.

33. "William Dudley Pelley: Racketeering among Indians," FBI Control Report, San Francisco Office, 19 March 1940, Files of the FBI (FOIPA). Also, Bell, *In Hitler's Shadow*, 90.

34. Franco, "Patriotism on Trial," 63.

35. "William Dudley Pelley: Racketeering among Indians," FBI Report, 19 March 1940; "American National Confederation Support for the American Indian Federation," undated Senate Committee Report, Office of Indian Affairs, RG 75, Box 15.

36. Ibid.

37. "Wake Up America!" July 1939, Office of Indian Affairs, RG 75, Box 17. This document was a synopsis of Towner's speech recorded by an unidentified agent of the BIA. See also, "William Dudley Pelley: Racketeering among Indians," FBI Report, 19 March 1940; Bell, *In Hitler's Shadow*, 90.

38. "Wake Up America!" July 1939.

39. Ibid.; "William Dudley Pelley: Racketeering among Indians," FBI Report, 19 March 1940.

40. "Memorandum: Nazi Propaganda among Indians," FBI Report, 8 July 1940, located in the file titled "James True" and released through FOIPA.

41. Laurence M. Hauptman, "Alice Jemison: Seneca Political Activitist, 1901–1964," *The Indian Historian* 12 (Summer 1979), 19; James S. Olson and Raymond Wilson, *Native Americans in the Twentieth Century* (Urbana: University of Illinois Press, 1984), 94.

42. "Testimony of Alice Lee Jemison," *Hearings before a Special Committee on Un-American Activities* (Washington DC: Government Printing Office, 1939), 2439. Also, Laurence Hauptman, *The Iroquois and the New Deal* (Syracuse, N.Y.: University of Syracuse Press, 1981), 41, 44.

43. Franco, "Patriotism on Trial," 62.

44. "Tribes Ask Congress to Let Indians Alone," *New York Times*, 1 August 1937, 3; Memo to the attorney general from Oscar L. Chapman, Acting Assistant Secretary of the Interior, 12 November 1940, and undated letter to the commissioner of Indian Affairs from Louis C. Mueller, Chief Special Officer, Office of Indian Affairs, Files of the Office of Indian Affairs, RG 75, Box 15.

45. "Ickes Mentioned by Witness," *New York Times*, 23 November 1938, 2; Alice Lee Jemison, the article stated, accused Ickes and other officials of communist inclinations. Her allegation centered on his affiliation with the ACLU, a "commie front" organization.

46. Untitled, unsigned, undated report to the Bureau of Indian Affairs, Files of the Office of Indian Affairs, RG 75, Box 15. The article did state, however, that the Salt lake Convention had recently concluded, thus placing the document's origin in that year.

47. Franco, "Patriotism on Trial," 71.

48. "To All Americans," *The James True Associates Bulletin*, October 1937, FBI Investigation File "James True," FOIPA.

49. Franco, "Patriotism on Trial," 59–60, 69.

50. Hauptman, "Alice Jemison," 16–17, 20.

51. "To All Americans," *The James True Associates Bulletin*, October 1937; "Testimony of Alice Lee Jemison," 2441.

52. "Testimony of Alice Lee Jemison," 2440.

53. Franco, "Patriotism on Trial," 60–61.

54. "Testimony of Alice Lee Jemison," 2440.

55. Ibid.

56. Ibid., 2442–43.

57. Ibid.

58. Hauptman, "Alice Jemison," 17.

59. Geoffrey S. Smith, *To Save a Nation: American Countersubversives in the New Deal and the Coming of World War II* (New York: Basic, 1973), 143–44; Hauptman, *The Iroquois and the New Deal*, 52.

60. "William Dudley Pelley: Racketeering among Indians," FBI Control Report, Washington Office, 15 January 1940, FOIPA.

61. Ibid.

62. William Dudley Pelley, *Indians Aren't Red!* (Asheville, N.C.: Pelley Publishers, 1939), 2. See also the *Asheville Citizen*, 7 June 1940.

63. Hauptman, *The Iroquois and the New Deal*, 139, 144; Memo to J. Edgar Hoover from Wendell Berge, Assistant Attorney General, 7 March 1941, and "William Dudley Pelley: Racketeering," FBI Report, 15 January 1940, FOIPA.

64. "The James True Associates," FBI Control Report, 11 December 1940, Washington DC, Office, FOIPA.

65. "Concerning Mr. True and His Peaceful Intentions," 19 June 1940, and letter to Edgar J. [sic] Hoover from Joseph Freeman of "New Masses Magazine," 12 August 1936, Files of the Office of Indian Affairs, RG 75, Box 6; "The James True Associates," FBI Control Report, 11 December 1940, FOIPA.

66. "Pogrom in September," 18 August 1936, Letter to Hoover from Joseph Freeman, 12 August 1936, FBI Report, "The James True Associates," 11 December 1940, Memo for the Director of the FBI from E. A. Tamm, "Regarding William Dudley Pelley," 7 October 7 1936, FBI files, FOIPA. Also, "Concerning Mr. True," Office of Indian Affairs, RG 75, Box 6.

67. Ibid. Also, "Senate Committee Report," Office of Indian Affairs, RG 75, Box 15; "Regarding James True Associates," FBI Report, 12 July 1941, FOIPA.

68. "Regarding the James True Associates," 12 July 1941 and "William Dudley Pelley," 17 June 1940, FBI Reports, FOIPA. Also, press release from the Office of Indian Affairs, 24 November 1939, and "Concerning Mr. True," 19 June 1940, Office of Indian Affairs, RG 75, Box 6.

69. "To Americans Everywhere," Circular from the James True Associates, October 1937, and "Statement of the Executive Committee of the General Jewish Council," 11 November 1940, FBI file "James True," FOIPA.

70. Undated, hand-written note from Collier to Ickes. This note demonstrates the thoroughness of Washington's investigation into Jemison's Nazi affiliation as it included her auto and motor identification numbers along with her license plate number. Also, "Senate Committee Report," and "Concerning Mr. True," Office of Indian Affairs, RG 75, Boxes, 6 and 15.

71. Letter to John Collier from Robert Marshall, U.S. Forest Service, Washington, 23 November 1938, and "Further Statement Upon Fifth Column Activities in Relation to Indian Legislation," 12 June 1940, Office of Indian Affairs, RG 75, Boxes 6 and 16, respectively.

72. Franco, "Patriotism on Trial," 80.

73. Letter to Collier from Robert Marshall, 23 November 1938 and "Further Statement Upon Fifth Column Activities in Relation to Indian Legislation," 12 June 1940.

74. Bell, *In Hitler's Shadow*, 90.

75. Ibid.

76. "William Dudley Pelley: Racketeering," FBI Report, San Francisco, 19 March 1940, and "Nazi Propaganda among Indians," 8 July 1940, FOIPA; Speech by Collier to the New York Rotary Club, 8 June 1944, Collier Papers, Yale University; "Senate Committee Report," Office of Indian Affairs, RG 75, Box 15.

77. Memo for the press from John Collier, 30 October 1940 and the Drew Pearson Column, *Washington Herald*, 4 May 1940, Office of Indian Affairs, RG 75, Box 6. See also Jemison's testimony before the House Committee on Indian Affairs, 13 June 1940.

78. "Regarding the James True Associates," 12 July 1941, and "William Dudley Pelley," 15 January 1940, FBI Reports, FOIPA; press release from the Office of Indian Affairs, 7 September 1939 and press release from the Department of the Interior, 26 April 1939, Office of Indian Affairs, RG 75, Box 7. An actual copy of the bill is located in FBI files.

79. Ibid.

80. Ibid.; also, Memo to Collier from Ickes, 23 November 1938, Collier Papers, Yale University. The $3,000 for $1 scheme had been discussed among AIF leaders, particularly by Jemison, for months prior to its introduction by Burdick.

81. Letters from Congressman Burdick to Harold Ickes, 28 April 1939 and 1 May 1939, Office of Indian Affairs, RG 75, Box 7.

82. Memo: "Nazi Propaganda among Indians," in FBI File "James True," 8 July 1940, FOIPA; "Newsletter," News Research Service, 18 December 1940, Office of Indian Affairs, RG 75, Box 15; Collier's speech to the New York Rotary Club, 8 June 1944, Collier Papers.

83. Undated letter to Walter Woehlke, Office of Indian Affairs, from Oliver LaFarge; letter to John Collier from Jesse Cornplanter, 12 June 1940, Office of Indian Affairs, RG 75, Box 6.

84. Franco, "Patriotism on Trial," 88, 98.

85. Letter to Captain Robert Coons, Joint Army-Navy Selective Service Committee, from John Collier, 18 October 1940; Memo to Harold Ickes from John Collier titled "Regarding Fifth Column Activities Among Indians," 6 June 1940, Office of Indian Affairs, RG 75, Box 6.

Chapter Three

1. Richard Neuberger, "The American Indian Enlists," *Asia and the Americas* 42 (November 1941): 629.

2. J. R. McGibony, "Indians and the Selective Service," *Public Health Reports* 57 (2 January 1942): 1; John Collier, "The Indian in a Wartime Nation," *Minority People in a Nation at War* (Philadelphia: American Academy of Political and Social Sciences, 1942), 29.

3. McGibony, "Indians and the Selective Service," 1; Robert Ritzenthaler, "The Impact of War on an Indian Community," *American Anthropologist* 45 (1943): 326; Duane K. Hale, "Uncle Sam's Warriors: American Indians in World War II," *The Chronicles of Oklahoma*, p. 410, 409.

4. "American Indians Fight the Axis," *New York Times*, 30 August 1942, 7; William Coffer, *Phoenix: The Decline and Rebirth of the Indian People* (New York: Van Nostrand Reinhold, 1979), 155.

5. Richard Neuberger, "The American Indian Enlists," 628–31; "Many Indians Sign Up for National Defense," *Indians at Work* 8 (March 1941): 10.

6. "Indians in the War for Freedom," *Indians at Work* 9 (April 1942): 6, 26.

7. Richard Neuberger, "The American Indian Enlists," 628–31; "Food and National Defense," *Indians at Work* 8 (August 1941): 20; "Indians Invest Millions in Bonds," *Indians at Work* 9 (May-June 1942): 31–32.

8. Thomas A. Britten, *American Indians in World War I: At Home and at War* (Albuquerque: University of New Mexico Press, 1997), 52–55.

9. Memo to Major Gareth Brainerd from Major R. R. Sedillo, Selective Service Manpower Division, 14 January 1941; letter to John Collier from Russell C. Chalton, state director of Selective Service, New Mexico, Selective Service System Central Files, RG 147, Entry 1, Box 136, File: "Indian Resistance, General, 1941," Military Field Branch of the National Archives, College Park, Maryland.

10. J. R. McGibony, "Indians and the Selective Service," 1; "American Indians Fight the Axis," *New York Times*, 30 August 1942, 7.

11. Carling Malouf, "Observations on the Participation of Arizona's Racial and Cultural Groups in World War II," *American Journal of Physical Anthropology* 5 (1947): 492; McGibony, "Indians and the Selective Service," 1.

12. Malouf, "Observations on the Participation of Arizona's Racial and Cultural Groups in World War II," 492.

13. Ibid., 493. Pulmonary problems proved the leading medical reason for the rejection of whites into the armed forces at Arizona recruitment centers, while respiratory complications most affected African Americans. Weight conditions, either excessive or insufficient, led the list in the rejection of Hispanics in the state.

14. Francis Case, "Sioux in the Service," *Congressional Record,* 77th Cong., 2nd sess., vol. 88, part 10 (Washington DC: Government Printing Office, 1942): A3727.

15. Ibid.

16. Memo for the Adjutant General from Wade H. Haislip, Assistant Chief of Staff, 17 May 1941; Letter to Oklahoma State Headquarters of Selective Service from Harry L. Deutsch, M.D., Stilwell, Oklahoma, 3 April 1941, Army Decimal File, RG 407, File 291.23, National Archives. Also, Carling Malouf, "Observations on the Participation of Arizona's Racial and Cultural Groups in World War II," 495.

17. Ibid.

18. Letter to Major Gareth Brainerd from Major R. R. Sedillo, 4 January 1941, Selective Service System Central Files, RG 147, Entry 1, Box 136, File: "Indian Resistance, General, 1941," Military Field Branch of the National Archives; "Indians at the Draft," *Indians at Work* 8 (November 1940): 28.

19. Britten, *American Indians*, 71.

20. Letter to William S. Iliff, Selective Service System, from John Collier, Office of Indian Affairs, RG 75, "Indians in World War II," Box 15, National Archives.

21. Letter to John Collier from Oliver LaFarge, 8 November 1940, Office of Indian Affairs, RG 75, Box 15.

22. Ibid.

23. Ibid.

24. Letter to the Secretary of War from the Acting Secretary of the Interior, 31 October 1940, Army Decimal File, RG 407, File 291.23, National Archives.

25. Letter to Clarence Dykstra, National Director of Selective Service, from Governor John E. Miles, New Mexico, 24 December 1940; Letter to the Commissioner of Indian Affairs from Superintendent Fryer, Window Rock, Arizona, 2 January 1941, Selective Service System Central Files, RG 147, Entry 1, Box 136, File: "Indian Reservations," Military Field Branch. Also, Letter to John Collier from Oliver LaFarge, 8 November 1940.

26. See Britten, *American Indians*, ch. 2: "Indian Soldiers and the Issue of Segregated Troops," 28–50.

27. Letter to U.S. Senator Hattie Caraway (Arkansas) from H. E. McGehee, 27 March 1941, Army Decimal Files, RG 407, File 291.23, National Archives.

28. Letter to Morris Burge, Acting Executive Director of the American Association on Indian Affairs, from John Collier, 26 October 1940, Office of Indian Affairs, RG 75, Box 15, National Archives; Letter to John Collier from Superintendent Fryer, 2 January 1941.

29. Memo to Chief of Staff from Brigadier General William E. Shedd, 10 November 1940; to Senator Hattie Caraway from J. A. Ulio, Acting Adjutant General, 7 April 1941, Army Decimal File, RG 407, File 291.23, National Archives.

30. The system as described was quickly altered once the United States entered World War II. Rather than regularly pull infantry companies and battalions off the front line to provide soldiers with rest, retraining, and the rebuilding of unit manpower and team cohesion, units tended to remain in combat zones and have replacements individually filtered through channels to the front. Commanders in the European Theater believed the replacement system to be the most effective method for maintaining constant combat strength, but the system did generate its own serious, unique problems-among them was the loss of unit cohesion. This issue serves as one prevalent theme throughout Stephen Ambrose's *Citizen Soldiers: The U.S. Army from the Normandy Beaches to the Bulge to the Surrender of Germany, June 7, 1944 to May 7, 1945* (New York: Simon and Schuster, 1997).

31. Letter to Collier from Major General E. S. Adams, 7 May 1941, Army Decimal File, RG 407, File 291.23, National Archives.

32. Burnett Hershey, "Indians on the Warpath," *The American Mercury* 59 (October 1944): 480; "Indians and the Draft," *Indians at Work* 8 (November 1940): 28; "Thirty Million Indians in North and South America May Be a Potential Force in Hemisphere Defense," *Indians at Work* 8 (December 1940): 15; "Detailed Figures on Indian Enlistments Show Extent of their Defense Efforts," *Indians at Work* 8 (April 1941): 19; "Records Relating to the Magazine *Indians at Work*," Records of the Bureau of Indian Affairs, RG 75, Entry 1005, Box 15, National Archives.

33. Oliver LaFarge, "Between the Two Wars Indians Have Gone Far Forward," *Indians at Work* 9 (March 1942): 13.

34. John Coffee, "American Indians in the War," *Congressional Record*, 77th Cong., 2nd sess., vol. 88, part 10 (Washington DC: Government Printing Office, 1942): A4386.

35. Ibid., A4385; *Annual Report of the Commissioner of Indian Affairs, 1942*, 239; John Collier, "Indians in a Wartime Nation," 30.

36. Ibid.

37. "Resolution," *Indians at Work* 7 (July 1940): 4.

38. Ibid.

39. Ibid.

40. Neuberger, "The American Indian Enlists," 630; *New York Times*, 30 December 1941, 38.

41. "Conference between representatives of the Office of Indian Affairs and the Superintendents and Members of the Tribal Council of the Colville Indian Reservation," 10 December 1941, Collier Papers, Reel 14, Yale University. Collier's estimate of the Polish population fell extremely short of actual numbers. More likely, he meant to refer to the number of Polish Jews who faced Hitler's brutality.

42. Interview of Cozy Stanley Brown in Broderick Johnson, ed., *Navajos and World War II* (Tsaile, Ariz.: Navajo Community College Press, 1978), 56.

43. Interview with Reverend James Martin Jr., an Osage from Tulsa, Oklahoma, Doris Duke Indian Oral History Collection, Norman, Okla. See also Vine Deloria's *God is Red* for a thorough explanation of Indian spirituality and its numerous points of contrast with Christianity.

44. Ibid.; Bruce Watson, "Jaysho, Moasi, Dibeh, Ayeshi, Hasclishnih, Beshlo, Shush, Gini," *Smithsonian* 24 (1993): 34–43; Johnson, ed., *Navajos and World War II*, 61

45. "Indians in the War for Freedom," *Indians at Work* 9 (April 1942): 30. Britten, *American Indians*, 51. Britten also argues that Indian soldiers who were sent to France in 1917 and 1918 were impressed with the cities they toured, the countryside, and the people they encountered. Travel overseas left an indelible imprint upon them and expanded their worldview. See also an earlier published article regarding Indian enlistment in the armed forces in World War I by Russell Lawrence Barsh, titled "American Indians in the Great War," *Ethnohistory* 38 (Summer 1991): 276–303.

46. See Tom Holm, *Strong Hearts, Wounded Souls: Native American Veterans and the Vietnam War* (Austin: University of Texas Press, 1996), 118–21. Holm also reveals that tribal and family traditions accounted for 75 percent of Indian enlistment during the Vietnam era. Sixty-two percent of the respondents cited the search for respect from other Indians as another major motivation for service in the armed forces and, particularly, in combat.

47. "Crows Honor Returned Tribal Hero," *Congressional Record*, 78th Cong., 1st sess., appendix, vol. 89, part 12 (Washington DC: Government Printing Office, 1943): A5642.

48. Tom Holm, "Fighting a White Man's War," *Journal of Ethnic Studies* 9 (Summer 1981): 75; James H. Howard, "The Dakota Indian Victory Dance," *North Dakota History* 18 (January 1951): 36.

49. *New York Times*, 26 January 1942, p. 9.

50. For example, see "Sioux Begin Sun Dance Today," 6 August 1945, 17; and "Army Frowns on Indian Wedding," *New York Times*, 19 September 1943, 24.

51. *Annual Report of the Secretary of the Interior, 1944*, 235–36; Harold Ickes, "Indians Have a Name for Hitler," *Collier's* 113 (15 January 1944): 58; "Honors for Heroism," a report compiled by John Collier, 1945, pp. 2, 4, Files of the Office of Indian Affairs, RG 75, Box 254, National Archives.

Chapter Four

1. "Many Indians Sign Up for National Defense," *Indians at Work* 8 (March 1941): 11.
2. Ibid.
3. Peter Farb, *Man's Rise to Civilization* (New York: E. P. Dutton, 1968), 122, 324–27.
4. "Indians Win Deferment for Their Rain Chief," *Washington Star*, 24 January 1941, news clipping, Files of the Office of Indian Affairs, RG 75, Box 16.
5. Farb, *Man's Rise to Civilization*, 325–27.
6. Letter to Superintendent Wilson, Holbrook, Arizona, from John Collier, 22 October 1940, Collier Papers, Reel 24, Yale University; Letter to William Zimmerman from John Collier, 22 October 1940, Office of Indian Affairs, RG 75, Box 16.

7. Letter to John Collier from Seth Wilson, 6 November 1940, Office of Indian Affairs, RG 75, Box 16; Letter to Collier from Seth Wilson, 24 December 1940, Selective Service Central Files, RG 147, Box 136, File "Indian Resistance," Military Field Branch, Suitland, Maryland.

8. Jere Franco, "Patriotism on Trial: Native Americans in World War II," (Ph.D. diss., University of Arizona, 1990), 120. Dr. Franco's dissertation is faithful to the Indian Bureau's determination regarding the cause of Hopi draft resistance; however, he does not place the Indians' argument in the larger, more appropriate, context of Hopi spirituality.

9. Ibid., 121.

10. Wilson to Collier, 24 December 1940.

11. Ibid.; Letter to Colonel Baker and Colonel Shattuck from Major Iliff, 18 July 1942, Selective Service Central Files, RG 147, Box 427, File: "Indians, 1942," Military Field Branch.

12. Leo W. Simmons, ed., *Sun Chief: The Autobiography of a Hopi Indian* (New Haven, Conn.: Yale University Press, 1942), 379.

13. Ibid.

14. John Collier, "Indians and the Draft," *Indians at Work* 8 (November 1940): 28.

15. Letter to John Collier from W. W. Shotwell, superintendent, Flathead Indian Reservation, Montana, 24 October 1941; Letter to Frank Knox from Harold Ickes, 18 August 1941, Files of the Office of Indian Affairs, RG 75, Box 16.

16. Letter to John Collier from Franklin Gritts, Farragut, Idaho, 30 October 1943, Office of Indian Affairs, RG 75, Box 16.

17. Helen C. Rountree, "The Indians of Virginia: A Third Race in a Biracial State," *Southeastern Indians Since the Removal Era,* ed. Walter L. Williams (Athens, Ga.: University of Georgia Press, 1979), 41.

18. "Draft Boards Told to Probe Ethnic Background of Indians," *Richmond (Virginia) Times-Dispatch,* 10 July 1942.

19. "The Gregory Petition," Legislative Records of King William County, 26 November 1842 and 12 January 1843, Virginia State Library and Archives, Richmond, Virginia.

20. E. Franklin Frazier, *The Negro Family in the United States* (Chicago: University of Chicago Press, 1966), 164–67, 184–89. The original was published in 1939.

21. Ibid.; see also Arthur H. Estabrook, *Mongrel Virginians: The Winn Tribe* (Baltimore, 1926) and Helen Rountree's original draft of "The Indians of Virginia," p. 24, File: "Indian Records," Virginia State Library.

22. "Indian Records," Virginia State Library.

23. U.S. Department of Commerce, "Population," *Fifteenth Census of the United States: 1930,* (Washington DC: Government Printing Office, 1933), 35, 37; "Population: Characteristics of the Non-White Population By Race," *Sixteenth Census of the United States: 1940* (Washington DC: Government Printing Office, 1943), 134, 136, 164–71, 266–75.

24. Theodore Stern, "Chickahominey: The Changing Culture of a Virginia Indian Community," *Proceedings of the American Philosophical Society* 96 (April 1952): 213; Noel P. Gist, *The Blending of Races: Marginality and Identity in World Perspective* (New York: John Wiley and Sons, 1972), 2012–20. Gist's work provides an excellent discussion of the identity crisis among the larger minority groups within the United States.

25. Max Stanton, "Southern Louisiana Survivors: The Houma Indians," 103, and Ernest C. Downs, "The Struggle of the Louisiana Tunica Indians for Recognition," 84, *Southeastern Indians Since the Removal Era*, ed. Walter Williams.

26. Letter to John Collier from Lawrence E. Lingley, general secretary of the Indian Rights Association, 26 February 1942; Letter to Judge J. Hoge Ricks from Robert Reeves, 28 February 1942, Frank Speck Papers, American Philosophical Society, Philadelphia.

27. Letter to Secretary Harold Ickes from J. L. Adams, January 1941, and Letter to James Price from J. L. Adams, 18 February 1941, "Indian Records," Virginia State Library.

28. Letter to General Lewis B. Hershey from Harold Ickes, 19 February 1941, "Indian Records."

29. Virginia Local Board Memorandum, 27 February 1941 and Letter to Commanding General, Third Corps Area, from Colonel Mills F. Neal, 28 March 1941, "Indian Records."

30. Letter to Commanding General, Third Corps, from Mills F. Neal, 26 February 1941; Letter to Mills F. Neal from E. R. Householder, 3 April 1941; Letter to Commanding General, Third Corps, from Adjutant General J. W. Boyer, 3 April 1941, Army Decimal File, RG 407, File 291.23, Military Field Branch of the National Archives, Suitland, Maryland.

31. Letter to Commanding General, Third Corps, from Mills F. Neal, 28 March 1941; Letter to General Hershey from Mills F. Neal, 26 July 1941, Army Decimal File, RG 407, File 291.23.

32. Letter to General Lewis B. Hershey from Mills F. Neal, 26 July 1941, Army Decimal File, RG 407, File 291.23.

33. "Memo 336: Proceedings for Classification of Persons Registered as Indians," Frank Speck Papers.

34. Ibid.

35. "Unregistered Men, 20 to 44, Will Sign Up on Feb. 16," 6 January 1942, 1; "Induction Call Sent to State Boards," 10 January 1942, 10; "220,000 Men Will Register," 11 January 1942, 11, *Richmond (Virginia) Times-Dispatch*. See also, Rountree, "Indians of Virginia," 39, and Gist, *The Blending of Races*, 199–200.

36. Letter to Governor Colgate Darden from O. Oliver Adkins, 28 August 1942, File: "Indians," Virginia State Library; Letter to the War Department from O. Oliver Adkins, 28 August 1942, Army Decimal File, RG 407, File 291.23.

37. Ibid.

38. "Disposition Form," 18 September 1942, Military Personnel Division, Army Decimal File, RG 407, File 291.23.

39. Stern, "Chickahominey," 212–14.

40. Letter to Kenneth W. Townsend from Helen C. Rountree, Old Dominion University, Norfolk, Virginia, 7 June 1990. Letter is held by this writer.

41. Interview with Chiefs Curtis Custalow (Mattaponi), Andrew Adams (Upper Mattaponi), O. Oliver Adkins (Chickahominey), and Assistant Chief Oliver Fortune (Pamunkey), Field Notes of Helen C. Rountree, 1975, File: "Indians," Virginia State Library.

42. Letter to Frank Speck from Charles Edgar Gilliam, 7 August 1943, Frank Speck Papers; Letter to Governor Colgate Darden from Lloyd Carr, 27 October 1942, Group 66, "Indians," Virginia State Library.

43. Letter to Dave E. Satterfield from John Collier, 6 May 1942, Office of Indian Affairs, RG 75, Box 16.

44. Ibid.

45. Letter To his Excellency Colgate W. Darden from the Council of the Pamunkey Tribe, 23 July 1942, File: "Indians," Virginia State Library.

46. Letter to Governor Darden from Lloyd G. Carr, 27 October 1942, Papers of Governor Colgate W. Darden, Virginia State Library.

47. Ibid.

48. Letter to Frank Speck from Otho S. Nelson, tribal chief at Indian Neck, Virginia, 31 October 1942, Frank Speck Papers; Letter to Kenneth Townsend from Helen C. Rountree, 7 June 1990.

49. Letter to Frank Speck from Charles Edgar Gilliam, 7 August 1943; Frank Speck, "Indian Notes," (1925), pp. 49–50, and "A Testimonial for Virginia Indians," Frank Speck Papers.

50. Ibid.

51. Letter to His Excellency, the President of the United States from Chief Otho S. Nelson, 19 November 1942, Army Decimal File, RG 407, File 291.23; Otho S. Nelson to Frank Speck, 2 December 1942, Frank Speck Papers; "3 Indians Are Sentenced in Draft Case," clipping, *Richmond (Virginia) Times-Dispatch*, Files of the Office of Indian Affairs, RG 75, Box 16.

52. Helen Rountree, "Indians of Virginia" (original draft), 43; Letter to Kenneth Townsend from Helen Rountree, 7 June 1990.

53. Maurice A. Mook, "Virginia Ethnology from an Early Relation," *William and Mary Quarterly* 23 (April 1943): 101; "Indians of the Old Dominion," clipping, *Richmond (Virginia) Times-Dispatch*, 7 July 1940, Papers of Governor Colgate W. Darden.

54. John Garland Pollard, "The Pamunkey Indians," 10, 16, and "Laws of the Pamunkey Indian Town," File: "Indians," Virginia State Library.

55. Ibid.

56. "Notes," Reel 10, and "A Testimonial for Virginia Indians," Frank Speck Papers; "Indians of the Old Dominion," Papers of Governor Colgate Darden.

57. "Notes," Frank Speck Papers; Letter to Governor Colgate Darden from Mrs. Letah Branch, 20 February 1945, Papers of Governor Colgate Darden.

58. "Memo for File," 26 March 1943, Reel 26, John Collier Papers.

59. Gilliam had been a longtime friend of Speck and had proven himself to be a "keen amateur linguist-historian"; Letter to Kenneth Townsend from Helen Rountree, 7 June 1990.

60. Letter to Frank Speck from Charles Gilliam, 7 August 1943, and "Notes," Reel 11, Frank Speck Papers. Nearly fifty years after his release, Oliver Fortune resided in Richmond and worked as a long-distance truck driver. "Quietly proud of having stood up for his Indian identity," Fortune seems to have been strengthened by his ordeal. Furthermore, Fortune credits both Speck and Gilliam for his own release from prison and turning public sentiment against Plecker. Letter to Kenneth Townsend from Helen Rountree, 7 June 1990. In 1991 this author solicited Mr. Fortune's comments regarding Plecker and his battle over race classification. All attempts failed. I was informed by one household member that Mr. Fortune did not wish to discuss the matter.

61. "Notes," Reel 11, Frank Speck Papers; W. Edwin Hemphill, ed., *Gold Star Honor Roll of Virginians in the Second World War* (Charlottesville, Va.: Virginia World War II Commission, 1947), 90.

62. U.S. Department of Commerce, "Population: Characteristics of the Non-White Population by Race," *Seventeenth Census of the United States: 1950* (Washington DC: Government Printing Office, 1953), 31.

Chapter Five

1. Peter Blaine Sr., *Papagos and Politics* (Phoenix: The Arizona Historical Society, 1982), 92–93.

2. "Papago Village Defies U.S. Conscription Law," *Arizona Daily Star*, 17 October 1940, news clipping, Files of the Office of Indian Affairs, RG 75, Box 16, National Archives, Washington DC. Blaine, *Papagos and Politics*, 91.

3. Ibid.

4. Blaine, *Papagos and Politics*, 100–1.

5. "Papago Village Defies U.S. Conscription Law," *Arizona Daily Star*, 17 October 1940. In 1917, a similar instance of draft resistance arose among the Goshute Indians who dwelled along the Nevada-Utah state border. As in the case of Pia Machita's tribe, the 150 Goshutes lived a rather isolated life and were virtually ignored by the Bureau of Indian Affairs. As a result, the tribe believed its members were not citizens of the United States and were not, therefore, subject to draft registration. For a detailed treatment of Goshute draft resistance, see Thomas Britten, *American Indians in World War I: At Home and at War* (Albuquerque: University of New Mexico Press, 1997), 67–69.

6. Ibid.

7. Ibid.

8. Blaine, *Papagos and Politics*, 101.

9. Ibid., 102–5.

10. Letter to John Collier from Dwight Gardin, 10 February 1941, Selective Service System Central Files, RG 147, Entry 1, Box 136, File: "Indian Resistance, 1941," Military Field Branch of the National Archives, Suitland, Maryland.

11. Ibid.

12. Letter to James McInerney, special assistant to the attorney general, Criminal Division, from John Collier, 20 February 1941, Selective Service Central Files, RG 147, Box 136, Entry 1, Military Field Branch.

13. "65 Seminoles Draft Prospects," 6 October 1940, p. 6 and "Seminoles Go in Hiding," 17 October 1940, p. 12, *New York Times*; Letter to the director of Selective Service from Vivian Collins, Brig. General, AGD, Office of the State Director of Selective Service, 11 June 1941, Selective Service Files, RG 147, Box 136, Entry 1; Letter to the attorney general from Herbert S. Phillips, U.S. attorney, 12 August 1943, Selective Service Files, RG 147, Box 816, Entry 1, File: "Indian Resistance, 1943," Military Field Branch.

14. Letter to Secretary of War Henry Stimson from Harold Ickes, 16 July 1941, Army Decimal File, RG 407, File 291.23, Military Field Branch.

15. Letter to Wendell Berge from Lt. Col. Glenn Parker, Alien Section of the Manpower Division, 24 September 1943, and Letter to director of Selective Service from Vivian Collins, 13 September 1943, Selective Service Files, RG 147, Box 816, Military Field Branch.

16. "Reds Say Arms Put Down Once, 'No Takum Up,'" *(Montana) Great Falls Tribune*, 18 October 1940, news clipping, and Letter to Captain Robert B. Coons, Joint Army-Navy Selective Service Committee, Washington, from John Collier, 18 October 1940, Files of the Office of Indian Affairs, RG 75, Box 16.

17. *Totus et al. v. the United States et al.*, 39 FS64, 1941, p. 7; Peter Farb, *Man's Rise to Civilization* (New York: Avon Books, 1968), 325–26.

18. *Totus v. the United States,* 7.

19. Ibid. Among the legal counselors representing Totus was E. A. Towner, who himself had earlier been the subject of FBI investigation for his alleged affiliation with Nazi propagandists inside the United States.

20. Ibid.

21. Ibid.

22. St. Regis Mohawk Council Resolution, 8 October 1940, Office of Indian Affairs, RG 75, Box 16. Laurence Hauptman, *The Iroquois Struggle for Survival: World War II to Red Power* (Syracuse, N.Y.: Syracuse University Press, 1986), 5.

23. "Indians Seek Draft Test," *New York Times*, 10 October 1940; 14 "Mohawks Resist Draft," *New York Times*, 14 October 1940; 14

24. Ibid.

25. Letter to Chief Clinton Rickard from Earl G. Harrison, director of registration, 23 October 1940, Army Decimal File, RG 407, File 291.23, Military Field Branch. Also, Letter to Representatives of the Mohawk Indians of St. Regis Reservation from John Herick, assistant to the commissioner of Indian Affairs, 12 October 1940; Collier statement in the *Buffalo Evening Star*, 15 October 1940, news clipping; Letter to the Chief of the St. Regis Mohawk Nation from John Collier, 16 October 1940, Office of Indian Affairs, RG 75, Box 16.

26. Press Release, 8 July 1940, John Collier Papers, Reel 31, Yale University, New Haven, Connecticut.

27. "Senecas Ready to Fight," *New York Times*, 16 October 1940, 9; "Say 1794 Treaty Exempts Indians," *New York Times*, 22 February 1941, 8. Hauptman, *The Iroquois Struggle for Survival,* 5.

28. *Ex Parte Green*, 123 FR 2d, (1941), 863; "Indians in Court Seek Rights as Free Nation," *New York Times*, 21 October 1941, 25.

29. *Ex Parte Green*, 862.

30. Ibid., 863. Laurence Hauptman, "Alice Jemison: Seneca Political Activist, 1902–1964," *The Indian Historian* 12 (Summer 1979): 18.

31. Ibid.; *United States of America, ex. Rel. Paul Diabo v. John B. McCandless*, Hearings on Petition, 19 March 1927, in the District Court of the United States for the Eastern District of Pennsylvania, Army Decimal File, RG 407, File 291.23, Military Field Branch.

32. U.S. Department of the Interior, Office of Indian Affairs, *Annual Report of the Commissioner of Indian Affairs, 1942,* 239.

33. Ibid., 239, 245.

34. Wilcomb E. Washburn, *The Indian in America,* (New York: Harper and Row, 1975), 51; Hauptman, *The Iroquois and the New Deal,* 56–57, 9.

35. "Decision of the Court," *Ex Parte Green,* Papers of Judge Jerome N. Frank, Group 222, Series 5, Box 78, Yale University, New Haven, Connecticut.

36. *New York Times,* 12 May 1941, 1; Washburn, *The Indian in America,* 51.

37. Helen M. Upton, *The Everett Report in Historical Perspective: The Indians of New York* (Albany: New York State American Revolution Bicentennial Commission, 1980), 79.

38. Ibid., 123, 4.

39. Ibid., 124, 4, 181, 82; Hauptman, *The Iroquois and the New Deal,* 6.

40. Upton, *The Everett Report,* 82; Barbara Graymont, ed. *Fighting Tuscarora: The Autobiography of Chief Clinton Rickard* (Syracuse, N.Y.: Syracuse University Press, 1973), 53.

41. *Ex Parte Green,* 862; Graymont, *Fighting Tuscarora,* 17.

42. *Ex Parte Green,* 862; *New York Times,* 15 May 1941, 14.

43. Telegram, Wilford Crouse to Franklin Roosevelt, 4 June 1941, and Letter from E. Watson to Wilford Crouse, 5 June 1941, Official File 296 (Indians, 1941–45), Franklin Delano Roosevelt Library, Hyde Park, New York.

44. *Ex Parte Green,* 862.

45. John Collier, "Iroquois Stand" (editorial), *The Washington Post,* 24 October 1941; "Iroquois Stand," *Indians at Work* 9 (November 1941): 35.

46. "'Decision of the Court' in *Ex Parte Green,*" Papers of Judge Jerome Frank, Yale University; *Ex Parte Green,* 864.

47. Ibid.

48. "The Opinion of Judge Thomas Swan," and "The Opinion of Harrie Brigham Chase," Papers of Jerome Frank, Group 222, Series 5, Box 95, Folder 751.

49. *Annual Report of the Commissioner of Indian Affairs, 1942,* 240.

50. "Six Nations Declare War on Axis," *Indians at Work* 9 (May-June 1942): 17; Hauptman, *The Iroquois Struggle for Survival,* 6.

Chapter Six

1. Bruce Watson, "Jaysho, Moasi, Debeh, Ayeshi, Hasclishnih, Beshlo, Shush, Gini," *Smithsonian* 24 (1993): 35.

2. Nash, *The American West Transformed,* 129; Oliver LaFarge, "Between the Two Wars Indians Have Gone Far Forward," *Indians at Work* 9 (March 1942): 11.

3. Insert for inclusion with the December 9, 1941, issue of *Indians at Work,* Records of the Bureau of Indian Affairs, File: "Indians at Work," RG 75, Entry 1005, Box 15, National Archives.

4. Duane K. Hale, "Uncle Sam's Warriors: American Indians in World War II," *The Chronicles of Oklahoma* 69 (Winter 1992): 411, 414; Neuberger, "The American Indian Enlists,"629; Ickes, "Indians Have a Name for Hitler," 58; "Six Nations Declare War on Axis," *Indians at Work* 9 (May-June 1942): 17; Charles L. McNary, "Our Indians at War,"

Congressional Record, 77th Cong., 2nd sess., vol. 88, part 10 (Washington DC: Government Printing Office, 1942), A3160.

5. John Coffee, "American Indians in the War," *Congressional Record*, 77th Cong., 2nd sess., vol. 88, part 10 (Washington DC: Government Printing Office, 1942), A4385; Hale, "Uncle Sam's Warriors," 412.

6. See the chapter titled "The Limits of Indian Sovereignty" in this book.

7. Collier, "The Indian in a Wartime Nation," 30; Virgil J. Vogel, *This Country Was Ours* (New York: Harper and Row, 1974), 334; Ickes, "Indians Have a Name for Hitler," 58.

8. "Honor for Heroes," report located in the Files of the Office of Indian Affairs, RG 75, Box 254, National Archives; Office of Indian Affairs, *Indians in the War* (Washington DC: Government Printing Office, 1945), 3.

9. Ibid.

10. "Two No. 1 Heroes Tell About War," *Chicago Daily News*, 24 April 1944, 4, news clipping, Files of the Office of Indian Affairs, RG 75, Box 253, National Archives; "Won Battle Alone and Gets the C.M.H.," *New York Times*, 13 April 1944, 5; *Indians in the War*, 2.

11. Albert Hemingway, *Ira Hayes, Pima Marine* (New York: University Press of America, 1988), xiii.

12. Interview of Arthur Stanton in Doris Paul, *The Navajo Code Talkers* (Philadelphia: Dorrance, 1973), 120.

13. Farb, *Man's Rise to Civilization*, 264. Farb states that the Pimas dwelled in Arizona for four thousand years, but other historians place the duration closer to nine thousand years. Regardless of their actual length of residency in that part of the United States, the point to be gleaned is that the Pima Indians were nonmigratory.

14. "Indians Fought on Iwo Jima," news clipping, Files of the Office of Indian Affairs, RG 75, Box 254, National Archives. The first American flag raised on Mt. Suribachi was quite small. Within a few hours after the fighting ended, Rosenthal learned that a larger flag was about to be hoisted in a reenactment of the original event. It was this staged raising that was captured on motion picture film.

15. Ibid.; Joseph Rosenthal and W. C. Heinz, "The Picture That Will Live Forever," *Collier's* 135 (February 1955): 65.

16. Hemingway, *Ira Hayes, Pima Marine*, xiv.

17. In conversation with this author, Grandee revealed his continued and heartfelt admiration for both Hayes and Stanton. He remains amazed that so many Native Americans freely and loyally served the United States given the history of Indian-white relations, and he genuinely cherishes the sacrifice made by the men who served in America's armed forces. The painting is as much an honor to America's servicemen as it is a tribute to Hayes individually. Telephone conversation between Joe Ruiz Grandee and Kenneth W. Townsend, 30 January 1999.

18. Paul, *The Navajo Code Talkers*, 119.

19. Stanley Vestal, "The Plains Indian and the War," *Saturday Review of Literature* 25 (16 May 1942): 9–10.

20. "A Choctaw Leads the Guerillas," news clipping, Files of the Office of Indian Affairs, RG 75, Box 254, National Archives; *Indians in the War*, 14–15.

21. *Indians at Work* 10 (July-August 1942): 17.

22. Ickes, "Indians Have a Name for Hitler," 58; Coffee, "American Indians in the War," A4385.

23. Elmer Thomas, "Indians as Soldiers," *Congressional Record*, 77th Cong., 2nd sess., vol. 88, part 10 (Washington DC: Government Printing Office, 1942), A4125–26.

24. Donald Peattie, "Lo Takes the Warpath," *The Reader's Digest* (July 1943): 78–80.

25. Burnett Hershey, "Indians on the Warpath Again," *The American Mercury* 59 (October 1944): 478.

26. Carl Hatch, "The Indian Question," *Congressional Record*, 80th Cong., 1st sess., vol. 93, part 11 (Washington DC: Government Printing Office, 1947), A1943.

27. Britten, *American Indians in World War I*, 99–100.

28. Jere Franco, "Publicity, Persuasion, and Propaganda: Stereotyping the Native American in World War II," *Military History of the Southwest* 22 (Fall 1992): 177.

29. Ibid.; "Thunderbird Men Back From Front," *New York Times*, 4 August 1945, 13; "Jonas Kills the Enemy Joins Up," *New York Times*, 26 February 1944, 6; "7th Army Indians in War Dance," *New York Times*, 25 July 1943, 30; "Indian Chief Leaps Ashore," *New York Times*, 16 September 1943, 5; Stephen Ambrose, *Citizen Soldiers* (New York: Simon and Schuster, 1997), 325.

30. "Annual Report of the Commissioner of Indian Affairs, 1944," *The American Indian and the United States: A Documentary History*, ed. Wilcomb Washburn (New York: Random House, 1973), 965–966.

31. Hershey, "Indians on the Warpath," 477.

32. Numerous similar stories filtered through the Allied ranks during the war; few were ever verified.

33. Richard Tregaskis, *Guadalcanal Diary* (New York: Random House, 1943), 32.

34. "Ceremonial Dances in the Pacific," *Indians in the War*, 12–13.

35. Paul, *The Navajo Code Talkers*, 16–17. An excellent presentation of selected Navajo veterans of World War II is Broderick Johnson, ed. *Navajos and World War II* (Tsaile, Arizona: Navajo Community College Press, 1978). This work is composed of interviews of eleven men and women who either served in the armed forces or in defense factories during the war years. Many of the interviews include recollections of pre-war years.

36. John Adair, "The Navajo and Pueblo Veteran: A Force for Cultural Change," *The American Indian* 4 (Winter 1947): 7–8.

37. Adair, "The Navajo and the Pueblo Veteran," 7.

38. Interview with a Navajo Marine in Paul, *The Navajo Code Talker*, 105.

39. Interview with Ray Blackbear, conducted by Julia Jordon, 2 February 1968, Doris Duke Indian Oral History Collection, T-184B, vol. 39, 223–24.

40. Interview with a Navajo Marine in Paul, *The Navajo Code Talkers*, 82.

41. Paul, *Navajo Code Talkers*, 82.

42. "5 Troopships Bring 6,124 Into Boston," *New York Times*, 4 August 1945, 12; *Indians in the War*, 3–6.

43. The experiences of World War I demonstrated the need for sophisticated programs. In 1924, the United States acquired the technology for encrypting and decrypting messages under the skilled guidance of Lt. Commander Laurence Frye Safford, USN. For detailed accounts, see John Toland's *Infamy* (New York: Berkley, 1982), Edwin T. Layton's

And I Was There (New York: William Morrow, 1985), and Gordon Prange's *At Dawn We Slept* (New York: Penguin, 1981).

44. "Many Indians Sign Up for National Defense," *Indians at Work* 8 (March 1941): 10; "Transmitting Messages in Choctaw," a report given to the commanding general, Thirty-sixth Division, from Colonel A. W. Bloor, commanding officer, 142nd Infantry, January 23, 1919, Special Research Histories, RG 120, Box 21, National Archives II, College Park, Maryland.

45. *New York Times*, 13 December 1940 and 16 February 1941; "Many Indians Sign Up for National Defense," p. 10; Elizabeth Sergeant, "The Indian Goes to War," *New Republic* 107 (30 November 1942): 709; John Collier, "Indians in the War for Democracy," 11 March 1942, Reel 32, Papers of John Collier.

46. Letter to the commandant, United States Marine Corps, from Philip Johnston, 14 September 1942, located in the appendix of Doris Paul's *The Navajo Code Talkers*. See also Peter Iverson's *The Navajo Nation* (Westport, Conn,: Greenwood Press, 1981).

47. Ibid; Henry Greenberg and Georgia Greenberg, *Carl Gorman's World* (Albuquerque: University of New Mexico Press, 1984), 60.

48. "Navajo Dictionary," (declassified DoD Dir 5200.9, revised as of 15 June 1945), 1–2, Marine Corps Archives, Quantico, Virginia; Murray Marder, "Navajo Code Talkers," *Indians in the War*, 25–27. In July 1971, surviving Navajo code talkers assembled for a reunion in Window Rock, Arizona. A record of that gathering was made. See Duke Indian Oral History Project, "They Talked Navajo: The United States Marine Corps Navajo Code Talkers of World War II, A Record of Their Reunion," (Window Rock, Ariz.: Navajo Tribal Museum, 1971), 1–58.

49. "Navajo Dictionary," 3, 4, 6; Greenberg and Greenberg, *Carl Gorman's World*, 59–60.

50. David Gomez, "Navajo Code Talkers," *New Mexico Magazine* (August 1990): 121. See also Margaret Bixler, *Winds of Freedom: The Story of the Navajo Code Talkers of World War II* (Darien, Conn.: Two Bytes, 1992).

51. Ibid., 125; "Navajo Code Talkers," 51–53, Service Research Histories, RG 120, Box 21, National Archives II. Eugene Roanhorse Crawford stood only a few yards from Ernie Pyle at the moment the journalist was killed on Ie Shima near Okinawa. "He was just a little ways from where I was," Crawford remembered.

52. Ibid. Thirty Navajos failed the communications course. Their inability to adapt to military life, a poor educational foundation, and failure to comprehend the code quickly eliminated most of these Indians from the program. In 1943, code training was transferred from Camp Elliot to Camp Pendleton. Also Greenberg and Greenberg, *Carl Gorman's World*, 63.

53. "Navajo Code Talkers," 51–53, Service Research Histories, RG 120, Box 21; "Code Talkers," Marine Corps Archives, Quantico, Va.

54. Greenberg and Greenberg, *Carl Gorman's World*, 62.

55. Memo to chief signal officer, Pentagon, from Colonel George L. Townsend, Army Signal Corps, 13 June 1943; Letter to assistant chief of staff, G-2, from Colonel Carter W. Clarke, General Staff, g-2, 8 October 1943; Memo to commanding general, Army Service Forces, from Major General Thomas T. Handy, assistant chief of staff, 18 October 1943; Memo to chief signal officer from Lt. H. C. Viken, Intelligence Branch, 30 December

1943; "Indians-Use in Communications Work," a report from Admiral Aubrey W. Fitch to commanding general, South Pacific, 15 January 1944, Service Research Histories, RG 120, Box 21, National Archives II.

56. Letter to Col. William F. Friedman from Paul Wheat, 10 March 1944, Service Research Histories, RG 120, Box 21.

57. "Report from Chief Signal Officer, South Pacific," 31 March 1944, Service Research Histories, RG 120, Box 21.

58. *Historical Statistics of the United States* (Washington DC: Government Printing Office, 1975), 1141.

59. Many tribal communities honored their sons who served in the war by publishing rosters identifying those who served and those who were killed or wounded in battle. The best example is Aren Akweks, *Six Nations Iroquois Confederacy Record (World War II)*, (Hogansburg, N.Y.: Akwesasne Mohawk Counselor Organization, 1946).

Chapter Seven

1. *Annual Report of the Commissioner of Indian Affairs*, 1942, 239.

2. Ibid.; Indians at Work 9 (July-August 1942): 18, 21; "Records Relating to the Magazine Indians at Work," Records of the Bureau of Indian Affairs, RG 75, Entry 1005, Box 15, National Archives; Interview with Myrtle Kincoln (Arapaho), November 1970, vol. 3, T-661, 3–4; Speech given at the Kiowa Veterans Day Celebration, vol. 3, T-641, 1–3, Doris Duke Indian Oral History Collection, Norman, Okla.

3. Letter to the commissioner of Indian Affairs from C. C. Graves, superintendent of the Blackfoot Indian Agency, Browning, Montana, 31 December 1940, Files of the Office of Indian Affairs, RG 75, "Indians and the War," Box 17, National Archives; "Crow Indians Offer All," Indians at Work 10 (July-September 1942): 12; Neuberger, "The American Indian Enlists," *Asia and the Americas* 42 (November 1942): 628–29; "Defense Fund Voted by the Klamath Tribal Council," New York Times, 28 February, 1941, 8.

4. Edward B. Liebow, "A Sense of Place: Urban Indians and the History of Pan-Tribal Institutions in Phoenix, Arizona," (Ph.D. diss., Arizona State University, 1986), 144; "Indians in the War for Freedom," Indians at Work 9 (April 1942): 6, 7, 11, 12, located in "Records Relating to the Magazine Indians at Work," Records of the Bureau of Indian Affairs, RG 75, Entry 1005, Box 15, National Archives; *Annual Report of the Commissioner of Indian Affairs*, 1942, 243; "Nineteen Pueblos Organize for War," Indians at Work 10 (July-September 1942): 11.

5. "Indians in the War for Freedom," 29.

6. John Collier, Address to the Tribal Council of the Colville Indian Reservation (Nespelem, Washington), 10 December 1941, Papers of John Collier, Reel 24, Yale University Library, New Haven, Conn.

7. John Collier, "Editorial," Indians at Work 9 (March 1942): 5 in "Records Relating to the Magazine Indians at Work," Records of the Bureau of Indian Affairs, RG 75, Entry 1005, Box 15, National Archives.

8. LaFarge, "Between the Two Wars Indians Have Gone Far Forward," 11, 14; "Records Relating to the Magazine Indians at Work," Records of the Bureau of Indian Affairs, RG 75, Entry 1005, Box 15, National Archives.

9. Letter from John Collier to Secretary Harold Ickes, 21 September 1942, Papers of John Collier, Drawer 3, Yale University; *Annual Report of the Commissioner of Indian Affairs*, 1942, 256; "Report of the Office of Indian Affairs, 1945," *Report of the Secretary of the Interior* (Washington DC: Government Printing Office, 1945), 247.

10. "Nineteen Pueblos Organize for War," *Indians at Work*, 11–14; *Annual Report of the Commissioner of Indian Affairs*, 1943, 280.

11. "Note on Possible Use of Negro Nurses in Indian Service," December 15, 1941, Papers of John Collier, Reel 25, Yale University.

12. "Indian Girls Now at War Jobs; Others Serving as Army Nurses," *New York Times*, 6 February 1943, 16; "Indian Women Await Foe," *New York Times*, 18 December 1941, 36; "Indian Women Harness Old Talents to New War Jobs," *Indians at Work* 10 (Fall 1942): 28.

13. "Indian Girls Now at War Jobs; Others Serving as Army Nurses," *New York Times*, 6 February 1943, 16; "Indian Women Harness Old Talents to New War Jobs," *Indians at Work* 10 (Fall 1942): 28; Grace Mary Gouveia, "'We Also Serve': American Indian Women's Role in World War II," *The Michigan Historical Review* 20 (Fall 1994): 153, 170–71.

14. Gouveia, "'We Also Serve'," 168–69.

15. Deborah Locke, "From Rabbit Snares to Riveters Guns: The Lives of Minnesota Ojibwe Women During World War II," (Honors Paper, University of Minnesota, 1990), 36–38.

16. Ibid., 39–42.

17. Gouveia, "'We Also Serve'," 160.

18. "Indian Girls Now at War Jobs,"16; "Indian Women Harness Old Talents to New War Jobs," 25–27; "Women Work for Victory," *Indians at Work* 13 (May 1945): 47–49; *Annual Report of the Commissioner of Indian Affairs*, 1943, 274; Deborah Locke, "From Rabbit Snares to Riveter Guns: The Lives of Minnesota Ojibwe Women During World War II" (Honors Paper, University of Minnesota, 1990), 36, 14–20.

19. "Indian Girls Now at War Jobs; Others Serving as Army Nurses,"16.

20. "Indians Now at War Jobs;" Locke, "From Rabbit Snares to Riveter Guns," 42–44.

21. "Indians Are Fit," *Indians at Work* 9 (March 1942): 13; "Indians Women Harness Old Talents,"25; "Indians Benefit From Indian Service Training," *Indians at Work* 9 (February 1942): 10.

22. Alan Sorkin, *The Urban American Indian* (Lexington, Mass.: D. C. Heath, 1978), 25, 42; Robert Ritzenthaler, "The Impact of War on an Indian Community," *American Anthropologist* 45 (1943): 325.

23. "Rail Note," *New York Times*, 6 June 1943, section II, 14; "Indian Girls Now at War Jobs,"16; "Annual Report of the Commissioner of Indian Affairs, 1943," *The American Indian and the United States: A Documentary History*, ed. Wilcomb E. Washburn (New York: Random House, 1973), 956–57; Ritzenthaler, "The Impact of War on an Indian Community,"326.

24. "Annual Report of the Commissioner of Indian Affairs, 1943," 956–57; Nash, *The American West Transformed*, 135; "Indians in the War for Freedom,"8; *Indians at Work*, 9 (March 1942): 17; William Coffer, *Phoenix: The Decline and Rebirth of the Indian People* (New York: Van Nostrand Reinhold, 1979), 148, 153; Iverson, *The Navajo Nation*, 49.

25. "Use of Indian Manpower," *Indians at Work* 13 (January 1945): 15–18; Nash, *The American West Transformed*, 136.

26. Although the Lumbees maintained a tribal structure and membership roster, federal recognition was not bestowed until autumn 1991.

27. William McKee Evans, "The North Carolina Lumbees: From Assimilation to Revitalization," *Southeastern Indians Since the Removal Era*, ed. Walter L. Williams (Athens, Ga.: University of Georgia Press, 1979), 63.

28. Laurence M. Hauptman, *The Iroquois Struggle for Survival: World War II to Red Power* (Syracuse, N.Y.: Syracuse University Press, 1986), 4–5.

29. "Annual Report of the Commissioner of Indian Affairs, 1943," 228; Alison Ricky Bernstein, "Walking in Two Worlds: American Indians and World War II" (Ph.D. diss., Columbia University, 1986), 133; Gouveia, "'We Also Serve'," 174.

30. Executive Order 8802 established the Fair Employment Practices Commission (FEPC) which was designed to protect African American opportunities for employment in defense plants. Boards were formed to hear complaints and make recommendations to assure fair treatment of all races associated with companies holding federal defense contracts. Attorney General Frank Murphy created the Civil Liberties Unit to guarantee the protection of civil rights to all citizens, but with particular emphasis on African Americans. Robert LaFollette's Civil Liberties Committee also served minority groups. Furthermore, the United States Census Bureau was desegregated and the Ramspeck Act on Civil Service, passed in 1940, prohibited racial discrimination in matters of employment.

31. Albert Russell Buchanan, *Black Americans in World War II* (Santa Barbara, Calif.: Clio Books, 1977), 29–30, 41.

32. Ibid., 43.

33. John Useem, Ruth Useem, and Gordon MacGregor, "Wartime Employment and Cultural Adjustments of the Rosebud Sioux," *Applied Anthropology: Problems of Human Organization* 2 (January-March 1943): 1, 4–5.

34. Ibid.

35. Ibid., 9.

36. "Indians Benefit from Indian Service Training," *Indians at Work* 9 (February 1942): 11; Lawrence R. Samuel, *Pledging Allegiance: American Identity and the Bond Drive of World War II* (Washington DC: Smithsonian Institution Press, 1997), 108–9.

37. Samuel, *Pledging Allegiance*, 109; *Indians at Work*, 9 (April 1942): 13; "Navajo Woman Weighs Scale," *New York Times*, 30 January 1942, 15.

38. "Indians Invest Millions in Bonds," *Indians at Work* 10 (September 1942): 31–32; *Annual Report of the Commissioner of Indian Affairs, 1942*, 238; Ickes, "Indians Have a Name for Hitler," 41–45; "Records Relating to the Magazine Indians at Work," Records of the Bureau of Indian Affairs, RG 75, Entry 1005, Box 15, National Archives.

39. "Food and National Defense," *Indians at Work* 8 (August 1941): 29.

40. "Jobless Youths Take Up Farming," *Indians at Work* 8 (August 1941): 30.

41. Ibid.; "At Cherokee the War Will Not Be Lost," *Indians at Work* 10 (July-September 1942).

42. Ibid.; *Annual Report of the Commissioner of Indian Affairs, 1943*, 241; *Annual Report of the Commissioner of Indian Affairs, 1946*, 366.

43. Ibid.; "Report of the Office of Indian Affairs, 1945," *Report of the Secretary of the Interior* (Washington DC: Government Printing Office, 1945), 240.

44. Ibid., 239; *Annual Report of the Commissioner of Indian Affairs*, 1943, 241.

45. Graham Taylor, *The New Deal and American Indian Tribalism: The Administration of the Indian Reorganization Act, 1934–1945* (Lincoln: University of Nebraska Press, 1980), 132; Fowler, *Arapahoe Politics: 1851–1978*, 197; *Annual Report of the Commissioner of Indian Affairs, 1944*, 239.

46. For example, three hundred families living in the Red Hill area of Horry County, South Carolina, were forced to sell their farm lands to the federal government so that pilots of the newly constructed Myrtle Beach Army Air Force Base would have a suitable bombing range nearby. Displaced families typically moved in with relatives until they were able to purchase suitable farmland elsewhere in the county.

47. Letter from John Collier to Secretary Harold Ickes, 22 June 1941, Papers of John Collier, Box 10, Yale University.

48. Allison Bernstein, *American Indians and World War II: Toward a New Era in Indian Affairs* (Norman: University of Oklahoma Press, 1991), 141–46.

49. *Annual Report of the Commissioner of Indian Affairs, 1945*, 238; *Annual Report of the Commissioner of Indian Affairs, 1946*, 365.

50. "Records Relating to the Magazine Indians at Work," Records of the Bureau of Indian Affairs, RG 75, Entry 1005, Box 15, File: "Indians at Work." Also "Indians in the War for Freedom," *Indians at Work* 9 (April 1942): 8.

51. *Indians at Work*, 9 (May-June 1942): 25–26.

52. For a thorough treatment of Japan's presence in Alaska and the Aleutian Islands and the forced relocation of Alaskan natives by the United States during the war, see Dean Kohlhoff, *When the Wind Was a River: Aleut Evacuation in World War II* (Seattle: University of Washington Press, 1995).

53. John C. Kirtland, *The Relocation and Internment of the Aleut People During World War II: A Case in Law and Equity for Compensation*, (Anchorage: Aleutian/Pribilof Islands Association, 1981), foreword.

Chapter Eight

1. *Annual Report of the Commissioner of Indian Affairs, 1942*, 255.

2. Memo to Harold Ickes from John Collier, 30 December 1941, Papers of John Collier, Reel 25, Yale University; Elizabeth Shepley Sergeant, "The Indian Goes to War," *New Republic* 107 (30 November 1942): 709.

3. "Department of Interior Appropriations Bill, 1943," *Congressional Record*, 77th Cong., 2nd sess., vol. 88, part 3 (Washington DC: Government Printing Office, 1942), 2994.

4. Ibid., 3001.

5. Ibid., 3001.

6. Letter to Milton Eisenhower from John Collier, 15 April 1942, Reel 25, Collier Papers; Sergeant, "The Indian Goes to War,"709.

7. Ibid.

8. Ibid.; "First Japanese Evacuee Colony is on Colorado River Indian Lands," *Indians at Work* 9 (April 1942): 13.

9. "First Japanese Evacuee Colony," 13.

10. Letter to Milton Eisenhower from John Collier, 15 April 1942, Reel 25, Collier Papers.

11. Letter to Bishop Shirley Nichols from John Collier, 22 April 1942, Reel 25, Collier Papers; Sergeant, "The Indian Goes to War," 709; "First Japanese Evacuee Colony," 12–14.

12. John Collier, "Address to the Residents of the Colorado Relocation Facility," 27 June 1942, Records of the Bureau of Indian Affairs, RG 75, Box 17, National Archives.

13. Memo to Secretary Ickes from John Collier, 9 October 1942, Reel 24, Collier Papers.

14. Letter to C. F. Palmer from John Collier, 9 October 1942; Memo to Secretary Ickes from John Collier, 9 October 1942, Reel 24, Collier Papers.

15. Letter to Mrs. Charles Dietrich from John Collier, 1 November 1943, Reel 12, Collier Papers.

16. Within military circles, there was serious consideration in the immediate postwar era of maintaining a special program within the armed forces for Indian code talking. By the early 1950s, however, the idea was put to rest.

17. Letters to Mrs. Charles Dietrich from John Collier, 1 November 1943, Reel 12, Collier Papers.

18. "The Apache Goes to War," *New York Times*, 23 October 1942, 20.

19. Rex Stout, "Senate Report 310: A Letter to Senator Elmer Thomas," *The American Indian* 1 (Fall 1944); Harold Fey and D'Arcy McNickle, *Indians and Other Americans: Two Ways of Life Meet* (New York: Harper and Row, 1970), 148–49.

20. Ibid. Although the IRA had been severely criticized by some opponents as an experiment in socialism, conceived by "pinkish" politicians, this particular line of argument proved rather muted during America's alliance with the Soviet Union. However, it was loudly voiced once more as the war drew to a close and in the immediate postwar period.

21. Letter to Mrs. Cutting from John Collier, 28 October 1943, Papers of John Collier, Reel 12; undated, untitled statement by John Collier, Reel 31; Yale University.

22. Undated, untitled statement by John Collier, Reel 31, Papers of John Collier, Yale University.

23. Oliver LaFarge, "The Brothers Big Elk," *The American Indian* 1 (November 1943): 17.

24. Rex Stout, "Writer's War Board Protests," *The American Indian* 3 (Spring 1944): 22–23; Jere Franco, "Empowering the World War II Native American Veteran: Postwar Civil Rights," *Wicazo State Review* 9 (Spring 1993): 34.

25. Transcript of radio address by John Collier, 1944, Reel 31; Collier's remarks as recorded in "American Indians Alarmed at Report from Home Front," *Star*, 28 October 1944, Reel 12, Papers of John Collier.

26. Skudder Mekeel, "The American Indian as a Minority Group Problem," *The American Indian* 3 (Fall 1944): 3–11; Mekeel, "An Appraisal of the Indian Reorganization Act," *American Anthropologist* 46 (1944): 209–17.

27. Thomas W. Cowger, "'The Crossroads of Destiny': The NCAI's Landmark Struggle to Thwart Coercive Termination," *American Indian Culture and Research Journal* 20:4 (1996): 121–22.

28. Ibid., 122.

29. "A Common Voice," *The American Indian* 8 (Spring 1954): 44.

30. "Urges Indian Vote in 2 States," *New York Times*, 21 September 1943, 26.

31. "Indian Affairs," Hearings Before the House of Representatives Subcommittee on Indian Affairs, 78th Cong., 2nd sess., 1944, p. 345.

32. Interview with Ms. Hazil Lohah Harper, Doris Duke Indian Oral History Collection, vol. 40, T-53A, 10–11.

33. Draft of a paper written by John Collier, Reel 31, Part 2, Series 3, HMI03, Papers of John Collier.

34. Letter to President Franklin Roosevelt from Secretary Ickes, 28 December 1942, Reel 14, Papers of John Collier; John Collier, "What the American Indians Will Do in the Future for Themselves and for Us," *Predictions of Things to Come*, Reel 32, Papers of John Collier.

35. "Memorandum Concerning the Foreign Relief and Rehabilitation Administration," 12 December 1942, Reel 32, Papers of John Collier.

36. Executive Order, "Providing for the Training of Civilian Personnel for Service in Occupied and Liberated Areas," January 1943, Reel 31, Papers of John Collier.

37. "To the Secretary of the Interior from the President of the United States," Reel 14, Papers of John Collier. No specific date cited, but the document is filed with 1943 materials.

38. Memo to Harold Ickes from John Collier, Reel 14, Papers of John Collier.

39. Memo to John Collier from Mr. Harper, 28 December 1942, Reel 14; John Collier, "Our Red Indians in the War for Democracy," (address to the New York Rotary Club), 8 June 1944, Reel 32, Papers of John Collier.

40. "To the Secretary of the Interior from the President of the United States," Reel 14, Papers of John Collier.

41. John Collier, "What the Indians Will Do in the Future for Themselves and for Us," Reel 32, Collier Papers.

42. Letter to John Collier from Archie Phinney, superintendent at Window Rock, Arizona, 1 September 1943, Reel 16, Collier Papers.

43. Letter to President Roosevelt from John Collier, 19 January 1945; Letter to John Collier from Franklin D. Roosevelt, 22 January 1945, Reel 16, Collier Papers.

Chapter Nine

1. Thomas Mails, ed., *Fools Crow* (Garden City, N.Y.: Doubleday, 1980), 153.

2. Letter to John Collier from Archie Phinney, Reel 16, Collier Papers.

3. Nash, *The American West Transformed*, 140.

4. Bernstein, "Walking in Two Worlds: American Indians and World War II," 242.

5. Mails, ed., *Fools Crow*, 153.

6. Report from the Bureau of Indian Affairs, 1 January 1944, and cited in Archie Phinney's article, "Problem of the 'White Indians' of the United States," 1 June 1945, Reel 16, Collier Papers. Also Bureau of the Census, "Non-White Population by Race," and "Occupational Characteristics," Seventeenth *Census of the United States: 1950* (Washington DC: Government Printing Office, 1953), 32, 72, 183, 215.

7. George Boyce, *When Navajo Had Too Many Sheep: The 1940s* (San Francisco: The Indian Historian Press, 1972), 229–30.

8. John Adair, "The Navajo and Pueblo Veteran: A Force for Cultural Change," *The American Indian* 4 (Winter 1947): 5–11.

9. Oliver LaFarge, "Address at the Annual Meeting of the Association on American Indian Affairs," *The American Indian* 4 (Fall 1947): 7–8; Frances P. Bolton, "Justice to the Indians," *Congressional Record*, 80th Cong., 1st sess., vol. 93, part 11 (Washington DC: Government Printing Office, 1947), A2720–21.

10. Ibid., 7, 9–10.

11. Oliver LaFarge, "They Were Good Enough for the Army," *Harper's Magazine* 195 (November 1947): 444–45.

12. Ibid., 448; Paul, *The Navajo Code Talkers*, 111; Nash, *The American West Transformed*, 146–47.

13. Evon Z. Vogt, "Between Two Worlds: A Case Study of a Navajo Veteran," *The American Indian* 5 (Summer 1949): 13–15.

14. Ibid., 17.

15. Ibid., 17–19.

16. Francis Case, "Indian Veterans' Chance for School," *Congressional Record*, 79th Cong., 2nd sess., vol. 92, part 10 (Washington DC: Government Printing Office, 1946), A2255; Karl Stefan, "Set the American Indians Free," *Congressional Record*, 79th Cong., 1st sess., vol. 91, part 13 (Washington DC: Government Printing Office, 1945), A4815; Harlan Bushfield, "The American Indian," *Congressional Record*, 79th Cong., 1st sess., vol. 91, part 12 (Washington DC: Government Printing Office, 1945), A3648.

17. William A. Brophy, "The Office of Indian Affairs," *Annual Report of the Secretary of the Interior, 1945*, 233–50.

18. U.S. Senate, *Hearings on Senate Resolution 41*, 80th Cong., 1st sess., 1947, 547.

19. Donald Fixico, *Termination and Relocation: Federal Indian Policy, 1945–1960* (Albuquerque: University of New Mexico Press, 1986), 28. Fixico convincingly traces the origin of "termination" to the earliest periods in Indian-white relations and provides a thorough and conclusive study of the course and conduct of the policies of termination and relocation following World War II.

20. See Francis Moul, "William McKinley Holt and the Indian Claims Commission," *Great Plains Quarterly* 16 (Summer 1996): 169–81.

21. Boyce, *When Navajo Had Too Many Sheep*, 229–30.

22. Iverson, *The Navajo Nation*, 50.

23. Boyce, *When Navajo Had Too Many Sheep*, 186.

24. Ibid., 190–91.

25. Interview of Alfred Dubray, Brule Sioux, by Herbert T. Hoover, 28 July 1970, "The Indian New Deal and the Years That Followed: Three Interviews," *The Plains Indians of the Twentieth Century*, ed. Peter Iverson (Norman: University of Oklahoma Press, 1985), 131.

26. For a detailed treatment of the NCAI in the 1950s, see Jere Franco, "Empowering the World War II Native American Veteran: Postwar Civil Rights," *Wicazo State Review* 9 (Spring 1993): 32–36; Thomas W. Cowger, "'The Crossroads of Destiny,': The NCAI's Landmark Struggle to Thwart Coercive Termination," *American Indian Culture and Research Journal* 20:4 (1996): 121–44.

Selected Bibliography

Government Documents

Bureau of Indian Affairs. *Indians at Work.*
Department of Commerce. *Statistical Abstract of the United States.* Washington DC: Government Printing Office, 1924.
Department of Commerce. *Statistical Abstract of the United States.* Washington DC: Government Printing Office, 1929.
Department of Commerce. *Statistical Abstract of the United States.* Washington DC: Government Printing Office, 1942.
Department of the Interior. *Annual Report of the Commissioner of Indian Affairs,* 1941–1948.
Ex Parte Green. 123 FR 2d., 1941.
Fitzpatrick, Edward A. *Selective Service in Wartime: Second Report of the Director of Selective Service, Lewis B. Hershey, 1941–1942.* Washington DC: Government Printing Office, 1943.
Great Plains Committee. *The Future of the Great Plains.* Washington DC: Government Printing Office, 1936.
"Indian Affairs." *Hearings before the House of Representatives Subcommittee on Indian Affairs.* Washington DC: Government Printing Office, 1944.
Office of Indian Affairs. *Indians in the War.* Washington DC: Government Printing Office, 1945.
"Testimony of Alice Lee Jemison," *Hearings before a Special Committee on Un-American Activities.* Washington DC: Government Printing Office, 1939.
Totus et al. v. the United States et al. 39FS64, 1941.
U.S. Congress. House of Representatives. 77th Cong., 2d sess. *Congressional Record.* Vol. 88, part 10.
U.S. Congress. House of Representatives. 78th Cong., 1st sess. *Congressional Record.* Vol. 89, part 12.
U.S. Congress. House of Representatives. 80th Cong., 1st sess. *Congressional Record.* Vol. 93, part 11.

U.S. Department of Commerce. "Population: Characteristics of the Non-White Population by Race," *Fifteenth Census of the United States: 1930.* Washington DC: Government Printing Office, 1933.

U.S. Department of Commerce. "Population: Characteristics of the Non-White Population by Race," *Sixteenth Census of the United States: 1940.* Washington DC: Government Printing Office, 1943.

U.S. Department of Commerce. "Population: Characteristics of the Non-White Population by Race," *Seventeenth Census of the United States: 1950.* Washington DC: Government Printing Office, 1953.

U.S. Marine Corps. *Navajo Dictionary.* Washington DC: Government Printing Office, 1945.

Manuscript Collections

Army Decimal File. Record Group 407. National Archives II, College Park, Maryland (formerly, Military Field Branch, Suitland, Maryland).

Doris Duke Indian Oral History Collection. University of Oklahoma, Norman, Oklahoma.

Executive Papers of Colgate Darden. Virginia State Library and Archives, Richmond, Virginia.

Frank Speck Papers. American Philosophical Society, Philadelphia.

Franklin Delano Roosevelt Papers (Official Files). Franklin Delano Roosevelt Library, Hyde Park, New York.

"Indians." Virginia State Library and Archives, Richmond, Virginia.

John Collier File. American Philosophical Society, Philadelphia.

Legislative Records of King William County, 1842–1843. Virginia State Library and Archives, Richmond, Virginia.

Papers of Jerome Frank. Yale University Library, New Haven, Connecticut.

Papers of John Collier. Yale University Library, New Haven, Connecticut.

Records of the Bureau of Indian Affairs. Record Group 75. National Archives, Washington DC.

Records of the Federal Bureau of Investigation. File: "Alice Lee Jemison." Department of Justice, Washington DC.

Records of the Federal Bureau of Investigation. File: "James True." Department of Justice, Washington DC.

Records of the War Relocation Authority. Record Group 210. National Archives, Washington DC.

Selective Service System Central Files. Record Group 147. National Archives II, College Park, Maryland (formerly, Military Field Branch, Suitland, Maryland.)

Service Research Histories. Record Group 147. National Archives II, College Park, Maryland.

Newspapers, Periodicals, and Journals

"A Common Voice." *The American Indian* 8 (Spring 1954): 44.

Adair, John. "The Navajo and Pueblo Veteran." *The American Indian* 4 (1947): 5–11.

Adair, John and Evon Vogt. "Navajo and Zuni Veterans." *American Anthropologist* 51 (1949): 547–68.

"American Indians Fight the Axis." *New York Times*, 30 August 1942, 7.

"Army Frowns on Indian Wedding." *New York Times*, 19 September 1943, 24.

Austin, Mary. "The Canoe that the Partridge Made." *Golden Book Magazine* 20 (October 1934): 417–18.

Barsh, Russell Lawrence. "American Indians in the Great War." *Ethnohistory* 9:38 (Summer 1991): 276–303.

Bushnell, John. "From American Indian to Indian American." *American Anthropologist* 70 (1968): 1106–16.

Cancroft, Richard. "The American West of Karl May." *American Quarterly* 19 (Winter 1967): 249–58.

"Civilizing the Indian." *The Nation* 138 (10 January 1934): 33–34.

Collier, John. "The Indian in a Wartime Nation." *The Annals of the American Academy* 223 (1942): 31–34.

_____. "The Indian Affairs Outlook." *American Indian Defense Bulletin* (8 May 1926).

_____. "The Vanquished Indian." *The Nation* 26 (11 January 1928): 38–41.

Cowger, Thomas. "The Crossroads of Destiny': The NCAI's Landmark Struggle to Thwart Coercive Termination." *American Indian Culture and Research Journal* 20 (1996): 121–44.

"Draft Boards Told to Probe Ethnic Background of Indians." *Richmond (Virginia) Times-Dispatch*, 10 July 1942, 4.

Franco, Jere. "Empowering the World War II Native American Veteran: Postwar Civil Rights." *Wicazo State Review* 9 (Spring 1993): 32–36.

_____. "Publicity, Persuasion and Propaganda." *Military History of the Southwest* 22 (Fall 1992): 173–87.

Gerken, Edna A. "Development of a Health Education Program." *American Journal of Public Health* 30 (August 1940): 915–20.

Gomez, David. "Navajo Code Talkers." *New Mexico Magazine* (August 1990): 116–22.

Gouveia, Mary. "'We Also Serve': American Indian Women's Role in World War II." *Michigan Historical Review* 20 (Fall 1944): 153–82.

Gower, Calvin. "The CCC Indian Division." *Minnesota History* 43 (Spring 1972): 3–13.

Guthrie, M. C. "The Health of the American Indian." *Public Health Reports* 44 (19 April 1929): 945–57.

Hale, Duane K. "Uncle Sam's Warriors." *Chronicles of Oklahoma* 69 (Winter 1992): 408–29.

Hauptman, Laurence M. "Alice Lee Jemison: Seneca Political Activist, 1901–1964." *The Indian Historian* 12 (Summer 1979).

Hershey, Burnet. "Indians on the Warpath." *The American Mercury* 59 (October 1944): 477–80.

Hoffman, Frederick L. "Are the Indians Dying Out?" *American Journal of Public Health* 20 (June 1930): 609–14.

Holm, Tom. "Fighting a White Man's War." *Journal of Ethnic Studies* 9 (Summer 1981): 69–81.

Howard, James H. "The Dakota Indian Victory Dance." *North Dakota History* 18 (January 1951): 31–40.

Ickes, Harold. "Indians Have a Name for Hitler." *Colliers* (January 1944): 41–45.

"Ickes Mentioned by Witness." *New York Times*, 23 November 1938, 2.

"Indian Chief Leaps Ashore." *New York Times*, 16 September 1943, 5.

"Indian Girls Now at War Jobs." *New York Times*, 6 February 1943, 16.

"Indians in Court Seek Rights as Free Nation." *New York Times*, 21 October 1941, 25.

"Indians in the CCC Camps." *Missionary Review of the World* 56 (December 1933): 611.

"Induction Call Sent to State Boards." *Richmond (Virginia) Times-Dispatch*, 10 January 1942, 10.

"Jonas Kills the Enemy Joins Up." *New York Times*, 26 February 1944, 6.

LaFarge, Oliver. "Address at the Annual Meeting of the Association on American Indian Affairs." *The American Indian* 4 (November 1947): 6–10.

———. "The American Indian's Revenge." *Current History* 40 (May 1934): 163–68.

———. "The Brothers Big Elk." *The American Indian* 1 (November 1943): 15–17.

———. "Revolution with Reservations." *New Republic* 84 (9 October 1935): 232–34.

———. "They Were Good Enough for the Army." *Harper's Magazine* (November 1947): 22–27.

Leighton, Dorothea C. "As I Knew Them: Navajo Women in 1940." *American Indian Quarterly* 6 (1982): 34–51.

Malouf, Carling. "Observations on the Participation of Arizona's Racial and Cultural Groups in World War II." *American Journal of Physical Anthropology* 5 (1947).

McGibony, J. R. "Indians and the Selective Service." *Public Health Reports* 57 (2 January 1942): 1–7.

Mekeel, Scudder. "An Appraisal of the Indian Reorganization Act." *American Anthropologist* 46 (1944): 209–17.

———. "The American Indian as a Minority Group Problem." *The American Indian* 3 (Fall 1944): 3–11.

Mook, Maurice A. "Virginia Ethnology From an Early Relation." *William and Mary Quarterly* 23 (April 1943): 193–208.

Morgan, J. C. "A Navajo Dissenter." *Christian Century* 51 (3 October 1934): 1379–80.

Murray, Paul T. "Who Is an Indian? Who Is a Negro?" *Virginia Magazine of History and Biography* 95 (April 1987): 215–31.

"Navajo Woman Weighs Scales." *New York Times*, 30 January 1942, 15.

Neuberger, Richard. "The American Indian Enlists." *Asia and the Americas* 42 (November 1942): 628–31.

Parman, Donald. "The Indian and the Civilian Conservation Corps." *Pacific Historical Review* 40 (February 1971): 39–57.

Ritzenthaler, Robert. "The Impact of War on an Indian Community." *American Anthropologist* 45 (1943): 325–26.

Rosenthal, Joseph, and W. C. Heinz. "The Picture That Will Last Forever." *Collier's* 135 (February 1955): 65.

"Say 1794 Treaty Exempts Indians." *New York Times*, 22 February 1941, 8.

"Seminoles Go In Hiding." *New York Times*, 17 October 1940, 12.

"Senecas Ready to Fight." *New York Times*, 16 October 1940, 9.

Sergeant, Elizabeth Shepley. "A New Deal for the Indian." *New Republic* 95 (June 1938): 151–54.

_____. "The Indian Goes to War." *New Republic* 107 (30 November 1942): 708–9.

"Sioux Begin Sun Dance Today." *New York Times*, 6 August 1945, 17.

Stern, Theodore. "Chickahominey: The Changing Culture of a Virginia Indian Community." *Proceedings of the American Philosophical Society* 96 (April 1952): 157–225.

Stout, Rex. "Senate Report 310: A Letter to Senator Elmer Thomas." *The American Indian* 1 (Fall 1944).

_____. "Writer's War Board Protests." *The American Indian* 3 (Spring 1944): 22–23.

"Thunderbird Men Back from the Front." *New York Times*, 4 August 1945, 13.

Townsend, James G. "Disease and the Indian." *The Scientific Monthly* 47 (December 1938): 479–95.

"Tribes Ask Congress to Let Indians Alone." *New York Times*, 1 August 1937, 3.

"Unregistered Men, 20 to 44, Will Sign Up on Feb. 16." *Richmond (Virginia) Times-Dispatch*, 6 January 1942, 6.

Useem, John. "Wartime Employment and Cultural Adjustments of the Rosebud Sioux." *Applied Anthropology* 2 (1943): 1–9.

Vestal, Stanley. "The Plains Indian and the War." *Saturday Review of Literature* 25 (16 May 1942): 9–10.

Vogt, Evon Z. "Between Two Worlds: A Case Study of a Navajo Veteran." *The American Indian* 5 (1949): 13–21.

Weeks, Charles J. "The Eastern Cherokees and the New Deal." *North Carolina Historical Review* 53 (1976): 303–19.

"Won Battle Alone and Gets the C. M. H." *New York Times*, 13 April 1944, 5.

Books and Dissertations

Akweks, Aren. *Six Nation Iroquois Confederacy Record (World War II)*. Hogansburg, N.Y.: Akwesasne Mohawk Counselor Organization, 1946.

Ambrose, Stephen. *Citizen Soldiers: The U.S. Army from the Normandy Beaches to the Bulge to the Surrender of Germany*. New York: Simon and Schuster, 1997.

Bell, Leland V. *In Hitler's Shadow: The Anatomy of American Nazism*. New York: Kennikat Press, 1973.

Bernstein, Alison Ricky. "Walking in Two Worlds: American Indians and World War II." Ph.D. diss., Columbia University, 1986.

_____. *American Indians and World War II: Toward a New Era in Indian Affairs* Norman: University of Oklahoma Press, 1991.

World War II and the American Indian

Billington, Ray Allen. *Land of Savagery, Land of Promise: The European Image of the American Frontier*. New York: W. W. Norton, 1981.
_____. *Westward Expansion*. New York: Macmillan, 1982.
Bixler, Margaret. *Winds of Freedom: The Story of the Navajo Code Talkers of World War II*. Darien, Conn.: Two Bytes, 1992.
Blaine, Peter. *Papagos and Politics*. Phoenix: The Arizona Historical Society, 1982.
Boyce, George A. *When Navajo Had Too Many Sheep: The 1940s*. San Francisco: The Indian Historian Press, 1974.
Britten, Thomas A. *American Indians in World War I: At Home and at War*. Albuquerque: University of New Mexico Press, 1997.
Buchanan, Albert Russell. *Black Americans in World War II*. Santa Barbara, Calif.: Clio, 1977.
Burnette, Robert. *The Road to Wounded Knee*. New York: Bantam, 1974.
Cash, Joseph, and Herbert Hoover, eds. *To Be an Indian: An Oral History*. New York: Holt, Rinehart, and Winston, 1971.
Coffer, William E. *Phoenix: The Decline and Rebirth of the Indian People*. New York: Van Nostrand Reinhold, 1979.
Collier, John. *Indians of the Americas*. New York: W. W. Norton, 1947.
Compton, James V. *The Swastika and the Eagle*. Boston: Houghton Mifflin, 1967.
Diamond, Sander A. *The Nazi Movement in the United States, 1924–1941*. Ithaca, N.Y.: Cornell University Press, 1974.
Dippie, Brian W. *The Vanishing American: White Attitudes and United States Indian Policy*. Middletown, Conn.: Wesleyan University Press, 1982.
Duke Indian Oral History Project. *They Talked Navajo: The United States Marine Corps Navajo Code Talkers of World War II, a Record of Their Reunion*. Window Rock, Ariz.: Navajo Tribal Museum, 1971.
Farb, Peter. *Man's Rise to Civilization*. New York: Avon, 1968.
Fey, Harold, and D'Arcy McNickle. *Indians and Other Americans*. New York: Harper and Row, 1970.
Fixico, Donald. *Termination and Relocation: Federal Indian Policy, 1945–1960*. Albuquerque: University of New Mexico Press, 1986.
Fowler, Loretta. *Arapahoe Politics: 1851–1978*. Lincoln: University of Nebraska Press, 1982.
Franco, Jere. "Patriotism on Trial: Native Americans and World War II." Ph.D. diss., University of Arizona, 1990.
Frazier, E. Franklin. *The Negro Family in the United States*. Chicago: University of Chicago Press, 1966.
Gessner, Robert. *Massacre: A Study of Today's American Indian*. New York: DeCappo Press, 1931.
Gist, Noel P. *The Blending of Races: Marginality and Identity in World Perspective*. New York: John Wiley and Sons, 1972.
Graymont, Barbara, ed. *Fighting Tuscarora: The Autobiography of Chief Clinton Rickard*. Syracuse, N.Y.: Syracuse University Press, 1973.
Greenberg, Henry, and Georgia Greenberg, eds. *Carl Gorman's World*. Albuquerque: University of New Mexico Press, 1984.

Hauptman, Laurence M. *The Iroquois and the New Deal.* Syracuse, N.Y.: University of Syracuse Press, 1981.

_____. *The Iroquois Struggle for Survival: World War II to Red Power.* Syracuse, N.Y.: University of Syracuse Press, 1986.

Hemingway, Albert. *Ira Hayes: Pima Indian.* New York: University Press of America, 1988.

Hemphill, W. Edwin, ed. *Gold Star Honor Roll of Virginians in the Second World War.* Charlottesville, Va.: Virginia World War II Commission, 1947.

Holm, Tom. *Strong Hearts, Wounded Souls: Native American Veterans and the Vietnam War.* Austin: University of Texas Press, 1996.

Hoxie, Frederick. *A Final Promise: The Campaign to Assimilate the Indians, 1880–1920.* Lincoln: University of Nebraska Press, 1984.

Iverson, Peter. *The Navajo Nation.* Westport, Conn.: Greenwood Press, 1981.

_____. *The Plains Indians of the Twentieth Century.* Norman: University of Oklahoma Press, 1985.

Jackson, Helen Hunt. *A Century of Dishonor.* New York: Harper and Row, 1965.

Johnson, Broderick, ed. *Navajos and World War II.* Tsaile, Ariz.: Navajo Community College Press, 1978.

Kelly, Lawrence C. *The Assault on Assimilation: John Collier and the Origins of Indian Policy Reform.* Albuquerque: University of New Mexico Press, 1983.

Kirtland, John C. *The Relocation and Internment of the Aleut People During World War II: A Case In Law and Equity for Compensation.* Anchorage: Aleut-Pribilof Islands Association, 1981.

Kohlhoff, Dean. *When the Wind Was a River: Aleut Evacuation in World War II.* Seattle: University of Washington Press, 1995.

Lewis, David Levering. *When Harlem Was in Vogue.* New York: Random House, 1981.

Levine, Stuart, and Nancy Levine, eds. *The American Indian Today.* Baltimore: Penguin, 1974.

Liebow, Edward B. "A Sense of Place: Urban Indians and the History of Pan-Tribal Institutions in Phoenix, Arizona." Ph.D. diss., Arizona State University, 1986.

Locke, Deborah. "From Rabbit Snares to Riveter Guns: The Lives of Minnesota Ojibwe Women during World War II." (Unpublished Honors Paper), 1990.

Lomawaima, K. Tisianina. *They Called It Prairie Light: The Story of Chilocco Indian School.* Lincoln: University of Nebraska Press, 1994.

Mails, Thomas, ed. *Fools Crow.* Garden City, N.Y.: Doubleday, 1980.

Meriam, Lewis, et al. *The Problem of Indian Administration.* Baltimore: The Johns Hopkins Press, 1928.

Naguta, Shuichi. *Modern Transformation of Moenkopi Pueblo.* Chicago: University of Illinois Press, 1970.

Olson, James S., and Raymond Wilson. *Native Americans in the Twentieth Century.* Chicago: University of Illinois Press, 1986.

Paul, Doris. *The Navajo Code Talkers.* Philadelphia: Dorrance, 1973.

Perrett, Geoffrey. *America in the Twenties.* New York: Simon and Schuster, 1982.

World War II and the American Indian

Philp, Kenneth, ed. *Indian Self-Rule: First-Hand Accounts of Indian-White Relations from Roosevelt to Reagan*. Salt Lake City, Utah: Howe Brothers, 1986.

_____. *John Collier's Crusade for Indian Reform: 1920–1954*. Tucson: University of Arizona Press, 1980.

Rosentiel, Annette. *Red and White: Indian Views of the White Man, 1492–1982*. New York: University Books, 1983.

Samuel, Lawrence R. *Pledging Allegiance: American Identity and the Bond Drive of World War II*. Washington DC: Smithsonian Institution Press, 1997.

Simmons, Leo W., ed. *Sun Chief: The Autobiography of a Hopi Indian*. New Haven, Conn.: Yale University Press, 1942.

Smith, Geoffrey S. *To Save a Nation: American Countersubversives in the New Deal and the Coming of World War II*. New York: Basic Books, 1973.

Sorkin, Alan. *The Urban American Indian*. Lexington, Mass.: D. C. Heath, 1978.

Stanley, Samuel. *American Indian Economic Development*. Paris: Mouton, 1978.

Szasz, Margaret. *Education and the American Indian: The Road to Self-Determination, 1928–1973*. Albuquerque: University of New Mexico Press, 1974.

Taylor, Graham D. *The New Deal and American Indian Tribalism: The Administration of the Indian Reorganization Act, 1934–1945*. Lincoln: University of Nebraska Press, 1980.

Tregaskis, Richard. *Guadalcanal Diary*. New York: Random House, 1943.

Upton, Helen M. *The Everett Report in Historical Perspective: The Indians of New York*. Albany: New York State American Revolution Bicentennial Commission, 1980.

Wyaco, Virgil. *A Zuni Life: A Pueblo Indian in Two Worlds*. Albuquerque: University of New Mexico Press, 1998.

Vogel, Virgil, ed. *This Country Was Ours: A Documentary History of the American Indian*. New York: Harper and Row, 1972.

Vogt, Evon Z. *Navajo Veterans: A Study of Changing Values*. Cambridge, Mass.: Harvard University Press, 1951.

Washburn, Wilcomb E. *The Indian in America*. New York: Harper and Row, 1975.

Williams, Walter L., ed. *Southeastern Indians Since the Removal Era*. Athens: University of Georgia Press, 1979.

Zeman, A. A. B. *Nazi Propaganda*. London: Oxford University Press, 1964.

Index